If You Wake Up,
Don't Take It Personally

Dialogues in the
Presence of Arunachala

If You Wake Up,
Don't Take It Personally

Dialogues in the
Presence of Arunachala

Karl Renz

www.AperionBooks.com

APERION BOOKS™

1611A South Melrose Dr #173

Vista, California 92081

www.AperionBooks.com

10 9 8 7 6 5 4 3 2

First edition

Printed in the United States of America

ISBN-10: 0-9829678-4-5

ISBN-13: 978-0-9829678-4-3

Library of Congress Catalog Card Number: 2011902670

Transcribed and compiled by Karen J. Quastler

Cover Painting by Karl Renz

Cover & book design by CenterPointe Media

www.CenterPointeMedia.com

For All Who Seek Truth

Table of Contents

January 17
Still the Happy Failure; or, the End of Intellect

January 18
The Problem That There Is No Problem;
or, the End of Worry and Boredom

January 22
You are That Which Is Home; or, the End of All Ends

Rollicking
Advaita

Vorsicht! Watch out! Karl Renz is as sure to madden as he is to delight—but people keep coming back anyway, because he is so right, or perhaps only because he is so entertaining. With Karl, every idea, every theory, every sacred idol of the mind, is fair game. Sooner or later, he will turn his attack to one of your most cherished beliefs, and his bite is sure to sting, but then, amidst all the fun and laughter and the relaxed atmosphere of acceptance that he generates, you will start to laugh at yourself, and the hardened misconceptions with which you perpetuate your suffering will begin to fall away.

Karl Renz is one of the foremost teachers of non-dual philosophy. "Non-dual" really means non-multiple—all that is knowable and unknowable and also the knower (and non-knower) of all these things are One. We use the term "non-dual" because, in One-ness, no experience is taken to be relative to its opposite, not even existence itself.

Karl is a teacher of non-duality; he recommends no specific technique and advocates no method. His talk will contradict itself, or run in circles, or simply converge into indecipherable paradoxes. The room is full of people determined to understand his system—struggling to figure it out, once and for all, write it down, memorize it, and then walk away "enlightened"—but there can be no figuring out, because any enlightenment you could "figure out" would be a mere idea. Karl always points to something beyond ideas and concepts, and *he takes you there*. Is Karl, therefore, enlightened? I have no idea. What is "enlightenment"? What is "Karl"? I do not vouch for Karl Renz; I vouch for the experience of non-duality that resonates in the words of this book.

As you read, you may begin to recognize a pattern in Karl's way of thinking, but don't try to be clever. Enlightenment is not a matter of cleverness. The important thing happening when you read is not the superficial meaning of Karl's statements, but something much deeper and more mysterious. The "Karl" we encounter in these pages has eliminated the idea of "personhood" in himself and in his perception of others. He looks at those who ask questions, and he responds, but for him, no one is looking, no one is being seen, no one is talking, no one is listening; instead, there is only That which he is, which is also you and everyone. He speaks only to That, not to the person, and by reading his words, his perspective *just might* become your perspective.

The emphasis is on "just might." Karl insists that neither he nor anyone else can do anything to enlighten you, and in fact he claims he can offer you nothing at all. Your true state, according to Karl, is always *in spite of* anything you have done, never *because of* anything you have done. He points out that any enlightenment that someone could give you, or that you could somehow achieve, would be an enlightenment not worth having, because what is given or achieved can be just as readily lost. An achieved enlightenment would, in his view, be a mere mental construct, and only your mind, not the real *you*, has any need for such a thing. Taking this general principle as his starting point, Karl proceeds to obliterate (sometimes with outright vulgarity) every concept of religion, piety, and sacredness that anyone has ever held dear.

But a word of caution is appropriate—though Karl might object. Do not fall into the common trap of renouncing all spiritual effort as mere vanity, and then, after a cup of coffee and a few exciting insights, imagine yourself to be enlightened. One frequently encounters such people wherever non-dual philosophy is being taught, but these intelligent souls have only substituted one persona for another. Non-dualism has been called a "lollipop for the mind," and with good reason; it offers a satisfying answer to every question. Nevertheless, if you want to reach the highest state, you must *strive* and then *strive some more*, just as so many others have done before you. Why? Because you cannot possibly do anything else. As a soul that God has chosen, it is your very nature to seek God with all your strength. But when finally you rest in the ultimate Truth, you see very clearly that all your seeking achieved nothing, it never actually happened, and God was there all the time, doing everything while doing nothing at all.

One who categorizes religious philosophies might place Karl in a school of thought known as Advaita Vedanta. *Advaita* means "non-dual," and the Advaita philosophy asserts that there is no true distinction between knower and known; the experience itself is the experiencer of the experience, while the eternal Source remains unaffected throughout the illusory flow of change. Advaita is rooted in the sophisticated musings of the Upanishads, Hinduism's philosophical distillation of its ancient Vedic scriptures, and hence, it is *Vedanta*, that is, "the end of the Veda." Some scholars suggest that Advaita Vedanta emerged as one of Hinduism's responses to Buddhism, and in many ways the ideas of Buddhism run parallel, but non-dual thought is much older than Buddhism and much bigger than its relatively orthodox formulation in Advaita Vedanta. Non-dual thought lies at the heart of heterodox South Asian traditions such as Kashmiri Shaivism, and it is also a fundamental principle in Jewish mysticism. Most important, the Advaita that Karl teaches is not confined to any religion; Karl simply speaks from his inner experience. Nor should we dismiss Karl's teachings as mere postmodern cynicism or the intellectual musings of a dry heart. True Advaita is pure love, a love grounded in the experience that nothing is different from one's own Self.

One of the leading classical teachers of Advaita Vedanta was Shankara (686-718 C.E.), and in modern times, the Advaita philosophy was powerfully restated and popularized by Ramana Maharshi (1879-1950 C.E.). At the foot of the holy mountain Arunachala in the South Indian temple town of Tiruvannamalai, Ramana Maharshi's hermitage continues to attract thousands of students and seekers, and the surrounding village is like the Agora of Athens in the time of Socrates. Under the warm tropical sun, amidst the dappled shade of flowering trees, on temple verandahs, and in the courtyards of noisy tea shops, teachers abound, presenting their competing versions of enlightenment. These are informal gatherings, publicized by word of mouth alone. The seekers are a relaxed mix of tourists and pilgrims, expatriates and native Indians. Many are road-worn veterans of the spiritual path, bringing with them the wisdom of many lifetimes dedicated to seeking God. They have experienced all the striving and the hardships, all the ecstasies and the dark nights of the soul, all the hopes and the crushing doubts of spiritual inquiry. And, at last, they have come to Tiruvannamalai to be told, and perhaps to realize, that they themselves *are* the thing they have been seeking, for Advaita teaches that in the midst of all the seeking and attaining, you—the true You—have always been content, enjoying an *absolute contentment* that is not relative to discontentment.

It is January in South India. Every day, the sky is the same clear, vibrant blue. Flowers bloom on every creeper, bush, and tree. The warm air swells with the sounds of birds singing, workmen shouting, and peddlers hawking their goods. On a rooftop, under a palm leaf awning, with the holy mountain's commanding presence as a backdrop, Karl chats and jokes, answers questions from newcomers and longtime admirers, and all the time points everyone to something beyond—while insisting he can do nothing at all to help you.

—Ya'akov ben Avraham

Compiler's
Notes

This book attempts to convey the delight and drama of a week of *satsangs* with Karl. It's a straight transcription, as true as possible to what was actually said, including all of the joking around, even when it may not be "G-rated." But this is part of the experience, and some may say that the surprise and the humor are every much as important as the philosophy.

Although I've inserted titles and headings for the sake of readability, during the *satsangs* there was no break in the flow of conversation. The first line of a new section is actually the very next utterance. Also in the interest of readability, I've removed *some* repetition and corrected *some* basic grammar. (Much of the original phrasing is unedited in order to leave open the meaning of the speech, preserve the fun of the banter, or allow the reader to "hear" the voices through the page.) Other than these minor changes, the transcript is complete.

People from many countries earnestly participated in these *satsangs*, and some regular participants are identified by name. Except for Karl's, however, all the names in this book have been fictionalized. In some cases, the nationalities of the participants are noted. Based upon recordings of the *satsangs*, I occasionally had to guess at a speaker's identity or nationality, and I apologize for any error.

One convention may be worth noting. Karl's only prop is his own hand, which he uses to symbolize the Self and three aspects or states of experience. When Karl refers to the Self, or what he calls "Heart," he holds up a closed fist. When he refers to the "I," or pure awareness, he raises his thumb. When he refers to the "I am," or formless, non-identified consciousness, he raises his thumb and index finger. And when he refers to the "I am so-and-so," or consciousness identified with form, he raises his thumb, index, and middle fingers.

The *satsangs* were held in the town of Tiruvannamalai, in the Indian state of Tamil Nadu. Tiruvannamalai lies at the foot of Arunachala hill and is the home of one of India's largest Shiva temples, Arunachaleswarar Temple, which is associated with the element of fire. For centuries, the area has been regarded as sacred and has attracted many mystics and sages.

From ten o'clock to noon, the *satsang* takes place on the roof of Ragini's, a private home and one-room diner that is a short walk from Ramana Maharshi's *ashram* (Sri Ramanasramam). A narrow stairway leads up to the roof. Although there's a canopy above, the sides are open to the breeze and bright sunlight. The roof space is completely bare of decoration. On the concrete floor are several mats, and five or six chairs are at the back for those who might be uncomfortable on the floor. A simple chair waits at the front for Karl.

A group of thirty to fifty people gather, a very international scene. Many know each other from their years of meeting at *ashrams* and spiritual retreats. The room has a relaxed atmosphere as people chat in several languages. Punctually, Karl enters and joins in the chat, greeting and asking after people's health. But soon the group quiets, waiting for the question and answer format to begin. The near constant background noise comes to the foreground—"three-wheeler" taxis and motorcycles, bicycle bells, children playing and crying, peddlers calling out their wares, workers shouting, hammering, and drilling, birds, cows, dogs, monkeys, etc.

With the first question, Karl speaks only to That which you are—with hammering logic, confusing contradiction, stern compassion, and joyful, often hilarious irreverence—and the room is transformed into a churn of the soul. Karl's *satsang* is not simply an elaboration of concepts, but an experience of the dance of Shiva, the Destroyer. And above all, in Karl's words, "It's Self-entertainment, all the way."

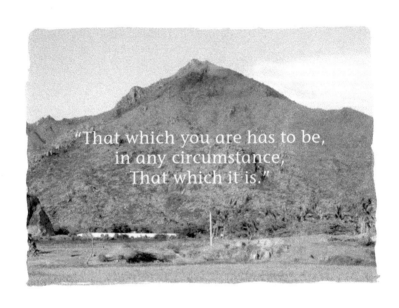

"That which you are has to be,
in any circumstance,
That which it is."

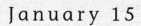

January 15

From the Oneness, Everyone Comes Back; or, the End of "Divine Love"

Breaking the Mind, Breaking the Heart

KARL: Morning!

MATTIAS: Morning, *Meister* (master).

KARL: *Meister*? "Morning, Master" to you! *Ein Meisterschreinerei* (a master carpenter's shop). *Wir wird gehobelt* (we will be made smooth; lit., planed like wood). [to various attendees] Hello! How's Mexico? Good. Hello, is France okay?

VICKI: [about the French man] Yes. He's coming back. No operation.

KARL: Maybe just seeing the hospital room, he changed his mind! [the group laughs]

VICKI: And having the doctor tell you everything that can go wrong.

KARL: Yeah, it's like the dentist. Okay. Oh, Francesco, after yesterday, you look shiny! He went to the hairdresser.

FRANCESCO: After he cut me, he asked, "You like this?"

KARL: [teasing] And you thought you'd better be quiet, or what? Ah, we go again. Without questions, I will continue talking about Francesco's affairs. [group laughs] You think now it's working?

A French WOMAN: I don't know. I am waiting for the question. Then I will see after. [group laughs]

KARL: Okay, let's see. Looks very promising. James, it sounded like you had something.

JAMES: I have a cold! [group laughs]

A German WOMAN: Today's an emotional carousel.

KARL: Merry-go-round. Mary goes round. Emotional merry-go-round!

A Mexican WOMAN: I have a question. What is the meaning of what Ramana said, that when the mind is broken, we fall into the heart? Many times I've tried to understand what this is. Is this like a *koan* that the monks do? What's the difference between "killing the mind" and "breaking the mind"? What's the meaning of "breaking the mind"?

KARL: You have a broken heart.

WOMAN: And what does this have to do with the "split second" that you talk about? Is the broken mind like the split second?

KARL: This is when the heart breaks.

WOMAN: You always say "heart."

KARL: When the heart breaks, you have a heartbroken existence. You are not in love with anything anymore. When the heart is totally broken, in that split second, there is no mind anymore. There is only mind as long as there is a heart—a lover and something beloved. But with the heart broken, there is no mind anymore, because you are not glued to anything.

So the breaking of the mind is actually breaking the heart. The heart is totally broken in the moment there is no lover and nothing beloved anymore. As the beloved is gone, the lover is gone, and being heartbroken, the mind is gone too. There is only mind because there is a lover and something beloved, something you care about. It is the same.

In that split second, you lose all the glue. You have no clue anymore. About anything. Your heart is broken, there is no lover and nothing beloved anymore, and even the idea of "love" is gone.

WOMAN: It is the same thing you have been talking and talking about.

KARL: Yeah, always pointing to That.

WOMAN: So what is this "split second"?

KARL: It breaks in a split second. You may dent it for a while, but then it pops up again. When it breaks, it breaks at once and not in slow motion. That's why it's called "heartbreak." At that moment, it's broken—it's a split second. There is no time. Everything else, like meditation, may bend it, but you cannot dissolve it. It breaks at once, because all the relationship ideas break at once. That's being heartbroken.

When you lose total love for yourself, there is no one left anymore. It's a split second. You drop out of that existence. It's not something you can come to by understanding, or anything. It simply comes by total resignation of loving love itself.

AIKO: Then what is all this about "opening the heart"?

KARL: That's a surgery, but it will not break the heart. It simply makes it open.

AIKO: Must it be open before it breaks?

KARL: No. "Open heart" is like "oneness heart," like bliss or a feeling of oneness. It cannot break anymore. It breaks here—being in love with the world and then losing that love. But not by going to that oneness or any landing place. It has to break here, now, and not in any special state.

[An explosion is heard in the background.]

AIKO: Can you dissolve in oneness? Is that a different way to lose the mind?

KARL: No. From the oneness, everyone comes back. What is love is oneness, and it always goes back to the separation of a lover and something beloved. Many people go from relative love to oneness love, but then a beautiful girl or man comes their way and they step into the same thing again. It's worth nothing anyway. That heaven of oneness is fleeting. It's promising a lot but it's not delivering.

AIKO: I have a *guru* and he's love itself.

KARL: Who says so?

AIKO: I see it.

KARL: Who sees it? Who defines it? Who makes the standards of love? You.

AIKO: It's my hope.

KARL: It's your opinion.

AIKO: It's my projection.

KARL: It's your longing, it's your devotion, whatever. It's you who make it. It's your imagination of what it has to be. Because you are longing for That, you make an image of it and then you project it onto the *guru*. But it's still relative love. Whatever love you can experience is relative. There's nothing wrong with it, I say. I just point out that you can go to the place of oneness and love, but wherever you go, you have to leave again.

That which you are has to be, in any circumstance, That which it is. What needs a special circumstance, like a definition of love, is dependency. Love that makes you dependant is, for sure, not the freedom you are looking for. So you frame it again, putting it into some beloved *guru*. It's okay, but just see, freedom is not that.

ROSA: Does the mind exist?

KARL: As the clouds are, it is. Do the clouds exist? For a while they exist; then it rains and they are gone.

ROSA: So it's a bundle of thoughts?

KARL: One thought surrounded by other thoughts. But whenever you want them to go, you make them real. The cloud will rain one day and then the cloud will be gone. That's the mind. Clouds come and go, water always produces another cloud.

ROSA: What does it mean when one says, "the mind drops to the heart," or "the mind resolves in the heart"?

KARL: That's when the heart is broken. Then it's the empty Heart. And only emptiness can contain the fullness of existence. In the fullness of existence, there is no place of mind anymore, because there is no mind in the fullness of That which is. In the broken heart, where Heart is totally empty of any idea of love or freedom, it can contain the totality.

But as soon as there's a definition of love, or one who defines *love* as "oneness" or "divine" or whatever, it's occupied. There's occupation and possession. There's one who defines something. This definer is mind. But in the emptiness of Heart, there's no place for any definer anymore. So this emptiness of Heart contains the absolute totality of existence—but not any idea. That first idea of "me," the "I"-thought, the ownership idea, occupies everything.

ROSA: And the closest—any word will be an limitation—is *stillness*?

KARL: It is That which is stillness, but that stillness doesn't know stillness. It's simply a pointer to That, that nothing ever happened to That. There is no coming and no going in it. It's so solid in itself. It is never in time or out of time. It has absolutely no definition. It's so absolute in itself that it doesn't even have to exist to exist. Way beyond the beyond!

KLARA: Karl, is that something like a *satori?*

KARL: It is, but it is not. What wakes up is still asleep. That idea of "awakening" makes you asleep, and what can wake up is still asleep. There was never one who was not awake and there will never be one who is awake. Both ideas make you asleep. Both come together and go together. There will never be any *satori* for what you are, but for that which needs a *satori*, there is a *satori*. But there is none.

THERESE: And Karl, for what you are, this split second doesn't matter either?

KARL: No. You long for it. It matters totally. Only that matters—to lose that love for yourself. There is nothing else. Everything else pales before your longing to go to the ruthlessness you are. That ruthlessness is emptiness of ideas, of one who is in love or not in love, of one who cares. That concernlessness is what you're longing for so much. That Self is sitting here longing for that concernlessness. That's all.

THERESE: And there is nothing to do?

KARL: In that split second, your heart will be broken totally. There will be no one left, because in the heartbroken heart, there is no idea anymore. So you have no glue anymore for anything. You have no relationship, because you see there is no second. You are absolutely alone. You cannot avoid it anymore.

You Are the Absolute Failure

THERESE: So, when I am on my deathbed and the split second didn't happen, then I am a failure?

KARL: You're always a failure! That's a failure, that you always will be a failure. You see that there's nothing to gain, nothing to lose. You are the total failure, because whatever you did didn't bring anything. You are the absolute failure, here and now, don't worry! [group laughs] You will always fail yourself.

GEORG: How can Self long for anything? If there's non-duality, how can Self long for concernlessness?

KARL: Simply by taking a phantom image as real. It creates an image of itself and then becomes trapped in that image by taking the image as real. What else is there to take something as real? Being the Source of imagination, only the Self can imagine something, and then step from that Absolute into some relative experience. If there is any experience, it is always the Self.

GEORG: The Self does all that?

KARL: Whatever is done, is done by That, and by not doing anything. It's a dream-like thing, so it's not doing anything, but still it is the Self experiencing the Self in a dream of itself.

GEORG: With no difference between dream and reality, *dream* is just a word. If it's experiencing anything, then it's experiencing something.

KARL: Whatever is experienced is experienced by the Self experiencing an aspect of Self. There is nothing but That.

GEORG: [laughing] Okay!

KARL: Thank you very much. [group laughs] Part of the experience is that you become a *jiva*, a little self, so that you can experience separation, that dream-like separation, and then you step out.

GEORG: It sounds a bit tricky to have all this duality inside the non-duality.

KARL: Yeah, all comes together as you realize yourself. All that is part of your absolute realization. In absolute realization, there's separation, one-ness, and awareness—as the trinity of your infinite body or whatever manifestation. You cannot *not* realize yourself, and part of it is separation. So what? To be That, it doesn't matter. That is what you are.

GEORG: So why should That give a damn? Why does it have this longing?

KARL: Why not?

GEORG: Yeah, why not?

KARL: If there's nothing to lose, my goodness, it can give a damn, but it doesn't give any damn at all. It can give everything by giving nothing. It has nothing to lose, my goodness!

GEORG: But what of this longing business?

KARL: Yeah, why not?

GEORG: [laughing] Why not!

KARL: What's the problem with longing?

THERESE: Because it keeps on creating a sense of failure.

KARL: Wonderful. Why not? Wonderful experience of being a failure. What's wrong with being a failure? Be happy. Happy failure. Who cares? [group laughs]

A WOMAN: And on the other hand, this longing is also you projecting that you gain something.

KARL: Yeah, why not? You have nothing to lose. Even there is no advantage in not longing. Why not long? You are the helplessness. You cannot decide to long or not to long, that's all. So why not?

VICKI: Longing hurts!

KARL: Phew! I tell you, even that hurting or whatever you experience is totally enjoyed by That which you are.

VICKI: But not by me!

KARL: The "me" is part of the enjoyment. The "me" never did enjoy anything! It's part of That which is enjoyed. That "me" is an idea and cannot enjoy anything. Whatever is experienced is experienced by that experience itself, the Absolute. The Absolute cannot *not* enjoy itself. It's joy itself, because there is a total absence of anything, of any idea of joy or no joy.

TOMAS: Then how can there be joy?

KARL: How can there be no joy? It's just a name for something which is joy because there's an absence of whatever. You are a total absence of any idea of one who has joy or no joy, and that is the Absolute enjoying itself by not knowing joy. So that joy doesn't know joy.

TOMAS: And doesn't experience it. If it doesn't know it, then how—

KARL: To be That is joy itself.

TOMAS: But joy itself is somehow defined by having an experience.

KARL: There is no difference. It defines itself in everything, but itself cannot be defined. It defines itself as "joy" and "no joy," as "war" and "peace," but whatever you define, comes out of the absolute Source, and the absolute Source cannot be defined. The absolute definer cannot be defined, but it defines itself in whatever you can imagine.

So imagination is the definition of the definer in the realization of what it is, but it's not the realization. It is still That which is realizing itself. It was never part of the realization. It's here, now, That which is realizing itself, not the reflection of it. Isn't it fun? [group laughs]

Come on! Enjoy yourself, or you will be enjoyed. That's all I am saying. Joy will be there, whether you like it or not. [group laughs] So you can be That which is enjoying itself, absolutely, or you can be enjoyed by it. What's the problem? Both are no problem.

TOMAS: So it's somehow like saying "yes" to everything.

KARL: No one says "yes."

TOMAS: Without saying "yes," but there is acceptance.

KARL: Who needs it? Who needs acceptance? Forget it. Forget the word. Acceptance itself doesn't need acceptance. What needs acceptance is not That which is acceptance. What to do?

It will not be *your* acceptance, I tell you. That's the whole problem! You cannot put acceptance in your pocket and take it with you for the rest of your so-called existence. That is the person—"me"—trying to be happy all the time and then trying to accept what is. But you can never accept That which is.

THERESE: But even this trying I can do nothing about?

KARL: Oh my goodness!

THERESE: No, I am asking.

KARL: Oh, yes, "I am asking"! You want to have a free letter or something? Absolution all the time. "I cannot do anything. I am not the doer. I cannot help myself." So that is okay too. "I'm not guilty!" But Thérèse is always guilty. She is guilt itself. [group laughs] There's the confirmation!

THERESE: [laughing] Happy guilt and happy failure!

KARL: Always picking on herself. With her sword. "I'm not guilty!" [group laughs]

THERESE: You know, when we were in Portugal, we never went there with all this kind of talk, and as soon as I see you, it's like something goes. For four months, there was no discussion inside, no moods, emotions coming up and down—

KARL: Oh, come on! No discussion with your beloved? [group laughs] As I always say, I can only sit here and blah, blah, blah, so that you see it doesn't make any difference. There is no problem, blah, blah, blah.

FRANCESCO: So why don't you tell us all something beautiful?

KARL: Oh my goodness. I'll talk to your hairdresser! [group laughs]

FRANCESCO: It's only blah, blah, blah! Talk, talk, talk. Yeah, you like it.

KARL: Yeah, I like it.

FRANCESCO: [teasing] It's German! [group laughs]

KARL: [teasing] Staccato. It's what Italians do.

FRANCESCO: It's boring.

KARL: Especially yesterday. You could not think anymore. I saw it. [group laughs] Totally there. I saw it in the reflection of their eyes.

FRANCESCO: What to do?

KARL: [to the group] You have to know, this is the *Brahmacharya* club here. [points to some men sitting on one side, including Francesco] Seven years, nine years, ten years of no sex. And then this young woman was sitting there with no underwear, and they saw everything. [group laughs]

FRANCESCO: Not only me. A lot of people saw.

KARL: Oh yeah, that other guy even went to sit from this side to that side. [group laughs] I tell you, existence is such a director.

FRANCESCO: It makes no difference. Who cares?

KARL: Aw, wasn't that nice, Francesco! You saw her, and straightaway you went to the hairdresser.

FRANCESCO: Maybe she'll comes back. [group laughs]

KARL: You were shaved, totally. Okay. [group laughs] It's dangerous to make like this.

LIZ: [laughing] Sometimes when you stretch, it's trouble. You're a stretch itself!

Grace Will Break Your Heart

MR. RAO: You said, "Try to accept what is, but you cannot accept what is." I do not understand. How can you not accept what is?

KARL: You cannot accept existence, because existence already is a crisis. Out of the first notion of existence, the crisis starts. You are in a crisis with that "I"-thought already. And then at, "I am," the crisis of, "I am so-and-so" starts. You cannot accept that. Because the longing, the one who *can* long, the possibility of longing, starts there. Maybe there is no longing, but the possibility will always be there in the first notion of existence. This you cannot accept.

But for That which is, there's no problem, because it is acceptance itself. There is nothing to accept, only to be That which is without a second. When you are That which is, without any idea of what you are and what you are not, when there is no second, then you *are* acceptance, because there is nothing left to accept. Not even the idea of "existence" is there. So then there is absolutely no necessity of acceptance, no need at all for That which you are.

So the total absence of any idea of whether to exist or not to exist is That, and then you are acceptance. But then there is nothing to accept anymore. That's why I am saying, you can never accept, as you are acceptance already. You cannot have more acceptance for what is—as you are already acceptance itself, there is nothing to gain by any relative acceptance.

What to do with it? You cannot add to the absolute acceptance that you are! And then, when you accept, what then? So what? It's all coming and going, fleeting shadows of acceptance. Then you reach some control system of acceptance and understanding, and then you will be crossed by a camel again, stepping on your feet. No way out. Only you may accept yourself as a person, but it will not be *your* acceptance.

But we cannot go further than this. This is the last thing. This is called *satori*. This is stepping out of wanting into, "not wanting." But that's all. You cannot break your own heart. It will be broken when it breaks, in a split second, not one second before, in spite of what happened before, with your acceptance or non-acceptance, whatever you have done or understood or not, it will break at that instant. That's all.

KLARA: What does "not wanting" mean?

KARL: *Not wanting* means "no wanting."

KLARA: Is it indifference?

KARL: Wanting no difference? Wanting to be indifferent? What an idea! [group laughs] Wanting to be indifferent, you still make a difference of wanting to be indifferent. Even the idea of "indifference" is different. Being totally attached to detachment. Oh my goodness. "Oh, I'm so detached!"

ROSA: Will you talk about grace?

KARL: Grace? I talk about you all the time! [group laughs] I only talk about grace. I'm always talking about That which is grace. What is grace is That which is Self. That which is grace is what you are. And you are looking for grace, that's your problem.

ROSA: I just wanted to hear what you say about grace.

KARL: But I cannot talk about grace, because you cannot find grace.

ROSA: Exactly. That's what I wanted to hear.

KARL: It's like every seeker is looking every place, in every dimension, for grace, but you cannot find it. Opposite! If grace is after you, you cannot hide. So when grace is after you, it will break your heart. Because grace is breaking all ideas; all concepts will be annihilated by grace. By the annihilation of all ideas, you become totally empty, and it breaks your heart.

This is like senselessness. You cannot cope with this; you cannot live by that. That senselessness, that emptiness of whatever ideas, you cannot deal with, you cannot grasp, you cannot exist in it. This will break your heart. It will break your idea of "existence." Your loving whatever objective idea of existence will be, by grace, erased. Eh-graced! [group laughs] It's grazing! Eating all the stupidity away.

GEORG: Disgraced.

KARL: [laughing] Disgraced!

MARY: What do you say about loving more and more, and still yet more, until we become worthy of—

KARL: Worthy?

MARY: Worthy of this breaking, this ultimate blessing.

KARL: You will never be pure enough, my dear!

MARY: Not becoming more and more pure, but loving more and more the truth.

KARL: Your love is too dirty! No one wants your love! Dirty love. The idea of "love" is dirty. More love is dirty. Quantity of love is dirty. Even the idea of "a quantity of love" is dirty. You are offering me a dirty idea. You are dirt itself in the moment you want to get love.

MARY: [softly] But love—

KARL: What love? "Let's talk about love, my dear!" [group laughs]

MARY: I wanted to know what you would say about it, and I got the answer.

KARL: You can never be ripe enough, or mature enough, by whatever you do.

MARY: Loving is not trying to get ripe. Loving is not trying—

KARL: What loving?

MARY: Loving is like—

KARL: Whose loving will it be?

MARY: Loving is not an, "I-me-mine." "I-me-mine" is not a loving. "I-me-mine" is a wanting.

KARL: Listen to you! You want to control what you are by loving yourself, wanting to become ripe for it. So you still want to control it by *you* liking to do something, to become something. What an idea! What a dirty idea. You want to control existence! By what? My goodness.

MARY: Thank you.

KARL: Welcome. Very welcome. It always sounds so beautiful.

MARY: I wasn't trying to sound beautiful.

KARL: Oh, come on! Forget it.

MARY: Okay. Thank you.

MONIKA: [singing] "All you need is love, da da da da da."

[Others join in singing.]

KARL: "Maybe I'm not the only one." "Let it be." [group laughs] One Beatle, one bead from that side and one bead from the other side.

A Play of Divine Love

MARY: Well, let's go into this a little bit more. I need to go into this more.

KARL: What?

MARY: Loving is a giving. It's not a wanting. It's not an asking. Real love is a giving.

KARL: What real love? Even the idea of "real love" is shit.

MARY: Divine love has no purpose.

KARL: What purpose? You want to put it in your purse. You want to define it, and that is putting it into your purse of your owning some understanding and some definition of love. You make it dirty. Whatever you tell, *whatever* you say about it, you make it dirty!

MARY: I have a reference for this.

KARL: What reference? You, reverent? You've become a referee for love?

MARY: Meher Baba.

KARL: Meher Baba! Ali Baba! Are you one of the forty thieves, or what? [group laughs] "Open sesame! By my beauty, by my heart, open sesame!"

MARY: There's no "my" in love.

KARL: So no *my* love? Well, it's still very mean. You are still meaning something.

MARY: I wanted to present this to you—that love, real love, is not contaminated by wanting.

KARL: Of course. Even to call it "real love"—

MARY: I mean—

KARL: Whatever you say, my goodness, forget it! Romantic bullshit.

MARY: No, this has nothing to do with that. "Romantic" is bullshit.

KARL: This is romantic bullshit; this is divine romance—even more bullshit!

[group laughs]

MARY: Real love is not for the faint—or weak-hearted. That's romanticism. This is something else.

KARL: Oh goodness. Always, "this is something else." Blah, blah, blah.

MARY: I won't, I won't— I thank you for the cutting. Because the speaking is always an "I-me-mine." But this is a concept that's really—

KARL: What? Still a concept.

MARY: —that is beyond.

KARL: In German, we say it's still a *Kotzept* (vomit; play on *Konzept* meaning "rough idea"). You have to break out.

MARY: Divine love is not a concept!

KARL: It is a *Kotzept*. You have to break it out. Vomit it out, here and now!

[group laughs]

GEORG: Concept, *Kassette* (cash-box; casket).

KARL: *Kassette*! You want to put love in the *Kassette* of your ideas.

MARY: It's a gift.

KARL: It's a gift, yes! *Gift* in German means "poison." It's totally poison!

[group laughs]

MARY: Divine love is a gift of God.

KARL: What God? What "God" are you talking about?

MARY: The One.

KARL: What One?

MARY: The Self.

KARL: What "Self" are you talking about?

MARY: Even Ramana says—

KARL: Even Ramana! Now you are even quoting Ramana! You want to get all the sources together just to make your point, or what? Ramana, Meher Baba, Tralala, Falala! [group laughs]

MARY: The true masters are all one and the same.

KARL: True master! What is a true master?

MARY: The true master is the Self realized.

KARL: The true master doesn't know any true master! What are you talking about? You want to be a true master. That's what you're wanting to be. "No, no, not me!"

MARY: [laughing] I don't, I really don't. But I do have a reverence for this divine love, this purposeless—

KARL: You're longing for whatever you can put into the pocket of *your* experience.

MARY: One can't long for it; it's a gift.

KARL: What gift? Ah, forget it. Be gifted.

ROSA: Are you saying not to talk about it?

KARL: You can talk about it, but you cannot talk it to "come" and you cannot talk it to "go away."

ROSA: It's to be.

KARL: I have no idea! Whatever your idea of it is is like dirt. Whatever you make out of it, whatever word you use, is dirt for That. That doesn't know anything about "divine," or Self, or any master.

MARY: Right.

FRANCESCO: [laughing] This is true.

MARY: This I feel. That's what I was saying. But I feel that you should know more of what I was saying.

KARL: Why should I know anything?

MARY: Oh, okay.

KARL: You want to control me, so that I should know something. No? You want my agreement. You are looking for confirmation.

FRANCESCO: Me too. [group laughs]

KARL: "Please confirm my idea of 'love'! Please, if you only could see my idea! How can I represent it to you? Please take it. Eat it from me!"

MARY: You know what? Really, it wasn't meant that way.

KARL: Okay. Don't worry.

FRANCESCO: "Don't worry. Be happy." "Tomorrow is another day."

KARL: Tomorrow may never come, thank God.

FRANCESCO: [laughing] The problem is, I come again.

KARL: [laughing] You come again, everyday. What to do?

Embracing Loneliness

KARL: Question? I'm not as bad as I look—maybe worse! Mexico, something?

Mexican WOMAN: In the case of saying, "no, no, no, not this, not this, not this," by denying everything, does something happen if you wait?

KARL: Maybe, maybe not. It's always a "maybe," a speculation. Whatever you can say, whatever you make up, is a speculation about it.

WOMAN: No, I really like it.

KARL: I can only talk about when the split second really breaks your heart. Then there is no heart anymore. That's all. Then you have no glue anymore. Because without the glue of ideas or "whatever," there is That. But That was always there.

MARY: So that's the divine love.

MONIKA: She comes again!

KARL: Forget it! Maybe if you drink enough wine, you are in the divine love.

MARY: Maybe I should use another word.

KARL: Yeah, maybe. Maybe, don't make it so special.

MARY: You used the word *peace*. You're not afraid to use that word.

KARL: Peace, yeah. Maybe it's more fitting.

MARY: Peace. Enjoyment. Love. Sing.

KARL: No, no. Peace is joy itself because there is no second. But there is no idea of peace.

MARY: There is no second in love.

KARL: Yeah, but this "no second" is still a second.

MARY: Hmm?

KARL: That "no second" of love, that oneness, is still a second.

MARY: There's no second in peace; there's no second in love.

KARL: I'm not talking about the, "no second" of oneness. I'm not talking about, "oneness love." I'm not talking about the love of God, loving himself—

MARY: The Self is peace itself, happiness itself, love itself.

KARL: But it doesn't know peace.

MARY: Peace itself, love itself.

KARL: But you can call it, "underwear itself." [group laughs]

MARY: Love itself too. Why should I shy away from the word *love?*

KARL: Because it's such a high icon, and it simply makes it too special.

MARY: Then say that.

KARL: You make it that. Just call it "the divine underwear," then I'm fine! [group laughs]

MARY: Why so shy? You're not shy with the word *peace.* You're not shy with the word *bliss.*

KARL: Whatever you say, I have to destroy it anyway. So forget it!

MARY: Maybe it's because *love* is such a misused word. It's not understood.

KARL: There's so much expectation in it. That's why it's called, "*Sat*-shit-*ananda,*" because you don't expect something coming out of shit.

MARY: In love, there's no expectation!

KARL: What? By putting this word onto something, there is expectation.

GEORG: Karl, grammatically, *love* has an object and *peace* does not. It's as simple as that.

KARL: Yeah, that's a point. There's only love when there is a lover and something beloved. Peace, not.

MARY: Okay. Then I'll add the word "*divine*" to *love.* [group laughs]

KARL: Forget "de wine"! My goodness. Don't drink so much. You still want to be drunk?

MARY: Rumi has said—

KARL: What Rumi? We have a rumor now. You make a rumor out of it. A rumor from Rumi, or what?

MARY: Rumi, Hafiz—they were not afraid of the word *love.*

KARL: So what? What does it mean?

MARY: They weren't afraid of the words *peace* or *love.*

KARL: You need confirmers from somewhere, now? Speak for yourself and not about who said something.

MARY: I know this is the truth. I'm just not gonna back down.

KARL: You know this is the truth?!

MARY: I'm not going to be reluctant to use this word.

KARL: We have to bow down to her now! She knows the truth. The only one I know who knows the truth. She's giving *satsang* tomorrow morning, nine o'clock, her place! [group laughs]

MARY: I'm not this truth. I do not feel that I am this truth. It's intuition. I'm not gonna back down from this. It's not speculation; it's not conceptualization. It's my very heart.

KARL: You are the mouth that found itself.

MARY: I won't bring it up again.

KARL: The divine speculation! [group laughs]

MARY: Intuition is not speculation. It's a whole other order.

KARL: What order?

MARY: What's the word *speculation?* There's the word *speculation,* there's the word *intuition,* there's the word *realization*—these are different things.

KARL: But they don't make any difference. You are still the devil who wants to make differences where there are none. [silence] Hallelujah. My goodness.

LIZ: I had this experience once.

MONIKA: Another comes.

LIZ: I sit here with you and it goes in my mind all over again. I once heard a verse about Shiva. It was a poem of some kind, not quite in a language I understood. But there was one line in it that was repeated over and over, and I finally asked the swami, "What is this line?" And he said, "It's not this, it's not this, it's not this." So when I sit here, everything is "not this," and it's such a relief.

KARL: That's why I am sitting here. Whatever comes up, it's, "not this."

LIZ: [teasing] And then I was enlightened. [group laughs] I'll hold *satsang.* Downstairs.

MARY: "Not this, not this, not this"—isn't that love? Isn't that the gift?

KARL: No. It cannot be given to you, not by any line, not by any beautiful words, not by "whatever"—it cannot be given to you. It's not a gift, not a transmission.

MARY: It's grace.

KARL: [sternly] It's not even grace.

MARY: That's what I mean by *gift*—"grace."

KARL: It's a joke "here and now" that grace is looking for grace at all.

MARY: Who can do *neti-neti* absolutely, but grace? And that's love.

KARL: Not even grace can do it.

MARY: And love has no expectation, so that's what I'm saying.

KARL: But you're still defining love.

MARY: This is no definition.

KARL: Of course it's a definition!

MARY: No!

KARL: Oh, come on. You are in a division.

MARY: Love has nothing to do with division.

KARL: Even the idea of "love" makes a difference.

MARY: What about "peace"?

KARL: The same. Whatever idea you make, it makes a division. Love makes no difference.

A WOMAN: Here I am, with this I have to live, my God! This is why I am in trouble. With all these concepts, it is a very lonely place.

KARL: That's why this is called "the embracement of loneliness," which is grace. There is no idea of love anymore, or anything. This is not bliss, this is not something—

MARY: That's what love is!

KARL: Forget it! It will break your heart, whether you like it or not.

MARY: Yes, love breaks the heart. [group laughs] That's love. Broken heart.

KARL: Whatever you say. My goodness.

MARY: All right.

KARL: Is everything okay there? Is something coming up?

FRANCESCO: [pretending to cry] A question, a question! [group laughs] Poor Karl!

KARL: Compassion from him! Thank you.

FRANCESCO: Welcome.

Any "Me" Is an Enemy

KARL: You're from Berlin? Just arrived?

KLARA: No, I am now in India for three weeks.

KARL: Everything fine?

KLARA: This is something, but I am just observing, and then it goes away again.

KARL: Oh, just spit it out. It's called, "spitting honestly." Someone called it, "core-splitting honesty." [group laughs]

KLARA: I just find that today, it's not so easy to laugh as it was yesterday. Something happened yesterday evening. My heart was hurting because I realized how attached I am to getting attention from others and to being seen. There was one sentence from another person that—pow!—I wanted to just explode or—

KARL: [teasing] You wanted to jump out of the basement and kill yourself?

KLARA: [laughing] No, I just felt how much it hurts. Then afterwards I read *Das Buch Karl* [a book by Karl Renz in German] about the war, and it helped me, just to see what's happening.

KARL: Yeah, sometimes this war is not so intense, but it is always war once you have the idea that you are in the world. It's always friendly fire.

A WOMAN: What's this?

KARL: In Iraq now American soldiers kill themselves by friendly fire. The other one is no different from you, so it's always friendly fire. But they shoot anyway.

GEORG: It's accidental.

KARL: Yeah, by accident they take you as an enemy, as you take them for an enemy, and so they shoot. But they call it "friendly fire."

MONIKA: But you're dead!

KARL: This is like the world. Everyone shoots, because they think there is an enemy. But being any, "me," there are enemies.

GEORG: Divine love!

KARL: [laughing] Divine love is always friendly fire and not caring about the other one. "It's *my* divine love!" That's why Jesus said that there will never be any peace on earth. As long as there is a world at all, there is war. As long as you are in any world and you see any world, there is war.

You are always at war with yourself. Whenever you make an image you take as real and not Self, there is war. Any moment there is a second one, there is war. Even if there is a world peace situation, there is still war.

Only That is peace which doesn't know any peace. Whatever comes out of it, even divine love, is war. So you fight for divine love, you fight for freedom. Look, Bush is sending so many soldiers into Iraq simply for the idea of "freedom," and out of that idea of "freedom," there is war. Out of the idea of "peace," there is war! Out of the idea of "love," there is hate. Even if you call it "divine love," there is still hate. Whatever you say—

MARY: Divine love has nothing to do with hate.

KARL: Oh, come on!

MARY: Love is of a whole other order. Should we make up another word?

KARL: What word?! There's just this word, this word!

MARY: I'll buy that. But let's not mix things that shouldn't be mixed in. Like, he was sarcastic about divine love.

KARL: Yeah, I am too.

MARY: Divine love has no ego. There's no "I-me-mine."

MONIKA: Who is there to define it? You're defining it!

KARL: Who needs that definition?

MARY: I don't know.

KARL: You still want to land on something. That's all.

MARY: Love is not for the faint-hearted or the weak, that's all there is to it. It has nothing to do with selfishness. I think, maybe, I don't know, there might be some laughter here coming from a place of weakness and misunderstanding.

MONIKA: Oh, that's enough. You call us weak and you're the strong one? [group laughs]

MARY: No!

KARL: You make war here and now.

MARY: Isn't this knowing at all?

KARL: Listen, you are fighting. For what are you fighting?

LIZ: For a concept.

GEORG: For "love"!

MARY: No, real peace—

KARL: What is this "real peace" you are fighting for?

MONIKA: Peace is an experience, not a blah, blah, blah!

KARL: Even Bush would say, "I am fighting for real peace and real freedom."

MARY: No!

KARL: [teasing] Yeah, you're American, I know! [group laughs] You want to bring that idea even to India.

MARY: Obviously, he's not! Bush is bullshit.

KARL: Bush is bullshit? I love Bush! [group laughs] What kind of divine love says, "Bush is bullshit"?

MARY: You know what I mean.

KARL: What kind of "divine love" are you talking about?

MARY: That has nothing to do with it. Divine love is related to truth.

KARL: You're talking about apartheid. You are so apart! That is an, "ab-heart."

MARY: I can't understand. I'm not understanding.

KARL: Talking about the divine love and then Bush is bullshit.

MARY: Divine love has nothing to do with Bush!!

KARL: Okay, forget it.

LIZ: Bush is fighting for *freedom* which translates to "oil."

KARL: [indicating Mary] Yeah, she wants to be in an oily situation. It's like the divine love is a mechanic and you go for an oil change.

BERTA: Cars can run on water, and Bush is killing all these people.

FRANCESCO: Why not?

GROUP: Francesco?!

FRANCESCO: It's a part of the joke. Why do you like Bush?

KARL: I don't know.

FRANCESCO: I like him too. He tries to do what he thinks is good.

KARL: I like Bin Laden too. [group laughs]

FRANCESCO: Me too. Why not? It's not a movie. It's not inside a movie. It's consciousness, is it not? Bush is coming from another way.

KARL: It's like when the towers came down, Allah came as Bin Laden. "There cannot be two!" and then Boom!

FRANCESCO: Just this.

KARL: Consciousness has fun, I tell you. To make it really like a big event, on September eleventh, there was Allah, the only one, saying, "I am the only God, there can be no two. There is no money too. There is no many at all. I have to show something. There is only one—Allah—the great one!" Bomb!! Divine love—Bomb! It all comes out of that divine love—Bomb! God himself makes sure there is no second one—Bomb! [group laughs]

MARY: I thought Ramana Maharshi was divine love.

GROUP: Oh, no!

MARY: Why? I don't understand. Help me to understand. What is there to understand?

THERESE: Get the CD! [group laughs]

MARY: [laughing] All right, I'll get the CD.

No Place to Land

ROSA: May I change the subject?

GROUP: Hooray! Bravo!

KARL: Thank you.

ROSA: I don't know—it's the first time I'm here—you are talking about the Self?

KARL: As an idea, a pointer, but the Self doesn't know any Self. There is only "Selflessness," you may call it, "lovelessness," "existencelessness." I am pointing to that, "idea-lessness," where all the icons—of divinity, of God—are gone, this Godlessness I'm talking about. You are That which is God, but God doesn't know any God, no second or whatever. That which cannot be talked about or defined—that's what I'm talking about.

This paradox cannot be solved. We talk about something that cannot be talked about. So we can talk about it, but it makes no difference. It's just pointing out that it makes no difference whether you talk or not.

For That which you are, it never makes any difference, whatever you say, whatever you define or don't define. There is nothing more or less. There is no quantity in it, of whatever idea of "divine" or anything. All this is gone. This is freedom which has no idea about freedom.

ROSA: Emptiness?

KARL: Not even emptiness. Even emptiness is too much. This is That which is emptiness, and this is That which is fullness, and this is That which is whatever you name, but it has no name.

ROSA: So there is also no center.

KARL: No. There is no *avatara* center, where you can go and buy an *avatar* idea. Whatever idea, it is not.

LIZ: Nothing to hold onto.

KARL: Even that is too much. Even nothing is too much. Everything is too less.

GEORG: Return to center. Address unknown.

KARL: Love letters. "Return to sender. Address unknown." Concepts come up and then "whoosh." That's all.

ROSA: That's your job.

KARL: Yeah, it's like harvest. Cutting ideas. Head-chopping.

A WOMAN: Pongal [Indian Harvest Holiday].

KARL: Today is Pongal. Kali day. Chopping heads. Core-splitting. *Kopf* (head)-splitting. Bone splitting. All the bones have to be spit out.

KLARA: Karl, I see you are in a form and you are talking with yourself, and you are making quite a funny impression on me. I think, "Do I want to go in that direction?"

KARL: For sure not! [group laughs] Better, don't. You will not arrive. There will never be any arrival.

KLARA: So absolutely nothing! There is not even nothing. It's a game with words, I know.

KARL: You are on a journey that never started and will never end. There is no place to land for the plane that you are. And there's no pilot.

KLARA: God!

KARL: You're still looking for the pilot, but there is none. It's auto-pilot. There's no landing place, no airport.

LIZ: What a nightmare!

KARL: You're a nightmare, whether you like it or not. Whatever dream you take as real becomes a nightmare. So whatever nice dream of love, or anything, is a nightmare. It's all dreaming. It makes you a dreamer. As long as there's a dreamer, there's a nightmare. A dreamer will always dream again another dream. A nice dream will always go back to an ugly dream. Happy dream, unhappy dream, whatever.

TOMAS: It doesn't even make sense to realize that one is a complete failure. It doesn't make any difference.

KARL: That's an absolute failure. You will fail anyway.

MARY: So in this, love has no purpose. So this fits.

KARL: Whatever. Make it. Keep it. Sit on it. Take it home.

MARY: Divine love—

[Mary keeps trying to make her point, but Karl doesn't pause.]

KARL: Sit it out. Do whatever you like. Falala. No one cares.

MARY: It should be given its proper place!

KARL: Yeah, you decide what is proper and what is not. Yeah, yeah, forget it. Thank you very much.

MARY: Divine love has no purpose, right?

KARL: Thank you very much for your love.

MARY: No, I don't have that love, that purposeless love. But that's love.

KARL: Ah, thank you very much.

ROSA: You are breaking her heart, right now.

MARY: [laughing] That's okay.

ROSA: That's your job.

KARL: That's my job. I am a heartbreaker.

FRANCESCO: Hey!

KARL: The absolute playboy.

A MAN: And we are in the "Heartbreak Hotel." [group laughs]

KARL: Yeah, the, "Heartbreak Hotel" on the funny hill of Arunachala! Heart itself.

Another MAN: Yesterday, you said that you make compost.

KARL: Yeah, everything together and then compost and then what comes out? Lotus. Out of compost, divine lotus. I have the divine *Lokus*?

THERESE: Yeah, *Lokus* is "toilet" in German.

KARL: That's right.

THERESE: Your language is something! [group laughs]

KARL: I tell you!

THERESE: [teasing] And how come the Germans are so serious this morning?! [group laughs]

KARL: [laughing] Don't ask me!

THERESE: What went wrong? [group laughs]

KARL: Am I not funny enough for you?

THERESE: You are the only one!

KARL: Oh, throwing stones! [group laughs]

MARY: Maybe this is a sign you're really free.

KARL: Of what?

MARY: Of your German birth. Because you're so funny.

KARL: I have no idea what you're saying.

MARY: [laughing] You're really free! Okay, I'll shut up.

KARL: Now she really wants to kill me. Offending me all the time. Whatever you call me, you offend me.

ROSA: [teasing] "German!" [group laughs]

KARL: "Oh, I have to accept that I'm a germ!"

MATTIAS: I can help you with that.

KARL: Germs are all over the place. There are more germs than people.

[indicating an Australian man] He is really lucky; there are only seventeen million Australians.

Australian MAN: Twenty million.

KARL: Oh, twenty. In the early eighties, there were only fifteen.

MAN: The government is thinking about giving couples five thousand dollars to have a child.

KARL: Same in Germany.

MAN: We're not into immigration.

KARL: The Germans have the same fear that they will die out. Eighty million Germans are now having to —! [group laughs]

MONIKA: Are you doing your bit, Karl?

KARL: Now in Germany, if you don't have children, you have to pay more tax. Like an extra tax for having no children. A single tax. They really make you. Germany becomes a pimp that makes you have sex. You have to have sex now. [group laughs]

MATTIAS: A non-*Brahmachari* country.

KARL: India was the same. It's a paradox. Twenty years ago, you were put into prison for abortion, years of imprisonment for abortion. But a few years ago, they changed it, and you got ten thousand *rupees* for an abortion. One day you'd be imprisoned, and the next day you'd get ten thousand *rupees* for the same thing.

GEORG: Only a transistor radio, Karl. It's not worth that much.

KARL: That's like, one day can totally change everything.

LIZ: One concept to the next concept.

KARL: This is actually consciousness. Unpredictable. It's really a bitch. You never know when it bites you. You may cuddle with a little puppy for a while. "My puppy, my puppy of acceptance." But then, you never know. Pow! It's beautiful.

You Will Never Reach Love

Australian MAN: Karl, I have a question. It's about the *Bodhisattva* thing. I've never had any conscious experience of it in this life. But some energy to do with it is coming up lately.

KARL: This is your idea of a *Bodhisattva*.

MAN: It's not even an idea, but that's all I can relate it to. I don't know what it is. I'm just "wording" it out in my head. But it's not even a word. I haven't even put words to it. There was a sense that it was a totally ridiculous idea, a ridiculous concept, for quite a few years. I was really damning it. But somehow, some sense, some energy arises in the body, a certain sense of selflessness, with an energy to do with it. I don't know. I could be right off the mark, but somehow, I sort of tie it back into that. I don't know anything about it, or whether you know.

KARL: Ramana talked about the Selflessness, then the helplessness. You just do, out of Selflessness, what has to be done, without questioning it. It is not someone doing it, or whatever, you realize yourself in doing it.

MAN: Even the idea of wanting *moksha*, even the idea of not coming back, not having rebirth, is just such a selfish idea.

KARL: Yeah. All that is gone in That. Because then no one ever came or will go. That's all I talk about, "no way out." Whatever you experience here is That which you are, one aspect of it, and you cannot leave what you are. This is as infinite as you are. The realization of what you are is as infinite as you are. This is *moksha*—to see that there is only Self. Only That is what you are. And there is no way out of it.

This is a total full stop. There is not even *moksha* anymore. This is *moksha*, freedom that there is no second, there is no way out of being what is. There will never be any reaching anything, such as an exit or love or whatever. There is no love for you. Whatever you have an idea of is simply gone. There is no way out of it.

All ideas are made of the idea of an advantage, to find a way out. By simply, totally stopping, and with seeing that there is no such thing as a way out for you to be what you are, you see That is what is.

You are energy, the Selflessness, inside. One may call it, like she's been calling it, or define it as, "love." But there is no love. There is simply the absolute "no way out." It doesn't know any love or freedom or anything, because it is a total absence of any way out of what you are. This is what is called "peace," this immense peace, but this peace has always been there, it has never gone. This is what is called, "peace of mind," but there is no mind anymore. Whatever is, is Self. *Whatever* is. Whatever energy, vibration, whatever, is That which is what you are.

There is no way out of it because there is no advantage in the next moment of controlling anything. Whatever you can control is what you are, so it makes no sense to try to control anything. This is senselessness of doing or not doing, because it produces no advantage—that is compassion. What you are talking about is compassion. It is compassion when there is no one left to have compassion or pity or anything. Pity is only there because you are longing for a way out. Then you pity yourself and you see others who pity themselves. But when there is no second anymore, you don't know.

This is so natural. It's nothing special. It's not, "divine love" or anything. It's your nature, and this nature has never been gone. What to do with it? Just have another coffee, that's all. Cheers! [drinks from his bottle of juice]

MAN: Cheers!

Here, Now, It's So Extreme Because You Are That Extreme, Absolute Existence

JUAN: Karl? "I am" in the world is loneliness.

KARL: Any idea of existence is loneliness.

JUAN: "I am" is lonely too?

KARL: It's a potential of loneliness.

JUAN: What we consider loneliness, or only when you're in the world?

KARL: Yeah, but what is this consciousness? Consciousness is awareness, pure "I"-awareness. Then the "I am"-ness is space, and "I am so"-ness is one aspect of that.

JUAN: But the "I" is lonely too?

KARL: That already is loneliness. Out of that loneliness comes "I am"-ness and then "I am so"-ness, defining itself. The "I," which is this [Karl holds up his thumb to symbolize this state of awareness], then "I am" [holds up thumb and index finger], what God called, "I am that I am," pointing to That which is the Heart of "I am," which is this [pulls his fingers in, holding up just his fist], Heart itself, which is Self itself.

JUAN: That's not lonely.

KARL: There is no loneliness in it, because there is no one who could be lonely.

JUAN: When manifestation arises—

KARL: Already this [holds up his thumb]. When this "I" arises, as a notion of existence, there is loneliness.

JUAN: But does it arise out of loneliness? Because otherwise, it wouldn't arise, I guess.

KARL: It wouldn't? It did arise, not because of something, but without any cause. There is no "I want to arise." There is nothing. There's a potential only, of absolute existence as it was arising. But it never was arising. Even that has no beginning and end.

There is no beginning and end of "I"-awareness, there is no beginning and end of "I am"-ness, and there is no beginning and end of "I am so"-ness. Even the world that is here, now, is as infinite as That which is Heart. Trinity is an absolute manifestation of That which is Heart. And so the manifestation is as infinite as the infinite Heart. Whatever is, is Heart. Nothing is there but Heart.

But That which is Heart doesn't know Heart and would never define it as such and such and such. All this is a dream-like definition. That which is dreaming, the absolute dreamer, as what is Heart, cannot be dreamt of, cannot be imagined. It cannot be defined by any big or beautiful names. They all don't fit. That which is beauty itself doesn't know any beauty.

For That which is knowledge itself, to be That which you are, there is absolutely not knowing what you are and what you are not. So there is an absolute absence of one who knows or doesn't know. There's even the absence of an absence.

This you cannot become by anything, as you are That already. Nothing is more natural than That, to be That which is Heart. But any definition whatever, *whatever* you say about it, is framing it.

JUAN: So the whole struggle is to get rid of loneliness, I guess?

KARL: No, in the total confrontation with that loneliness—being that—you sink into That which is Heart. In this absolute confrontation, there is seeing that there is no second and nothing will ever give you what you are. Becoming that awareness itself, which becomes aware of being lonely, in that absolute loneliness, you sink into That which is Heart, and you are That which is Heart. In that absolute confrontation with what you are, by being absolutely loneliness itself, out of that "alone," you become "all one."

This is like a total transformation. In that extreme of loneliness, there is no one lonely anymore. In that extreme of loneliness, no one can remain as separate, as you become That which is loneliness. But loneliness itself doesn't know loneliness.

[pointing to Mary] She is talking about being extreme love, but by being extreme love, you don't know love anymore. It's all concepts. Don't listen to it. Nothing can make you what you are. Even extreme concepts are concepts.

Here, now, it's so extreme because you are that extreme, absolute existence. You cannot lose it. You are it, and you can never leave it. By whatever extreme, you can never become it. It cannot get more extreme than it is here and now. This is extreme realization of That which is the extreme Self! [Mary screams with laughter. The rest of the group is silent.]

AIKO: I can understand her. I have the same problem with words. I am in love with "love." And we don't want to leave it because it is so beautiful.

KARL: Yeah, it's a beautiful prison.

AIKO: It's a trap.

KARL: That oneness is such a beautiful trap. I am here to point to that trap you are in. You are trapped in the beauty, in the idea of "beauty." But this is a temporary trap. You will drop out of it again. Don't worry. [group laughs] This temporary heaven is hell. You have to see heaven as hell. So don't worry. Heaven will be gone and hell will be back.

LIZ: The opposite of love is hate. It comes, it goes, it comes, it goes. You do drop out of the illusion.

AIKO: Yeah, but you can nourish it. Endlessly.

KARL: By effort, you can stay with it a bit longer. If you pay a bit more attention to oneness, you can stay a bit longer.

MARY: That's not what I was saying, by the way.

KARL: Yeah, yeah, yeah. You never said anything.

MARY: Okay, that's true.

THERESE: It seems like we try to make a difference between "loneliness" and "aloneness." Loneliness has suffering in it, and aloneness is a place where—

KARL: You make aloneness "all one." There is no one alone anymore. There is no loneliness. Whatever. It's all blah, blah, blah. Just forget it. Forget it and be happy.

That's why everyone is pointing to the deep sleep state, because in it, there is no such thing as "divine love," or any idea of whatever. But you still say, "Ah, wonderful," even though you don't know what is so wonderful. There is a total absence of an absence of "me," of one who defines anything. Even to call it "deep sleep" is a definition, but in deep sleep, there is no definition of deep sleep.

So be That which is in deep sleep as That which is here, now—Absolute. Absolute from any idea of "to be" or "not to be," in spite of knowing or not knowing, in spite of defining yourself or not defining yourself, you are. Never because. So be That, here, now, what you are in deep sleep, absolutely independent of any idea of existence or non-existence.

SOFIA: But Ramana said that it is beyond deep sleep.

KARL: Yes, but deep sleep is already not so bad. [group laughs]

MARY: So, is that a key?

KARL: Pointer! They call it a "pointer," but no pointer can make you what you are. That's another pointer. [group laughs] Forget Ramana. I don't want to hear anything about Ramana anymore. Here and now. And no Ali Baba.

MARY: Okay, how about an image?

KARL: What image?

MARY: The Kaaba, the Temple of Truth. You don't like the word *truth*. What word can I use? There was the Kaaba, Ramana said, others have said, and there's infinite ways of coming to this one Kaaba, infinite, from infinite directions.

KARL: What an idea, that you can go there.

MARY: But there's only one way in.

KARL: What way in? No way in.

MONIKA: The dirtiest thought on earth.

MARY: There's only one way in.

KARL: No way in. There's only one way out—no way out.

MARY: Okay. So that's the ultimate and last concept.

KARL: Ultimate? There's no ultimate.

MARY: [starting to laugh] It's too much!

KARL: "Ulti-mate." The ultimate mate? The ultimate love. [sings] "My soul mate. I met my soul mate—in heaven."

[Mary is giggling more and more. Others are noticing. Then she cracks up laughing. The whole group erupts with laughter.]

KARL: She went through it.

GROUP: She went through it! She is finished! She got it. [laughter and sighs of relief]

KARL: The devil is in love with his own grandmother.

[Mary continues to laugh.]

Erasing the Questioner

VICKI: I have a question. From this [holds up fist], comes this [thumb up], and then this [fingers up]?

KARL: You never left this [holds up fist]. That's the point. This [thumb up] is already a phantom dream. The dreamer is "I" [thumb], "am" [thumb and index finger up], "dreaming" [thumb, index, and middle fingers up]. It's all boom, boom, boom [thumb and fingers in and out, in and out].

You never went from there [fist]. You never went to there [thumb], there [thumb and index finger], or there [thumb, index, and middle fingers]. All this is dream-like. You never left That which is home [fist], because you are home itself. You cannot leave home, because there is no one at home. This [thumb] is the first tenant, "I." Out of that tenant, come tendencies.

VICKI: So all this [wiggles fingers] is this [fist]?

KARL: All is this [fist]. You are the absolute dreamer who dreams a dreamer. This is the dream of a dreamer. Already a dreamer is a dream, but you are that absolute Heart. The dreamer, as "I," comes out of that Absolute, as a dream already. Part of the dream is "I," then out of that comes "I am"-ness, as consciousness, as the Creator. And out of that Creator comes all that you can create. All three, this trinity of Father, Holy Spirit, and Son, is all a dream. Only Heart is.

Even on the cross, Jesus pointed to the Heart of existence. When he was on the cross he said, "Father, why have you forsaken me?" He was pointing out that not even the Father can help you, as you are on the cross of existence itself. There is no father who can help you. That Godlessness, which is Heart itself, doesn't know any Heart. No one can help That which you are.

The beauty of it is that you never needed any help. In essence, you are all of this—you are God, the Father, the first idea of "awareness," Source, the "Father" idea; you are the "I am" as Holy Spirit; and you are the "I am so"-ness as Son, as Jesus. You are all this, in essence, as you are the *I* of the "I," the *I am* of the "I-am," and the *I am so* of the "I am so." You are always That which is existence itself, what is Heart of whatever is and is not.

In this sense, you are That which is emptiness and you are That which is fullness. But you are not emptiness and you are not fullness. So be That, as you cannot *not* be it. By whatever you try, you cannot leave what you are. There is no advantage to be here, there, or there, and no disadvantage.

Whatever idea of advantage, or whoever tells you this is like "awareness" or something special, whenever you make a landing place, you are separating yourself from something else, from That which is separation. Whenever you make a landing place, you separate yourself from That. By making emptiness what you are, you separate yourself from fullness. Whatever you define, whatever "divine" idea you have, is separation. But you cannot separate yourself.

NATARAJAN: Why do people say the process of Self-inquiry works when we know the right answer in advance? It's so confusing for my mind.

KARL: For the mind, everything is confusing. Because it is confusion.

NATARAJAN: When I hear of Self-inquiry, it's supposed to be this innocent search into yourself, looking at your thoughts, asking, "Who are you?" What's the point, when we know the answer?

KARL: But this is a senseless question. You can only look for something that you know. Otherwise, you wouldn't look for it. You can only *not* know because you know it. You can only look for something because you already know what you're looking for. Otherwise, you wouldn't look for it.

NATARAJAN: This I couldn't do.

KARL: The moment that you get that, you are not there anymore.

NATARAJAN: So how does Self-inquiry work?

KARL: It works like this.

NATARAJAN: I don't understand. I feel very stupid.

KARL: Yeah, in the absolute non-understanding, you understand. In the absolute stupidity, in the absolute darkness, in the absolute absence of light, of knowing or not knowing, you know. As you see in a split second, in spite of knowing or not knowing, you are, never because. In spite of stupidity, in spite of ignorance, in spite of whatever relative knowledge or understanding or insight, whatever you can name, you are—never because.

This is what "Who am I?" is always pointing to, that mystery, that "in spite." Questioning the questioner all the time with "Who am I?" and getting no answer, never ever, it becomes an answerlessness. And in the answerlessness, the questioner gets annihilated. It's a nice concept.

This was the way of Ramana—"Who am I?" In the question, you burn out, because in the question, there is no history. When there is absolutely no answer to the question, you cannot make a history of an answer. You cannot make something of it if you cannot experience a history. You cannot experience the answer of the question mark, the mystery, which is always after "Who am I?" That "Who am I?" is always there. So there is no time and even non-time—there's the total absence of an idea which comes through an answer. There is no answer that it can give you, because there is no answer. This absolute absence of any answer erases the questioner.

NATARAJAN: So it's an unanswerable question, like a *koan.*

KARL: It's a *koan,* an absolute *koan.*

NATARAJAN: I went through my mind. There was an answer, "I am the Self." Then I start to imagine what the Self is.

KARL: Again it starts. *Whatever* you define. That's why I'm always hammering, even the concept of divine love. All these answers mean nothing. They will simply make a history out of it. Whatever answer you give, it's history. It's time-bound. It's framed. The mystery, the total question mark, the absolute absence of anything, sometimes sounds very beautiful, blah, blah, blah. But it's still blah, blah, blah. Because only the absolute "no answer"—that's the only answer. This is annihilating the questioner.

Twenty-four hours a day, three hundred sixty-five days a year, whatever second there exists, the question should be, That which you are. This question is meditation itself—meditating about the meditator himself and not getting an answer. And then you will see, there will be no expectation after a while. There is nothing to expect.

In meditation, there is "I am" meditating about what is "I am," but without expectation of an answer. Without the answer, there is only meditation but no meditator. That is meditation. Everything else—whatever is doing something for an answer, where there is expectation of getting something out if it—is not meditation.

NATARAJAN: No need to close your eyes?

KARL: No. That's why I really like Buddhism. You have to open your eyes. You have to see. You have to meditate about That, but not with closed eyes. You don't want to escape. You have to face That which is—not to escape it with closed eyes into some nice, cozy oneness, or emptiness, or whatever. Face it! This is what you are.

You have to see the form and the non-form in the same moment. You see that That which is form is formless and you are That which is seeing that form—you are the Source of both. You are emptiness and fullness, or That which is form and non-form, as both are there as what you are, space-like and That which isn't even form. But you are not form and you are not even space.

Whatever you define, you cannot find. It's always like this. "Who am I?" is like, "Who is seeing?" You cannot find it. There is nothing. There is no one to find. In that not finding yourself, you find that you cannot be found in anything anywhere, anytime. So, in absolutely not finding yourself, you rest. But this is not like a place you land. This is absolute not knowing. This is the total freedom of not knowing, not of some definition of whatever "divine tralalala." [group laughs] "Thank God no one knows that my name is Rumplestiltskin."

ANNA: When you speak about infinite realization, is this a dreaming realization?

KARL: Whatever you can realize is a dream.

ANNA: And I am a part of that dream?

KARL: That is realization—that whatever you can realize is a dream. That which is realizing itself, you can never realize. Whatever you can realize is not what you are. Sounds good, huh?

ANNA: Very good. [group laughs]

KARL: So there is no ending to it. Self-inquiry of that consciousness is infinite. That "I am" meditating about That which is "I am" is the realization of what you are, and it will never stop because it never started. So you cannot wait for anything to come, because there will be nothing that will ever come for That which you are. There will never be an answer for the question "Who am I?"

But the "Who am I?" question will still be there as "I am who?" or "Who am I?" These are two directions, and they will always vary. One says, "I am who?" and the other says, "Who am I?" "I am who?" "Who am I?" This is infinite. This is the realization of what you are, coming out of starting to dream.

Waking up to awareness, the dream starts. Out of "I" comes, "I am who?" and then, in one moment in time, comes, "Who am I?" That's all. The spider wakes up to awareness, spins a network of the universe, and then withdraws it again.

But it never left the Heart. All is Heart, as Heart is what you are. This you cannot leave. There is nothing to leave. All that is, is what you are. It is called "immense peace," and it's as solid as solid can be, because it is unmovable. It's in spite of whatever you know or don't know, in spite of whatever comes and goes, in spite of any idea or no idea of what you are. Hallelujah.

The beauty of this is you don't have to like yourself to be yourself. You don't even have to love yourself to be yourself. Imagine! You may even hate yourself. It makes no difference. Imagine! It makes no difference. We all have to sit for a while. Don't worry. It's a sit-in. Ha.

Some more questions? No? Okay. Thank you very much.

A WOMAN: May I just make an announcement? In case anyone doesn't know, you may order *satsang* recordings on CD from me.

GEORG: Wrong day! [group laughs]

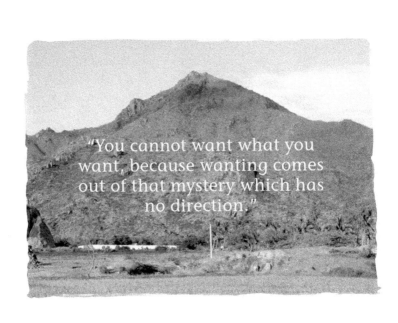

"You cannot want what you want, because wanting comes out of that mystery which has no direction."

January 16

Without a Second, There is Freedom; or, the End of "Free Will"

The Directionlessness of Self

KARL: Hallo!

BERTA: Karl, I brought some friends, so make a good impression. [group laughs]

FRANCESCO: Please!

KARL: She's warning me, if I don't do it, she'll beat me up again. [group laughs] "How dare you not be good today! Better be good today!" Otherwise, I cannot show my face again in Amsterdam!

BERTA: Ya!

KARL: That's really asking for something! Who knows? Come in! Come in, Brazil! Come in, then you can look out. *Merci Beaucoup. Danke schön.* What can I do for you?

MRS. ANGELINA: I have no idea!

KARL: Me neither, so we are in the same boat. I don't know how to help you, and you don't know how to be helped. That sounds good.

ANNA: Karl, could I start with a question? Actually, many times I have wondered, whether being in the being—

KARL: Being in the being?

ANNA: Being in the being, is it so, that that will also have an influence or an effect or something like that on the personal structure of the normal person?

KARL: No, it cannot, because there is no person anymore. Never was.

ANNA: You know what I mean.

KARL: I know what you mean. There was a structure before, but there was no person. That's all. What can change then?

ANNA: Not change, but sort of influence, sort of effect, because it's interrelated.

KARL: There is no cause and interrelation between That which is the essence of what you are and That which is realization of it. You cannot make an influence. It has no cause and effect. It may change something, but not because of that. Whoever said, "Because of this, something changed"—it was not that.

ANNA: But it's also not an automatic—

KARL: Side-effect?

ANNA: Side-effect, yeah.

KARL: Of a disease? The enlightenment disease? And you have side-effects? That is what enlightenment is, really, that awakening from identified consciousness to non-identified consciousness. Out of this you can make side-effects, out of that identified consciousness as a person then becoming cosmic consciousness. Then you can say there are energetic changes and other things to talk about.

That you can talk about, but not about That, because That is in spite of "whatever," never because. But whatever is because of something you have done, *sadhana*, Self-inquiry, or whatever, you go from identification to non-identification, from separation to oneness, all that you can go to—about *that* you can talk and make side-remarks.

ANNA: But the manifestation of the form as such, as we are all, in a sense, is it not, let me say, sort of automatically manipulated?

KARL: Automatically manipulated? [group laughs] How can there be an automatic manipulation? I have no idea what it means.

ANNA: Actually, basically, not.

KARL: Only when it's not automatic, there's manipulation. When it's automatic, then there's no manipulation. It doesn't fit together.

ANNA: Then let's say "natural."

KARL: But when it's natural, there is no manipulation either. When it's natural, everything is natural, so nothing gets manipulated by anything. You cannot put these two together.

"Manipulation" is a concept coming out that "me-controller" idea of an advantage, and then you have the idea that you take everything as *your* doing. But these are ideas. Nature never manipulates nature, because there are not two. It needs two for manipulation.

But as there is only one nature, it cannot manipulate itself. So it stops. When there is only consciousness, there is the end of manipulation. There is no side-effect anymore. There is no influence whatever from one to the other.

ANNA: I see, it's just a thing like seeing the manifestations and seeing the absolute consciousness. They are not two, I know that, but it's a sort of business—that is that, and this is this.

KARL: That's your concept.

ANNA: It's another concept. Yeah.

KARL: Consciousness in whatever form or shape is still consciousness, and consciousness that is formless is still consciousness. Pure consciousness, awareness, is simply the trinity of "I"-awareness, "I am"-ness as formless, and "I am so"-ness as form. This all is consciousness, which is the realization of That which is Self.

So you cannot say there is any manipulation in the whole game. There is not even an interrelation, in a way, because there is nothing relating to something else. Consciousness is simply as solid as solid can be.

ANNA: But if you take the example of the spider and the web, this is actually the same, and the web can be done in such and such a way.

KARL: But there is no one who decides it. It's a directionlessness of Self. There's a freedom of direction, there's a freedom of will, so you may say it's a natural spinning. But there is no manipulation in anything, as there is no direction in anything. There is no will at all, not even God's will.

ANNA: It just happens, just like that.

KARL: It is as it is. But not because of anyone who wants anything. You cannot want what you want, because wanting comes out of the mystery which has no direction. You may say that the totality of the moment is dictating the next moment, and moment by moment is dictated by that totality. But not by any wish or by any seeing what to do. There is no concept of how it has to be. It simply realizes itself, moment by moment, not knowing why. There is no "why" in it.

ANNA: And one can't even say, "influence."

KARL: No.

ANNA: A sort of conscious, unconscious influence.

KARL: You may say there's a *karmic* consciousness, like an action-reaction chain, that you can see. When there is an action, there's a reaction. But That which is acting and That which is reacting are no different. And there is no intention in action, and there is no reaction in reaction. There is meditation of "I am"-ness as consciousness meditating. This is like realization of That which is Self. But there is no intention in anything.

All this is Self-experience or Self-realization; there is nothing that is not. The Self cannot decide how to realize. Helplessness is what is your nature. You are in a total helplessness or hopelessness. Selflessness, which has no direction, can never decide what comes next.

ANNA: So it's just remaining in helplessness, and that's all.

KARL: Yes. Simply see that whatever is, is already there. Nothing comes and nothing goes. When nothing comes and nothing goes, when there is no birth and death, whatever comes and goes is not coming and not going. So then who is there who has to control something that's not even there?

Maybe here, now, the only thing that can die is the idea of "birth"—which includes ideas of coming and going, of dying, of mortality and immortality, of infinite and finite—these all die in the split second that you see that nothing is ever born, so nothing will ever die.

But no one can take that, because in a split second, you are gone. You are living out of the idea that you were born and may die. But in that split second you see that nothing has ever happened to what you are, or will happen, and you see that you are not born so there is no death for you, because existence never comes and never goes. What then? That's *Zen*. No, *Zazen*.

MATTIAS: Is there a certain order, although there is no intention, for dropping these three—the "I," the "I am," and the "I am so-and-so"—or can it happen altogether—gone?

KARL: Every night they drop together.

MATTIAS: But you are saying that, first there is the personal consciousness [holds up thumb, index, and middle fingers], or consciousness as an imagined person, and then there is the universal consciousness [holds up thumb and index finger], and then there is "I" [holds up thumb], and I thought this was happening somehow before—

KARL: No, it's not dropping, actually. By "dropping," it is meant that you see that there is nothing that can drop. It needs something to be born that can drop, but as you see nothing came and nothing will go, this is a total drop of it. That's the total drop of all three of these. If you are talking about first dropping, "I am so-and-so" and go to, "I am," that's all in the realm of effort, *sadhana*, and the interaction of consciousness.

MATTIAS: But there is no need so that this recognition can happen?

KARL: Not out of need. It never comes out of need. There is no rule in it. It is always unique. But I tell you again, every night it drops. You know it so well.

CHARLES: Even the awareness drops?

KARL: Yeah, of course. You cannot remember deep sleep. Awareness drops. You go back to That which you are. It's a natural thing. As you fall into sleep, you die into That which you are. Let die what can die, as it was never there, and you go to that place that is your nature where nothing happens. Never. Everyone knows it so well. This is nothing new that I'm telling you here. Every night you go to That which is your nature.

When you wake up, you go to that which wakes up. You love what wakes up, and then you get involved in that, so you are born. Every morning, you give birth to the idea that you are born again. In deep sleep, there is no one left who has any idea of being born or not born. There's simply no question.

But every morning you take the crazy idea that you are born, again as real. So the joke starts again every morning! And then the whole day, you want to get out of it! [group laughs]

MATTIAS: Is it true that something really extreme has to happen in order to recognize it?

KARL: For sure not.

MATTIAS: Nothing? No death experience, nothing terrifying?

KARL: All that belongs to the realm of moving from, "I am so"-ness to "I am"-ness and back. This comes and goes; the ping pong movement is always there. From identification to non-identification, there are extreme experiences—of love, of diving into the "whatever."

"The cosmic 'whatever' went into me and exploded into the star system! And then I came back. I found the pearl and now I want to share it!" [group laughs]

MATTIAS: I don't mean that. I mean in an extreme situation, like an accident or as you reported in your book.

KARL: Every night you have this accident. Don't worry. It's an extreme accident in which everything drops in front of you, and you are again without any glue to "whatever." In the morning, the glue wakes up again. You have a clue that you exist. You have an idea of "existence." Then you are glued on that again. So you fall in love every morning with your existence. And at night, you fall out of it.

So, as I always sit here and tell you, you cannot *not* fall in love with what you are, as you are not different from what wakes up, what is in front of you. You cannot *not* love what you are. You have to be, in spite of that lover and beloved, what you are, not because some lover and beloved has to go.

It will always happen again. Every morning. Otherwise, there was Jesus, there were so many sages, there was Buddha, all this—if it really would help to know yourself, there would be nothing left! Huh? Isn't that it? So many selves sitting here, and it didn't help! Still sitting here!

MATTIAS: I was wondering about this. So many sages in India for centuries and centuries, and nothing happened.

KARL: Even in Europe, there were so many! Go to the churches and see the statues of saints and holy people. But that's the beauty of it. It cannot be controlled by any knowing or not knowing. This will go on forever [holds up fingers and then folds them back into fist, over and over, to symbolize infinite movement between states of consciousness]; there is no way out of it. As infinite as you are as the Absolute, that is how infinite is realization. There is no stopping it, because it never started. So what?!

CHARLES: [holding up his fingers and then making a fist] Is this again and again?

KARL: There is not again and again. There is at once! There is a solid block of realization. And nothing comes and goes.

CHARLES: Who sees that?

KARL: There is no seeing. You are That. There is no seeing in it. The seeing is part of an aspect of that realization, but there is no seeing in it. There is simply, absolutely being That. It's what is meant by *I Am That*. Finished.

What Is Karl? You Must be Joking!

BERTA: Hey, but Karl, you also wake up in the morning.

KARL: No, no, no. That's not true. I never wake up, because I never went to sleep.

BERTA: All right, I'm going to come watch you tonight! [group laughs]

KARL: You will only see this body sleep, but you won't see Karl, as you don't see Karl here. You only see a body image, that's all. An idea of an image. The rest you have to speculate. You have to make a speculation—there is a Karl in some "whatever." What is Karl? A space-like entity? A cloud? An idea? What is Karl? A body? Do you know who Karl is? Then you know me.

BERTA: Well, I see your body-mind structure.

KARL: Yeah, that you take as Karl. That's all

BERTA: You call it "Karl."

KARL: No, I am not calling it "Karl." I am calling it "Me-steak." [slaps his leg] This is my steak. But I don't take it as a "mis-take." I'm not being mistaken to take that steak as me, as what I am. It's there, so I enjoy it. It will be eaten up by existence soon enough.

So nothing goes to sleep at night. There's simply the dropping of the "body" idea, and then some "I am" idea, and then the awareness goes. And then there is That which you are, without it, in spite of it. And then in the morning it wakes up again. Because you cannot *not* wake up.

KRISTOPH: So this means that you do not lose consciousness when you fall asleep?

KARL: Even consciousness drops, because even consciousness is part of it.

KRISTOPH: I don't understand. You get unconscious?

KARL: No, there is no one who is unconscious. There is simply That which you are without any experience of experience or non-experience. Both are gone.

KRISTOPH: But do you stay present?

KARL: There is no presence because That which you are has no presence. It needs two for presence. It needs one experiencer for presence. No one stays in anything. There is a total darkness, mystery, whatever; there is absolute non-experience.

There is no history. There is absolutely no time or non-time in all that.

KRISTOPH: And this is all the time?

KARL: It's here, now. This is what I am.

KRISTOPH: Always?

KARL: There is no break. That's what I meant. It is never asleep and never awake and nothing you can name. The sleeping, the waking, whatever you name, is in it, but it is never in something else. It's a statelessness in which all the states appear. Itself, it has no state. It's a false state, or statelessness, wherein all the "I," "I am," and "I am so-and-so" states appear. All this is a realization of "I am so-and-so"—the state of awareness, the state of "I am"-ness, and the state of "I am so"-ness. But they all appear within that statelessness of Heart, which is whatever you cannot define in any sense. With the first "I," with the first word, you create the whole thing every morning.

KRISTOPH: And how did it happen that you came to that experience, to the true state?

KARL: I never came to it.

KRISTOPH: You always were there?

KARL: I never lost it. It was always there in every moment of every experience. As "I am so-and-so," as "I am"-oneness, even as "I"-awareness, I was still prior to that. In spite of the light, I am. Not because.

KRISTOPH: Yeah, but how about earlier in your life, before—

KARL: It was never my life, so I cannot talk about it. There was the life of this body, you mean. There is a moment-by-moment history of this body-mind organism. Wonderful. There was a time, there's still a time. We can talk now about it now. It needs the illusion of time to make that experience of me and others. This body, other bodies, can appear only in that illusion, or that dream, of time.

KRISTOPH: I'm trying to get it, but I don't.

KARL: I know what you mean, that I'm mean! [group laughs] If you were really interested in that answer, you'd be more—

KRISTOPH: More insistent? But I don't think I can solve it with my mind, that I can get it by my mind through discussion. I feel I need to dive into myself. At some time, it was there, but I lost it or something, so it's not complete.

KARL: I wouldn't say it like this.

ANNA: Could we put it in terms of *sahaja samadhi*, which is a continuous state, and *nirvikalpa samadhi*, which is a state that can come and go?

KARL: All the states, *samadhis*, are in spite of it. That statelessness, whatever is Heart, is in spite of any ideas of *samadhi*, of fleeting states. Whatever you can talk about are fleeting states. Even awareness is a fleeting state.

ROSA: Have you been conscious always of where you are?

KARL: There was never anyone who was conscious, and there was never anyone who was unconscious. So it's futile to talk about what is not there. What to talk about? When there was never anyone who was unawakened, how can we talk about anyone who is awakened? There's here and now no one who is more or less than you.

ROSA: So this is a big joke.

KARL: This is the first joke, and out of that joke, you are joking. You must be joking!

ROSA: That's great, because I was always very serious. [group laughs]

KARL: That is the real joke. That's why I say there is a split second with absolutely no before or after. This [holds up his fist to symbolize Heart] is in spite. There is no awakening, awakening from what? There is simply no way out. Absolutely no way out. But even that is not there. You just have another coffee, because nothing has changed.

There is simply "Aha." Because That which is awareness, or That which is perception itself, is always as pure as at that moment, because in the split second you go to eternal existence. Back to Adam and Eve, or whatever, and you see there was always that perception, pure as it was, in no sense. Always in no sense. There are sensations coming and going, and ideas, but that was, is, as it was. There was no time and even non-time.

ROSA: So I am watching a movie now?

KARL: You are the movie!

ROSA: Yes, I am in it.

KARL: No, you are not *in* it. You *are* the movie. No one was ever in the movie.

ROSA: But you are now in my movie.

KARL: Ah, you are guilty that everyone is here! It's all *your* movie. We found her. You only have to kill her, and everything will be fine. [group laughs] "*My* movie!" If you want to get rid of the movie, kill her. Cross her. We found Jesus again. Cross her.

ROSA: But I'm not going to suffer. [group laughs]

KARL: You will be nailed anyway.

ROSA: That's what you are doing now!

KARL: I'm nailing you on the cross of existence and telling you that you cannot leave what you are, as you are that absolute existence. In horizontal time, in vertical time, and even in That which is the Heart of awareness, you cannot leave what you are. So I am nailing you, here and now, again, as Jesus was nailed.

ROSA: So I'm liberated?

KARL: That's liberation—being nailed on existence. The only way out of that drama you are in is *being* the drama, as the drama doesn't know any drama.

ROSA: I like it.

KARL: Be it. Because if you don't enjoy yourself, there will be no other Self who enjoys you.

ROSA: [laughing] There are many who don't enjoy me.

KARL: Many? Where? What many?

ROSA: Many in me.

KARL: Many in you. Many ideas of yourself. Many images of yourself. But you are not an image.

ROSA: I'm getting rid of them with you.

KARL: Rid of the images? Nothing has to go for That. You simply become that absolute Source from where all the images appear. But yourself, you're not an image. That's why I'm pointing to that split second where you see that you cannot imagine yourself. Whatever came out of an imaginative world, of awareness, light, whatever experience, you are not.

THERESE: So what is all this work, like you find everywhere, the work on the images?

KARL: You keep the images alive. That's called *dharma*-keeping.

THERESE: Again, it's Self-entertainment. But—

KARL: But, but, but—

THERESE: Just—

KARL: There is no just. There is no justice.

AIKO: But I think there is a lot of promise to come somewhere—

KARL: This is fine. It's part of the joke. You laugh about your joke, because you are the trap and you step into your own trap of wanting to gain something. You are the inventor of religion. Whatever religion there is, is because of you, because you have the idea that some knowledge or "whatever" can add something to your nature. You create a religion, all that you can imagine. You are the *dharma*-keeper himself. You are the inventor of the idea of "purity," so it makes you dirty. You are the inventor of "divinity" so it makes you shit. Whatever is, is because of you.

If you want to complain, you find the one! [group laughs] It's fun to complain about yourself, what you have done. So what!

AIKO: [laughing] In no sense.

KARL: In no sense, yeah. So it's not innocent. It's in no sense.

THERESE: Nonsense!

KARL: It's total nonsense, even before nonsense. Absolute nonsense. Just take one letter out.

Prior to guilt, you are absolutely guilty, so that takes the guilty one away. Because no one can take that guilt of being absolutely responsible for That. Only when you are That, there is no one who can be responsible. But no one can take that responsibility of being the Source of whatever is and is not.

Hmm? Anyone here who can take it? I think that everyone here can take it because, as That which you are, there is no problem to take it. But no person, no idea, can take that responsibility. Is there any idea here left that can take it?

As what you are, nothing is more easy than to be what is. But as that which is an image, you can never become That which is the Source of the image, you can never become That which is the image. So there's no way to become what you are.

Heart Is All There Is

BERTA: If there is no way, then we are sitting here for nothing.

KARL: That's fine. Imagine if you would sit here for something?!

BERTA: But I like to have a goal, actually.

KARL: Yeah, you are a goal-keeper. I know. Without a goal, there would be no Berta. Berta will fight for a goal as if for life.

BERTA: It's true.

KARL: Yeah, I tell you. That's the survival system of an image. Without the image of a goal, the image cannot stay. It fears death; it fears existence. It's in an existential crisis, and out of that crisis, it has to have a goal, it has to have a reference point, because without a reference point, it's simply not there. It simply disappears. What a joke—the Almighty, which is Berta, fearing itself, the goallessness.

BERTA: In Amsterdam, I was dying with no goal and I also didn't have the energy to make a goal. And then in the end, I almost didn't have the energy to walk. There was no point in anything.

KARL: Maybe you would be the first Bench Baba of Amsterdam! [group laughs] Maybe you missed it again, Berta!

BERTA: I think so.

KARL: Bench Baba was a holy man [in Tiruvannamalai] who simply laid on a bench for fifty or sixty years, just counting "one, two, three." Total senselessness. But he was a total pointer to That which you are. Many students came from all over India just to see him counting "one, two, three." Like me. [laughs] I'm always counting "one, two, three." [holds up thumb, index finger, and then middle finger]

THERESE: "Karl Yoga"! [group laughs]

MATTIAS: But you added something. There's the three states and the disappearance into the fist. So you have four—four states.

KARL: Does it make the hand different when it opens or it closes? It's still the hand. It's still the Heart. The Heart opening to this [holds up thumb, index finger, and then middle finger] is still the Heart. And closing in at night [closes fist], it's still the Heart. You never lost your Heart. You cannot lose what you are, as you are Heart itself.

So, even as "I am so-and-so," you never lost what you are in what is still the Heart. So all is Heart. Whatever is, is Heart. You cannot lose what you are. At night, you simply go back to the potential. And out of that potential, in the morning, you wake up again to that realization, Self-experience, all the way. You can only experience what you are, in your infinite aspects and forms, and all is Heart, as Heart is all there is.

KLARA: What do you mean when you say "Heart"?

KARL: I mean what I mean! [group laughs]

KLARA: Yeah, what do you mean?

KARL: I'm not talking about the physical heart, or the spiritual heart. I'm talking about the Buddha-nature you are, which cannot be defined, which is the essence of existence—whatever you call it, it is not. But That is what you are. You cannot give it a name, a form, a shape, an idea. Because whatever you could define it as is an image, it cannot fit.

Whenever you define it, you're wanting to frame the Heart, but Heart cannot be framed. You cannot imprison Heart, because Heart is all there is. When there is only Heart, there is no imprisonment for anything. So you cannot imprison it by knowing it or by not knowing it or by whatever idea you have about Heart. You cannot frame it.

That is freedom itself. Freedom, realizing itself in "whatever" is still freedom. Freedom in the idea of being imprisoned is still freedom. Because freedom imprisoned by freedom is still freedom. So Heart in Heart is still Heart.

So, as there is only Heart, and That which is freedom itself is Heart, freedom means there is no second Heart. There is no second edition of existence. As you exist, you cannot doubt, because even in doubting you exist.

This existence, which is totally "in no sense," has no second. Without a second, there is freedom. Without a second, you cannot control anything, not even yourself. There must be two in order to have a controller and one who is controlled.

That is paradise. Paradise means there is no second to control. You cannot control anyone; you cannot be controlled by anyone. So whatever controls you is what you are. Then who cares if you are controlled by what you are? So what? You cannot step out of the absolute control which is the realization of what you are.

That helplessness is sitting here, talking about what you cannot talk about again and again, for centuries, even ages. I have no idea how long this has gone on. It will never stop. The Self never gets tired of talking about the Self. Never, ever will it be satisfied by talking. That is the beauty. You cannot satisfy something that is satisfaction itself. It's so complete. You cannot make it more—or less. So you can talk and talk and talk and sing and sing and sing, blah, blah, blah, and it's totally irrelevant. That's beautiful, that joy!

KLARA: But why don't I feel that?

KARL: Why don't *I*?! There is no feeling. This is being it! It will be not *your* feeling, that's all. You cannot put this feeling or experience in your pocket and say, "my experience of existence." You cannot experience existence. You have to exist. This you cannot own as an experience. It will never be *your* experience.

So now you can hear and see there is no "mine." It will never be *my* experience as *I* cannot own existence. What an idea! Even the idea that there is *my* consciousness—what an idea!—as if you could own consciousness! What bullshit!

AIKO: I feel flat! [group laughs]

KARL: Rolled over.

JUAN: Karl, the idea of "impersonal existence" is so frightening somehow.

KARL: For a person, yes, but not when you are That. There is nothing to be feared. Jesus said that you shouldn't fear what you are. What an idea to fear what you are?!

Jesus was saying that he's an absolute man, he's absolute consciousness, and he's absolute awareness, as he's the Heart of existence, existence itself. So what to fear? But he's not awareness, he's not "I am," and he's not "I am so-and-so"—as he is Heart in whatever circumstance. Heart is all there is. So what to fear? Do you fear to be Heart?

JUAN: The personal fear is great.

KARL: It's too heart. Too hard. Too soft, maybe. You fear to be soft, too fragile, because you have learned that you have to defend yourself, because there is a second, there is a world, there is "me" and the world. "I have to defend myself." So you create armor around yourself, you build a fortress. "Don't touch me!" Then *you* even want to be detached from everything. You do all these techniques and meditations to be, "de-touched." "Don't touch me!" [group laughs]

FRANCESCO: You can laugh!

KARL: But then there is one moment when you fall in love with whatever, a woman or a man, and then the helplessness comes. "Oh, hoo, no!" Then you are really in trouble. Because you see, you cannot *not* fall in love if this happens. The total armor breaks down, falling in love that moment, and whatever you have done to be detached—"oh, shit" again. [group laughs]

Many have that experience. First, dropping out of identification, going to oneness, "I am not doing anything! I am detached! No one can touch me anymore! I'm out of it. The game is over for me. Now, I'm out"—and then, "Oh, no!"

THERESE: So many times when I wake up, there's a feeling like I didn't sleep. There are so many dreams. Suddenly, there is an attack of images.

KARL: Attack of the clones?

THERESE: So many dreams.

KARL: It's a nice title of a movie, *Attack of the Clones*. Every night, she has an attack of the clones. You are cloning yourself, imagining yourself, and then you get attacked back by echoes of your creation.

THERESE: I mean, when I wake up, I feel I could write movies, I tell you.

KARL: Yeah, why not? So what, then? It's a night circus? "Circus Thérèse!" Soon they will tape your brain at night, the dreams, and make movies out of it. Nightmares. Power movies. Love movies. Emotional movies. Devotional movies. Look at it, it's all here. Out of that dream comes everything.

A WOMAN: So, the second you wake up, the dreams appear as real?

KARL: You may say the body is still in that state; it's all part of the body. All those images come out of the energy of "I am"-ness, or whatever formless body, the energy which is sitting here. There's a memory effect, and there's echoes of information and dreams and movies, echoes of the day, echoes of the night dreams. It's all echoes.

WOMAN: It's still very much identifying with it.

KARL: What's wrong with identification? When there is no one who can be identified, what's wrong with identification? Why do you feel you need to be unidentified to what you are? Who needs that to change?

But with the dream come experiences of happiness and unhappiness, of heaven and hell. All is included in the total program of your imagination, because it all comes in the package of polarities and the shadows between it, the variations of shades and "whatever." But it's all you and all by you, you are the absolute Source of all that. This is all That which is your realization, whatever it is. And there is no way out of it. It makes no difference if you go to this state or that state, that dimension or that understanding. As all the understanding and non-understanding is because you are, and they are all there because you are That which is the absolute Self.

So what has to come and what has to change? There is no advantage in anything. This "person" is only there because you have the idea of an advantage in understanding or even knowing yourself, that there would be an advantage for what you are.

This first advantage idea is simply an image, a phantom. Even the idea of "consciousness" is promising you something that it cannot deliver. Even consciousness cannot make you more happy than you are. It cannot give you more knowledge, as you are That which is knowledge already. And there is consciousness promising you something more, or less—promising you that if you just meditate enough you will disappear and then you will be happy. You have to go so that you can be happy!

A MAN: Yeah, that's a weird one, isn't it?

KARL: It's a nice problem. You never solve it. [group laughs] "Oh, if I only had this blank mind! If I only controlled thoughts, I would be happy!"

ROSA: I have a blank mind often.

KARL: Every night you have a blank mind.

ROSA: [laughing] No, no, sometimes—

KARL: Is this Alzheimer's? [group laughs]

ROSA: Maybe something like that. So it's not dead.

KARL: No, you are not dead.

ROSA: [laughing] Not yet.

KARL: No, it's not the absence of something. In his writings, Wei Wu Wei always made it really hard. "It has to be the absence of the presence of an object, and even the absence of the absence of the presence of any object and image of what you would call the only presence of That which is Self, but this presence has no presence because there is no Self to experience that presence of that presence of that omnipresence of that Self!" [group laughs] Sounds good, huh?

ROSA: So it's not even *neti-neti?*

KARL: It's neti-*neti-neti.* [group laughs] It's actually *no* no. It's an *absolute no* to no. You become a no-no.

ROSA: But then there is a yes.

KARL: Yeah, that's a yes. So it's an absolute yes to existence, and this is acceptance. An *absolute no* no—an *absolute no* to no—and that's an absolute yes. And then you are That which is existence in an absolute acceptance, as that yes is as absolute as a no-no. But as long as there is one who says "yes" or "no," you're in trouble. So no-no includes yes, but yes alone always has an opposite.

ROSA: So it's a yes to no-no?

KARL: It's a no-no. [group laughs] Has to become a no-no.

FRANCESCO: This is basic.

KARL: Nitty-gritty. A no-no. Then you are full on.

ROSA: But I can't say "I am no-no," because then I can fall into the trap.

KARL: As I said, you have to *be* the no-no. The absolute no-no, in the absolute absence of that no-no. If you are that paradox, it's like the *koan* again. When you are the *koan*, there is no *koan* anymore. But as long as there is one who has a *koan*, the *koan* you cannot dissolve. The moment you drop that, you are the *koan* and there is no *koan* anymore. There is total understanding, because you are understanding, but as long as there is one who wants to understand the *koan*, you will never dissolve the *koan*.

So you sit in front of a wall and meditate on the *koan*, "Who am I?" This is a *koan*, because you cannot dissolve that. The *koan*, "Who am I?" drops when the meditation of the meditator drops. When both are in the mystery, you become the mystery. The dropping of that is simply like a side-effect.

By being what you are, everything drops, because there never was anything before or after what you are. So nothing drops because there is nothing to drop. No ocean, no wave, nothing to come, nothing to go.

ROSA: What is the effect of drugs?

KARL: Drugs? It's like meditation. The intention of taking drugs is to go to that "I"-lessness, to that blankness, to that non-doership, that irresponsibility. You are simply spaced out by whatever drug you take. Meditation is the same. As long as meditation is because of that, meditation becomes a drug. It's all a drug. Whatever you do, whatever you long for, you want to have this drug for being happy all the time, or you want to step out of the misery of that intention. With a drug, the one who has an intention drops, it's simply gone.

ROSA: So if I don't want to hear you anymore, I close my eyes and meditate. So that is then my escape.

KARL: I don't know. Yeah, you can try. [group laughs] Anyway, I'm not talking to ghosts. I am always talking to That understanding which is already there, so it doesn't matter. It's not in your hands anyway. Whether you give attention or not, it's not *your* attention anyway. So don't worry. Escape.

ROSA: I am now proud that I understand this.

KARL: Welcome.

ROSA: It's fun.

KARL: It's really like this. Whatever understanding that can come, will go again, so what to do with it? So again, in spite of understanding or not understanding, you are That. Never because. It will never be *your* understanding anyway. Because when there is understanding itself, there is no "me" left. It will not be in *your* presence. When you are That which is home itself, there is no one at home. So you'd better not look for it. Because when there is home, you will not be there.

BERTA: I know a nice joke about this. There were two madmen, and one madman goes to visit the other—

KARL: "Enlightened ones!" Last time, you said, "Two enlightened friends."

BERTA: Oh, okay. [group laughs] Made them laugh anyway!

KARL: Enlightened is a better joke.

BERTA: So one enlightened one rings the bell and the door opens and the other one says, "I'm not at home!" "Oh," says the first one, "I'm happy that I didn't come!" [group laughs]

KARL: "Wake me up before you go." Everything okay? Hi! Have a question? Something?

KRISTOPH: Not now.

KARL: Not now. Now, later. *The Power of Now* later. [group laughs] Maybe you?

Grace Without Mercy

A British WOMAN: I was just wondering, well, what do you do? I mean, yeah, the paradox and the polarities and all that sort of thing, and when you're here you don't know you're here because you don't exist.

KARL: I didn't say that you don't exist.

WOMAN: Well, you don't know about it.

KARL: I just told you, you cannot—

WOMAN: It doesn't matter! It's just so many *words*, and they don't help. [group laughs]

KARL: I hope so, I hope so! I actually say, I hope it doesn't help. Because imagine if I could help you. You would be something I could help!

WOMAN: I imagine that I'm moving toward trying to understand.

KARL: Yeah, I know! That's the problem.

WOMAN: That has something to do with moving in a direction, which you can call helpful or whatever. I don't know whether talking about it is of any use at all, and yet, here I am.

KARL: That's a problem.

WOMAN: It's just irritating! [group laughs]

KARL: That's granted. I'm not here to make anything clear. It's more like a confusion that gets bigger. That's the point. Maybe you can get to the experience that—in spite of order or not order, in spite of understanding—you are, and not because of anything. You are even the total confusion of not knowing what you are and what you are not—and you still are what you are. It doesn't matter.

WOMAN: So then this "by-product," as you call it, is that an accident?

KARL: My talk goes to That, so that, by words, That which is understanding already can simply be there, without that ghost "me."

WOMAN: I don't understand what on earth you're talking about! [group laughs] Sometimes I do, but I mean, you talk very fast.

KARL: Yeah, I tell you!

WOMAN: And you're German! [group laughs]

MATTIAS: In German he talks even faster!

KARL: He says, just be lucky that I am not talking in German, then it would be double speed.

British WOMAN: So the frustration is that it goes round and it's as if something should land, but it never does.

KARL: But that "not landing" is landing. Then you may absolutely see there is no place to land. I am like just a flying carpet with no landing place. A magic carpet. No one sits on it. I am just a carpet that has no place to land.

WOMAN: I like the whole thing you talk about that you don't sleep at night. You know, so, I wake up. Is there any choice in that matter?

KARL: No, you cannot *not* wake up to what you are.

WOMAN: So I do what I do and he does what he does.

KARL: No, that's the very point. You cannot want what you want, and you cannot first want what you do before you want what you do.

WOMAN: Say that again. [group laughs]

MATTIAS: In slow motion!
KARL: Slow motion. Einstein was always pointing to that, he could only bear humanity by seeing that humanity cannot want what humanity wants. So, all the wars, disasters, all the ugly stuff and evil things, he could only bear with "whatever," his fragile heart—
British WOMAN: Yeah, he was horrible to his wife!
KARL: Yeah, I tell you. He was so frustrated that he could not help himself. But acceptance came within him to see that he could not want what he wants. So whatever "came," came out of the totality, as a total order.

It's like a demand, you have to do it. You have no choice. You cannot be other than what you are, even as a body-mind organism. There is no other way.
WOMAN: Even whatever understanding his was, beating up on his wife is included in that?
KARL: Everything. Whatever.
WOMAN: Pisses me off.
KARL: Yeah. Peace is "peacing" you off.
WOMAN: Well, I don't give a shit about people's understanding, I care more about if they're kind to each other, to be honest.
KARL: You what?
WOMAN: I care more—
KARL: I know.
WOMAN: I care more if somebody is kind to somebody else than if they're enlightened.
KARL: If they are enlightened, they are not kind. I hope not. Because the ruthlessness that comes with this, the concernlessness, is not nice.
WOMAN: So what do you do about that?
KARL: I have no idea. That compassion is so blind, so radical, and so without caring. This concernlessness, this ruthlessness, is not nice. This is grace without mercy. There is no mercy and no kindness and no bliss in it. It is so radical—you cannot imagine.
WOMAN: I'm having difficulty with that.
KARL: Of course, you have to, because you will be erased.
WOMAN: What do you mean?
KARL: You will be annihilated by the grace that you are, because it will simply take the idea of "you" away. So you don't like it, for sure. You can never

like it—to be killed by grace. How can you like it? You don't have to like it, to be it.

You create standards. "If I had a choice, I'd rather like this coming as a nice, kindly, 'whatever,' understanding." But in the stories I hear, it is often like disaster, despair, always frustration, depression—all that coming to the nitty-gritty of existence, to the total nakedness of being. And then it simply is there, the total absence of any idea of what you are, not by any heavenly experience of nectar coming, floating into your so-called existence.

WOMAN: It seems this is often through some kind of extreme suffering. Is this what you're talking about?

KARL: Yeah, it's like Saint John of the Cross and "the dark night of the soul."

WOMAN: Many.

KARL: Yeah, many. The stories are full of this.

WOMAN: Why is that?

KARL: Because this is a total depression, a vacuum of sense. It's a total senselessness of existence, and no one can bear that. In that vacuum, in that desert, in that void of sense, you simply freak out, because you have no hold anymore.

WOMAN: Everything collapses.

KARL: Everything is collapsing. You have no landing place, no place to go to, nothing. This is unbearable for a person. But that is the only way out of that idea.

WOMAN: That's the only way?

KARL: Yeah, absolutely.

WOMAN: Is that what happened to you?

KARL: Yep.

WOMAN: You went into an extreme of suffering?

KARL: Absolutely.

WOMAN: So why don't you talk about it?

KARL: The "me-graine"?

WOMAN: It's interesting. You had migraines?

KARL: It's called "me-graine." The "me" was grained.

WOMAN: That to me is interesting. What happened to you in, whatever it was, I don't know, in that implosion, in that going down? I'm interested as a human, on a human level.

KARL: Normally, I don't speak about it because there is no use for it, because it's simply like a story. I have to really make an effort to go back to, whatever, experiences, because in spite of them, there was always That which I am. I have no idea. But we can talk about it. It makes no difference. So, maybe in the late seventies, there are these experiences of light, "life experiences," you may call them, which are really death experiences. You die. Totally. In "whatever." This darkness of existence is eating you up, and you remain at that, and then there is perception that is pure light, or "whatever."

WOMAN: Did it happen through your life circumstances?

KARL: No.

WOMAN: Did it just kind of happen in the middle of the night, or whatever?

KARL: In the middle of night. In a dream.

WOMAN: It was nothing to do with anything that was happening?

KARL: No, it was like a Castaneda technique, to find your hands in a dream. You make a lucid dream where you control your hands. You remember that you are dreaming and you lift your hands and look at them.

FRANCESCO: This is good.

KARL: That's very good. You may die with that.

FRANCESCO: Oh, okay.

KARL: Then you start dying because that awareness wakes up. You become aware that you are aware. And then something is, like, triggered. I don't know. Then that darkness comes and eats you up. Because you die in it. You simply die, but "aware" dying.

British WOMAN: The "me" dies?

KARL: Whatever form, whatever idea, dies.

WOMAN: Is that very painful?

KARL: You fight like hell. You fight for your life as nothing ever, this is your survival system. You fight against that with whatever is your energy, and then after hours, when everything is gone, there's a moment of resignation and then you simply resign yourself into That. "Okay." And then it—wah!—all becomes light. Before, it's like you fight against yourself, against that darkness of being beaten, eaten up. But then there is a moment of total acceptance, of death. Then suddenly, you are that light. You went through the eye of the needle because you became nothing, and then out of the ashes, the phoenix rises again. You are that light.

Actually, this is only the start. This awareness happens then, because you always wake up as the body, then the form comes back with, "all this." Then all the migraines, body experiences, side-effects happen. But this is all part of consciousness going from identification to non-identification, from the form to the non-form, from the form of energy to energy itself.

With all these changes, every cell in your body becomes aware of the awareness. So it wakes up to That which is energy. It becomes very painful. Body aching, migraine, and all that, what you may call "*kundalini* rising," blah, blah, blah, until the snake is totally awake, like this column of light.

WOMAN: What is the point of it?

KARL: I have no idea. That is what I mean. That's all we can talk about. This is all phenomena. It's still in the time frame of coming and going.

WOMAN: It does seem like there's a pull. I feel a pull to that.

KARL: Yeah, because it's interesting, because you're so in love with your experiences, you want to make it more of a collection of experiences, of excitement. You are excited by that, of course, because you want to collect interesting experiences. You long for some experiences to collect, for a cold night. You want to collect something, whatever you can dream about.

WOMAN: So you don't think that the purpose of this existence is just Self-recognition?

KARL: No, for that wanting, it has nothing to do with Self-realization. It's part of that dream.

WOMAN: Whatever name you put to what you describe—I don't mind what words you use—is that not somehow the purpose, the thrust of where everything is going?

KARL: No you may say that longing, what you are longing for, is always That. But it's not by any experience. Even by those experiences I just explained. Not by any experience can you become That.

Even to come to Arunachala here, to come and meditate in a cave, and go into the light of Arunachala, then you see that this is the center of the universe, out of that light the whole universe comes and disappears. It's always like creating . . . creating, like the infinite Source of light, becoming some forms and non-forms, and all that you can imagine, coming out of the mountain. But the beauty of it is to see that and still be prior to it. That is the beauty of the mountain. It's an absolute pointer. It shows you that you are not even the light, that you are prior to the light, so whatever comes out of the light, you are not.

WOMAN: I can't understand.

KARL: This is not part of understanding.

KRISTOPH: Intellectually? Or how do you get it then?

KARL: No, no.

KRISTOPH: I've also had these experiences, but I don't have the realization. So what is the difference?

KARL: I don't know. For me, it's simply the absolute evidence that That which I am is prior to whatever I can experience. Even the experience of awareness as the primary light of the universe is because I am, but I'm not because of it. This is like the split second that I am, in spite of the experiences or the experiencer, what I am, and never because of anything. Even the extreme experience of that light, of that awareness, cannot help me.

So I really see the helplessness I am. This is total resignation of any idea of help, this is dropping out, being totally heartbroken by hopelessness and seeing no land anymore. In anything. Not even the light of awareness, of knowledge, Source of the universe, can help me. So the total helplessness is there. And then, so what? Have another coffee.

It's such a paradise, because you drop out of all hopelessness, and whatever you can imagine, as you can never imagine what you are. You become the freedom itself, which you can never imagine. You are totally untouchable by whatever you can experience or not experience. Isn't it beautiful? It's such a joke that you could ever expect something coming out of whatever you can experience!

MATTIAS: It's a relief, I find. I was sitting in a cave this morning, and I really experienced this wanting to get somewhere. I thought I'd just sit there, but then all this effort to be a meditator, to get something, was there.

KARL: As a person, there is no way out.

MATTIAS: I could not meditate anymore.

KARL: Again, I want to really point out that That which is consciousness—the "I am" consciousness of Brahma—has to create, and part of creation is longing for oneself, always meditating about That which is "I am." This is the realization of whatever is consciousness. And there is no beginning and no end to it. This is the functioning of consciousness—"I am" meditating about That which is "I am." There is no way out. This will never end.

MATTIAS: Yeah, no matter what I do, even if I decide to not meditate, it's the same thing.

KARL: Not doing is the biggest doing you can do. What to do? That which is consciousness is as infinite as what you are. Infinite consciousness never has any beginning or end. Consciousness means "I am" meditating about That which is "I am." This is consciousness.

MATTIAS: When you are saying that, this is a big relief. I don't feel somehow that something will annihilate me, but I feel fine. It's joy! It's joy!

KARL: No, maybe you find out that you cannot be annihilated by anything, because there is nothing to annihilate. You see that nothing will be gone, because there was nothing to go. This is as solid as it can be. There is no coming and going in it. So nothing ever happens. *Nichts passiert* (nothing happens). No passing. So you'd better get used to what you are because it will take awhile.

But you will never get used to That. No one can take That. As much as you try, by understanding, by loving, by divine love, "pralala," you cannot take That. By no means. You can never become what you are by any understanding, nor can you take it to be the absolute, infinite existence. No one can bear That. And when you are That, there is nothing to bear. It's such an easiness. It's such an effortlessness in itself to be That. But at the moment you want to *become* it—any moment you want to become That—you suffer. It's like committing suicide. Any moment you want to become what you are, you are committing suicide.

Getting Over Adam and Eve

MONIKA: But Karl, why do you think the original split happened?

KARL: Original sin.

MONIKA: Original sin?

KARL: Yeah, that's in the Bible. At the moment you want to know who you are, you step out of the paradise of being knowledge itself. It's the idea that, by any more or less knowledge, you can add something to the knowledge that you are. So you step out of the timelessness you are, into that which is time and non-time, "whatever," this frame.

MONIKA: Why did this first happen?

KARL: There is no "why." You just step out. You cannot *not* step out. You cannot *not* fall in love with yourself.

MONIKA: Is it like expansion and contraction of the universe?

KARL: No, simply, you cannot *not* fall in love with yourself. You simply wake up to imagining awareness as light, as you cannot *not* wake up to that awareness. And out of that awareness, you fall in love with "I am" and "I am so-and-so." This is the nature of it. You cannot *not* do it. You are the helplessness. You cannot avoid anything! Your helplessness means you are That without a second. It means there is no control. There's absolute controllessness, because there is no second to control.

The beauty of "no second" is that there is no second who can control you. Whatever is there is an imagination of separation and oneness, and whatever ideas are there are because you imagine something. And all those imaginary sensations cannot touch what you are. That's all. They are simply dream-like imaginings. And you are That, but they will never change what you are, as they can never touch or move you one inch.

An Italian MAN: So is the mistake we make to make a separate world in it?

KARL: No, you are not in it. You are it. The crazy idea that you take this [Karl slaps his own leg] as being born, as your limited existence, you cannot avoid. But now, you as the Self, place yourself in front of That, whatever is sitting here, just to be reminded, "Hey, come on, this cannot be! You're joking! You must be joking to take that as real, as being born!" Ha ha ha. [Karl laughs, but all others are silent.]

MAN: But there is no difference? When this drops in the night, it's not separate from what I am now?

KARL: No. It's here, now. You simply fall in love every morning with an image—"me"—and then you are again in the relationship with yourself. And that relationship with yourself means there are two selves, and this is unbearable.

At the moment you take any image as a second, as real, you create a second self. That there is separation, that there is a second at all, is unbearable. There will never be any acceptance of that second. So, out of that, you long to erase it. Whatever you do, you want to make it go away, you want to kill that which is not you.

But the more you want to kill that image, the more it becomes alive. And at the moment you see it's only imagination, there was nothing to kill. You cannot kill an imagined thing. So what? It's simply okay. "I cannot kill an image. I cannot do anything with it. So what?" So you rest in that absolute peace by seeing that there is nothing to kill. And then you find there never was any second for That which you are. It was simply like an idea which comes out of the blue.

British WOMAN: But still it goes on happening. You go on relating and making mistakes and having successes—

KARL: Yeah.

WOMAN: And it goes on happening anyway, whether you have that second or not, huh?

KARL: Doesn't matter. That's the beauty of it. Even the experience of dropping out doesn't matter. You cannot drop out of what you are. That's all. This is a total dropping out, but no one was ever in. So what to do? If you are That which is, what to do?

WOMAN: Then it doesn't matter much if you go out and murder someone or if you go out and give *satsang*?

KARL: Why, I'm a killing machine! [group laughs]

WOMAN: Like, same.

KARL: Same, same. This choicelessness of being, this helplessness that is sitting here, this *Sitz Karlchen* (seat of little Karl), this name, this personal whatever—if this person had an advantage idea, I would not sit here. I would simply go to some holiday place somewhere, as a person would do, and lie in the sun, and have a nice margarita at night, or whatever.

WOMAN: So you don't choose. How come you sit here?

KARL: Can you tell me? I have absolutely no idea. But I just gave up wanting to know it. That's all.

WOMAN: Somebody just asked you?

KARL: Yeah, and there was some resistance, and when the resistance was broken, I was sitting here. So there was even resistance to sit here. Because before, for years I thought, "I would never sit in front of bloody seekers sucking around here, wanting to get something!" [group laughs]

WOMAN: Do you have preferences? Would you rather be sitting on a beach as you said, really?

KARL: Right now, if you ask me, if I could just make like this [snaps fingers] and I could sit there, I would sit there. But as I cannot do it, I would rather sit here. I am too lazy to make all the effort. I'd rather be moved by existence, and be totally lazy, moment by moment in that acceptance, and I let existence work, as existence does so anyway.

WOMAN: And that works?

KARL: It works.

WOMAN: You do go and shit when you need to shit, and when you're done you get up?

KARL: Yeah. You know, mostly the toilet woman in an ashram gets enlightened. Because she sees it only comes when it comes. [group laughs] But not under pressure. Under pressure is always constipation.

In Germany, it's very famous now, "family constipation." [group laughs] Bert Hellinger. You get over your mother, you get over your father, and then you're free. You get over your grand, grand, grand—you get over Adam and Eve.

The Absolute Joke That You Could Escape This Existence You Are

AIKO: Well, it seems like all these people that dropped or collapsed, did all they could do before they collapsed.

KARL: They did what?

AIKO: They did many things, very intensely.

KARL: But every one said it *was* in spite of that. It's not needed.

FRANCESCO: Are we to understand that we don't need this?!

KARL: It's not out of need. It's simply that they could not avoid it.

FRANCESCO: Are you really saying this?

KARL: There's a difference. There's no necessity, but you cannot avoid all the steps before. That's different than needing it. You don't need it, but you cannot avoid doing it. That's something else.

THERESE: And you think you need it.

KARL: Yeah, that's an idea that you need it, that's all.

AIKO: So with this idea, you can lift whatever you hear?

KARL: You cannot avoid what you are, because this is your realization as the personal experience, moment by moment. Having this personal experience is part of your realization. There's nothing wrong or right with it. You cannot avoid that part of your infinite nature.

AIKO: It's like you're running and running out.

KARL: You cannot run out. You cannot run out of energy because you are energy.

MONIKA: Then this idea of "predestination" comes again.

KARL: So what? It's fine.

MONIKA: Can predestination be a frame?

KARL: No, that's another idea only. The main thing to see is that there is no one who has any predestination. Predestination or not.

MONIKA: Predestination happens.

KARL: It's simply to tell you, just to show you, if there is predestination, you cannot change what already comes. Because then you rest, maybe, in that "okay." But even that doesn't help. You always get up again, and try to, "whatever," control it.

MONIKA: It has to be okay anyway.

KARL: Out of an "okay" always comes a "not okay" again. You have to live with it. Even to call it "predestination" is trying to control it, because by understanding it as predestination, the freedom or peace that comes, depending on that idea. So, whatever you do, you make yourself dependent on that understanding of predestination. You cannot step out of it. No way out.

That detachment is so totally attached to that detachment. When I am asked what you do, I say—Be totally attached to what you are, be that absolute being, as you cannot *not* be attached to what you are. Being attachment itself, you cannot leave what you are.

In absolute identification, there is no separate identification anymore, and the separate one simply drops—but that cannot be done. The absolute identification that you are That cannot be *done*—you have to *be* it! But it's not by any understanding, not by choice, not by anything, as you are That anyway, as you cannot *not* be it, that's all! So be it!

MATTIAS: *Fertig* (finished).

KARL: *Aber fertig* (but finished)! So it's not a question, as you ask me, "How can you become it?" You cannot *not* be it; you never left what you are, you

cannot go back. As you have never forgotten what you are, you cannot remember it. So what to do?

FRANCESCO: Yeah, what to do? Every day after two hours, I understand
nothing! [group laughs]

KARL: Ah, that sounds good.

JUAN: Karl, you had this experience of light, right? An experience of being
eaten by darkness and all that, and after that, it was easy for you to realize
this—the Heart of existence.

KARL: No. It was by the way, in spite of it.

JUAN: But it feels like I am identified with the body and mind, and you
want me to jump straight to That.

KARL: I don't want you to do anything. I just tell you, in spite of those experiences, you are, and not because of them. You may have such experiences
or not, but it needs one who cares, and you only care because you think
there is a way to it. You want to have the experience that makes you become
again, blah, blah, blah.

It may happen or not, but in spite of that, you are—not because. So you
cannot avoid whatever longing you have for the next step, whatever *sadhana*
or *tapas* or exercises you do, they will be done. But in spite of that, you will
be what you are—not because.

So in spite of that, I am sitting here and talking, being totally irrelevant.
That was what Buddha was saying in the *Diamond Sutra*. He made it totally
clear that there was never any Buddha on earth and there never will be.
He said that he'd preached for forty years and said no word to anyone. So,
totally irrelevant.

And even Ramana said it, when he was asked what was the realization of
Ramana. He said that there was no such thing as Ramana who ever realized
the Self. Self is ever-realized, so what is there to realize?

There will never be any image that realizes That which is the Source of
itself. That which is the Source of whatever image is ever-realized.

So you'd better be That which can never be realized because it's already
realized. You cannot add more realization to That which is the realization
of what you are anyway. You cannot make it more—or less. By any understanding, by any insight, by any separate knowledge, there is no adding
something to that absolute knowledge you are.

And as the last shirt has no pockets, whatever you get in this lifetime will be gone when this body is gone. You are so proud of your collection of insights and experiences and understandings, and it all will be gone at the moment this body is gone. The memory effect will be gone, that's all. We are so proud. "I have done twenty-five years of *Vipassana* tralala!" [group laughs] But what then? "I am a master black belt, ninth degree!" But so what?

So I stick to the sticks. In German, we say, *Das letzes Hemd hat keine Taschen* (the last shirt has no pockets). Just live as that—have nothing, gain nothing, nothing to get, nothing to come—because the last shirt has no pockets. And you will be surprised. When this body is gone, you will still be what you are. Whether you like it or not, there will be no end when this body is gone.

PETE: When the body is gone, is there still this? [holds up fist, raises thumb, index, and middle fingers, then closes fist again, and then raises thumb, etc.]

KARL: Yeah, yeah. It always starts again.

LIZ: Even when the body is gone? I thought death was the way out.

KARL: No. [group laughs] The only way out is to see that there is nothing born. The only way out of that idea is to see that there is no one ever who is born. The only thing that can die is the idea of "death." By seeing nothing was ever born, nothing will ever die—there is no way out, my dear. "I just was hoping, maybe ten years more, then I'm over it!"

LIZ: There's some days when it's so frustrating, and there's some days when it's all right.

KARL: Fantastic.

LIZ: So what, I don't know. Or maybe I do know? Or maybe I am?

KARL: You have to know what you don't know, that you don't know it.

LIZ: Sometimes, you just give up.

KARL: Yeah? You never give up. Because there is nothing to give up. You cannot give up what is not even there. And you cannot give up giving up.

AIKO: Oh, you're so hopeless!

KARL: But still smiling! [group laughs] I tell you hopelessness is the big laughter, the laughter of the universe laughing about the joke that you could ever think you could escape That which you are. It's really an absolute joke that you could ever have the idea that you could die, that you could escape that existence you are. What an idea!

LIZ: Well, the idea is, even though we're saying that we're not born and we don't die, the idea is that when we die, we quit looking because there we are.

KARL: You what?

LIZ: The concept I have is that, when we die, we can quit this wanting to know because there we are.

KARL: You cannot quit falling in love with yourself.

LIZ: That's fine. But I don't want the other stuff, the questions.

KARL: Yeah, but that love is wanting to know yourself. By that love, you want to know what you love. By falling in love with yourself, you create an image of a beloved, and that you want to know, because you want to know what you love. There is no way out. And you cannot *not* fall in love with yourself.

You cannot imagine what you are. So that imagination is the realization of what you are and you cannot *not* realize yourself. You cannot *not* imagine yourself. And by that imagination, you imagine a lover and a beloved. This you cannot avoid.

You have to be—in spite of the lover and the beloved—what you are. In spite of coming and going, the lover and beloved, and all those ideas—you are what you are—not because something has to go. You don't need anything to go because there is nothing to go.

LIZ: I believe that this moment, but the next moment—whoosh—it will come back, like a snake, coming back in.

KARL: Yeah. That's why you're sitting here.

LIZ: Wearing you out.

KARL: I think it's impossible. Many have tried. [group laughs] For hours and hours. Weeks after weeks. Day by day, they are trying to suck me out, but there is nothing to suck, nothing to wear out.

LIZ: Good. I won't feel guilty.

KARL: Otherwise, it's impossible.

The Silence You Are Cannot Be
Disturbed by All the Noise of India

AIKO: So you could do this for eight hours, not for two?

KARL: Oh, I did it in Santa Fe? Nine to five, and then seven to nine. I'd do it for weeks, day by day.

FRANCESCO: Oh, my God.

KARL: Yeah, oh my God.

FRANCESCO: Good boy.

KARL: Good boy? Feel sorry for the listeners! [group laughs] I don't have to listen to what I say. That's why I am saying it.

MATTIAS: That's why people talk.

KARL: Yeah, so they don't have to listen.

MONIKA: That's why Ramana didn't speak.

KARL: But he didn't listen, either. What is this fairy tale that he didn't speak?

MONIKA: He didn't speak much, no? [group laughs]

KARL: A stone doesn't say so much either.

LIZ: But it says something.

KARL: Yeah, it says, "I am a stone," if you look at it. Who has this idea that silence has to be there by not speaking, not saying something? As if silence needs non-speaking. What an idea!

LIZ: What an idea here in India!

KARL: Yeah. You will see, you walk through the streets, and the silence you are cannot be disturbed by all the noise. That's India for you! All the catastrophic, chaotic noises coming from everywhere, every morning at four, the temple there, blah blah blah here. After a while, you say, "Okay! If I don't go, okay."

No, I am always pointing to That which is silence itself. You can talk or not talk. That talking or not talking, who cares? Consciousness talks anyway. Even by not talking, you talk so much. You cannot stop talking.

AIKO: [laughing] Obviously.

KARL: Obviously! Look at it! The whole thing comes out of talking. Talking with yourself. Having the idea and imagining, and out of the first word, *I*, comes all the universe. Out of that talking with yourself, the Self-entertainment, you create the whole universe. And then you say, "Be quiet!"

FRANCESCO: No. Just speak slowly. [group laughs]

GEORG: Speak limit.

SOFIA: Speak in Italian.

FRANCESCO: No, no. That is too much. Because then I could understand. [group laughs]

KARL: If you really would understand what I say—

FRANCESCO: It's too much.

KARL: He is very happy that I speak so fast and in English. The angel language, language of the angels, Anglo Saxon. In German, we say *Engel-land*, the land of the angels.

FRANCESCO: Yeah? Look at this! Such a place.

KARL: And it's very narrow there, that's why it's *Enge-land* (narrowness land). [group laughs] You can do everything out of a word. Something from Brazil?

JUAN: I rest my case. [group laughs]

KARL: "Judge, I rest my case." Now you have to question the witness.

MONIKA: There is no witness.

KARL: Yeah, that's what I mean. You have to question the witness. [group laughs]

MARY and THERESE: That's what we're doing! We're questioning you!

KARL: [joining in the laughter] This is "Who am I?"—questioning the witness. Who is witnessing the witness? So it's like "Who am I?" is "Who is the witness of the witness?" What is perceiving the perceiver? Is there a difference? Who is there, then? And you step back and back and back. Who is wit? *Wit* is "white." Witness of blankness. There was white light, then there's a witness. If there's no more questions, I just make puns. [group laughs]

FRANCESCO: You may rest your case.

KARL: But if you analyze the language, it's really great! *Wit* means "white," like pure light, and *witness* then is, "that pure awareness of whiteness," being a witness of that pure awareness. It's great! Go to the root of language.

It's all Self-made. Imagine! If the Self can talk with itself, then we have Babylon. Out of Babylon came all of the different languages. They became an all sandwich-like language.

THERESE: And *babiller* in French is "babble"—blah, blah, blah.

KARL: In German too.

THERESE: And when a baby starts to talk, it is *babil* (prattle).
KARL: Blah, blah. Babble. Babble on. Babylon.
MARY: *Babble* means "to talk nonsense."
KARL: But it's like you talk different languages, because you don't under-
stand what the other one says. You're lost. Too many people anyway. Two is
even too much.
FRANCESCO: You only need one.
KARL: Yeah, out of one come two.
FRANCESCO: You!
KARL: Me!

Nothing Is More Negative Than Positive Thinking

ROSA: When I watch you, I see you are always joking and laughing.
KARL: They call me "Mr. Teflon." [group laughs] In Berlin, a lady meant
it like an offense. "You are like Teflon. Nothing sticks to you! You are still
laughing. I can blame you, I can do "whatever," and you are like Teflon.
Nothing sticks to you." Oh, it sounds good.
ROSA: You are too happy. There is something wrong. [group laughs]
KARL: Too happy? In America, they say, "For a German, you have humor.
Something is wrong with you."
MONIKA: [laughing] Yes!
KARL: "You are too happy. You cannot be German, because German means
something else."
ROSA: But what about suffering? You know, this is the path to enlighten-
ment.
KARL: Yeah?
FRANCESCO: Uh, oh! [group laughs]
KARL: Enjoy your ride.
THERESE: I don't join you there.
KARL: Maybe you will find some guests to suffer with you.
ROSA: Lots. Lots! [group laughs]
KARL: But I wish you suffer your last supper then. For the crucifixion, the

end of suffering, may you suffer and then become the last supper. You will be eaten up.

ROSA: Exactly. But is it necessary?

KARL: What?

ROSA: To be eaten up.

KARL: No, it's not necessary, but unavoidable. [group laughs] It's the same as sitting here—you don't have to come, but you cannot avoid it.

ROSA: It's cruel.

KARL: It's very cruel. You are very cruel with yourself, my dear. You like yourself too much. That makes you so cruel. Yeah, you're so in love with yourself that you are so cruel with yourself, because love is war. In love and in war, there are no rules, so you are so cruel.

ROSA: So "love yourself" is really not good advice. [group laughs]

KARL: I wouldn't say so.

KAATJE: Why not love yourself?

KARL: Because there is no Self to love. How can you love yourself, as there was never any Self to love? First, you have to create an image of yourself that you can love. You want to dance with some partner, and you create a partner. Then you forget that the partner is no different from what you are, because you only imagined a second one. Then you dance with someone and take the second one as real. So then you are out of That.

But by seeing that, by your imagination, you created a dance partner, then you dance with the imagined partner for whatever time of that realization. It's Shiva dancing with himself, creating the whole universe. Then Shiva forgets that he imagines a second, and steps into that trap of imagination and becomes a *jiva*, a little self. And out of that little self, taking that image as real, you suffer. And then I am sitting here telling you, "Hey, my goodness! Almighty!" And then again, you say, "Okay."

But you cannot avoid again falling into the same trap. You always, by love, open this same trap and you step into the trap of taking the imagined second as real, and then you dance again. Unavoidable. You cannot *not* dance. And you cannot say "no" to the invitation of yourself for dance. *Du kannst dein selbst keinen Korb geben* (you can't reject yourself, turn yourself down).

If existence wants to dance, existence will dance, whether you like it or not. In spite of that there's no necessity to dance, you dance.

KAATJE: So it's best to accept everything.

KARL: To see that there is no way out, that there is dancing. There is knowing, there is not knowing, so that realization is whatever can be. You cannot *not* realize yourself. And part of the realization is whatever you can imagine, you are That which is realizing itself but itself cannot be realized.

KAATJE: Say it again?

FRANCESCO: This you don't ask! [group laughs]

KARL: You are That which is realizing itself, but That which is realizing itself cannot be realized.

KAATJE: I see.

KARL: It's easy. You are That which is imagining everything, but itself, it cannot imagine That which is imagining everything. So, itself, it cannot be imagined. So that is life itself, but whatever comes out of that absolute life, whatever you imagine as life, is imagination. But That which is life itself, cannot be imagined.

So be That which cannot be imagined by not knowing, by not understanding, by being what nothing can be done to. That's freedom itself, because not knowing what you are and what you are not, is paradise.

The rest is being a sufferer, or whatever you imagine. Whatever you imagine you are, you are, you become. So if you imagine yourself to be a sufferer, you suffer. If you imagine yourself to be That, you are That. If you imagine yourself to be a mountain, you are a mountain. Whatever you imagine, you become.

THERESE: But you have no choice on your imagination.

KARL: As I said.

MATTIAS: Tomorrow you may wake up as a mountain. [group laughs]

KARL: Maybe today she woke up as a mountain, but Thérèse is fine enough right now.

THERESE: I'm so happy to be a happy failure! I'm still enjoying the happy failure idea. [group laughs]

KARL: Failed again! That's the best thing. Oh, failure! Failed again! The nature of the failure—failing. *Fehler* (mistake).

MATTIAS: Or loving, which is the same. Failing or loving.

KARL: Loving?

MATTIAS: New dictionary. *Failure* is "loving."

KARL: Out of loving, you fail.

LIZ: I failed at loving.

KARL: Out of loving, you miss. Or whatever. Yeah. Some more little questions?

JUAN: Karl, if you imagine to be a sufferer, you're a sufferer; if you imagine to be an enjoyer, you're an enjoyer—but you cannot control it.

KARL: You have to be, in spite of being a sufferer and suffering, only That which you are. It's unavoidable. You cannot avoid what you are, that which is, whatever aspect of existence, you are. And you cannot *not* imagine yourself as it, and by imagining it, you become it. And then there is the sufferer, the suffering, and that which is suffered about.

But you are That which is the sufferer, That which is the suffering, and That which you suffer about. You are always that experiencer, that experiencing, and what is experienced—as you are whatever is. You cannot *not* experience what you are. And by experiencing yourself, you become an experiencer experiencing what is experienced. But there is no difference. There is no separation between the experiencer, the experiencing, and what is experienced. It's all the realization of what you are as consciousness.

JUAN: But I'd rather experience myself being the enjoyer rather than the sufferer.

KARL: But that is part of the imagination.

LIZ: You're saying there's no control.

KARL: No.

LIZ: I was hoping if I imagined myself—

KARL: That's a different story. That's like giving an order to the universe, or this mystic—

LIZ: Controlling.

KARL: Yeah.

MONIKA: Positive thinking!

KARL: Nothing is more negative than positive thinking. You put your blackness, your darkness in your bag and then say, "Oh, my open heart! Embracing everything—Me! I just came from heart surgery, and now I have an open heart! I came from that *guru* and he opened my heart and now I'm embracing everything!"

FRANCESCO: This is not in your case.

KARL: Not in my case?

FRANCESCO: No, no.

KARL: Oh, I break your heart.

AIKO: The other day, you told me, "Embrace the devils, embrace the gods!"

KARL: Yeah, but you cannot do it. As you are the devil, you cannot embrace yourself. [she laughs]

Total embracement is being That which is the devil. So there is nothing to embrace. But this is absolute embracement. By being That which is the devil, by being That which is heaven, by being That which is hell, that is absolutely embracing whatever is. But not by one who is embracing it—by being it!

I'm not asking you for an act of embracement, I'm asking for absolute embracement by being That which is. By being That which is the devil, by being That which is God, by being whatever you can imagine you are. This is an absolute embracement of being That which is. This is not a separate or relative embracement of one who is embracing the world with an open heart. "Oh, you still have a closed heart, my dear! Oh, I'm so sorry about you." I'm not talking about that. I'm talking about that absolute embracement, by being it, by being That.

LIZ: Acceptance. Just accepting that we're all of these things. Is that what you mean?

KARL: No, by being it! That is absolute acceptance itself. But you cannot accept it. You have to accept that it doesn't need any acceptance, and that you cannot accept it. You aren't anyway, because you live with the idea that you can accept something or not.

SOFIA: No controller then.

KARL: Yeah.

MATTIAS: And that we can imagine we can—that's also an illusion, because as a person we don't exist, so it's not ours.

KARL: Whatever.

MONIKA: Anyway, it doesn't work.

KARL: It's not even God's. There's no institute.

MATTIAS: It just is. God's Loving Institute.

KARL: "God Loving Institution. Care-taking Institute of God. Brahman will help you."

ROSA: So I have a question now. Maybe it's stupid. But there are no stupid questions, only stupid answers.

KARL: Don't worry. There are only stupid questions and stupid answers.

Don't worry.

ROSA: So I have no decision, really. I cannot make a decision. The decision is already made.

KARL: I have no idea.

ROSA: So am I free?

KARL: You? No.

ROSA: Is it avoidable? My decision—is it avoidable or is it unavoidable?

KARL: Both are concepts. Both need one who needs to know it, and one who cares about free will or no free will.

ROSA: So I don't care?

FRANCESCO: You ask this? Funny question.

KARL: No, I would say That which you are is concernlessness and doesn't care if you care or not. There was never anyone who cared about caring. Free will or no free will, a decision or no decision, always depends on there being one who could have one. So both are concepts.

If you see both are concepts, and both are there or not, you may experience free will and you may experience no free will, but still the experiencer will be there as a separate experiencer of having or not having free will. So it makes no difference. So even no free will is evidence that you exist as having no free will.

There is no way out in seeing that there is no free will. Because it's simply like an exchange of concepts. Maybe it's good psychotherapy; your life may be easier because you lose your, whatever, guilt feelings, so you have a better personal life. There is nothing against it. But if you talk about That which you are, it makes no difference.

So there is no advantage in seeing that you have no free will. Because if there would be an advantage in seeing that there's no free will, it still would need one who could have an advantage, one who could need an advantage. What an idea!

So that advantage of seeing that there is no free will and going to that impersonal consciousness is still a disadvantage because it needs one to have an advantage. Forget it. Both are concepts. Find the one who could have one.

ROSA: So, it's not to be found?

KARL: So not finding what you are, in whatever—you rest—but never, ever, can you find any concept, image or landing place of an idea or frame of concepts. By not finding, you are that freedom, because that freedom cannot be found, because there is nothing to find for that freedom. Freedom means there is no second, there is no object, there is no relative, there is no idea, there is no concept about That which is freedom. So That which is freedom has absolutely no idea about what is and what is not freedom.

I'm talking about the absolute absence of the concept of "freedom," not about any understanding of free will, no free will, blah, blah, blah. All this is the realm of consciousness. In consciousness, we always step back into stupidity and ignorance, which is so in love with itself. It always creates the lover and beloved again, and then steps back into ignorance. So it will come to the understanding, and that understanding you can become, or you can go to, but you will leave again. Finally, you have to be absolutely, in spite of whatever you can understand or not understand.

You *are* in spite, of consciousness, as you are even prior to that concept of "consciousness," or energy, as That which is energy doesn't know energy. That which is consciousness doesn't know consciousness. And That which is consciousness, as the Heart of consciousness, doesn't even know Heart, or anything, it has absolutely no idea about consciousness, awareness, or whatever you can name and frame it with words and concepts.

In what you are, there is Selflessness, even, Godlessness. That which is God, as what you are, has no idea about God. So, for what you are, there is no God. There never was and never will be. For what you are, which is grace, there will be no grace. So you'd better not wait for it. Hallelujah! I think this is a good goodbye. Thank you very much. *Namaste.*
GROUP: Thank you! *Namaste.*

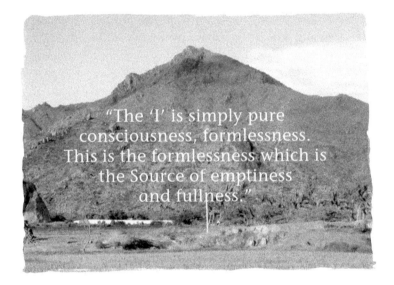

"The 'I' is simply pure consciousness, formlessness. This is the formlessness which is the Source of emptiness and fullness."

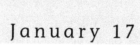

January 17

Still the Happy Failure;
or, the End of Intellect

The Ghost in the Bottle

KARL: Shall we swap today?

A MAN: No, no. You sit there. This is okay.

KARL: Thank you very much. Welcome. Is everything okay?

A WOMAN: Is the microphone on?

KARL: Yeah, it says "on," but sometimes, you never know. Okay, who is on today?

KAATJE: I have a lot of questions. I don't know where to start, though. [voice wavering] I just arrived here three days ago, and I have this constant feeling that I want to cry all the time.

KARL: Cry, cry!

KAATJE: [tears start flowing] It's so beautiful. The people I've been meeting, and—I've been carried from this, like I'm not doing anything at all. Everybody, everything takes care of me. I didn't even know who you were, I never heard of you, and everybody was astonished that I hadn't heard of you [group laughs], and I didn't know what to expect when I came here yesterday, and I've been in this constant state of—I don't know how to [sobs]—I don't know—

KARL: Welcome it. Just say "hello." Yeah. What to say?

KAATJE: What to say!

KARL: Sounds very good. So just enjoy it.

KAATJE: I do. I feel I am not doing anything also. It just happened to me. Everything is happening to me. So beautiful! So beautiful!

KARL: What have you done right then?

KAATJE: Nothing. I've done nothing.

KARL: [to the group] You see?! [to Kaatje] Actually, you don't deserve that. [group laughs]

THERESE: [teasing] Starts now. Was too sweet until now.

KARL: No, the beauty is she has nothing done for her. That's the beauty of it. In spite of whatever.

KAATJE: In spite of. Yeah.

KARL: So enjoy it.

KAATJE: I will. I do. I'm so grateful, so grateful. [weeps] I'm so overwhelmed.

KARL: You waited so long, huh?

KAATJE: Who knows? I don't know.

KARL: The beauty is that it's never too late. There is no time for it. It happens when it happens.

KAATJE: Yeah.

KARL: Until the last minute of this body, anything can happen. What to do?

KAATJE: I don't expect anything. Whatever happens—

KARL: —may happen.

KAATJE: May happen.

KARL: Sounds good. There is a total welcome.

KAATJE: Yeah.

KARL: So what to say then?

GEORG: Welcome!

KARL: Welcome! But if you have any question, just tell me.

KAATJE: I will.

A Spanish MAN: Karl, you've been talking about the "I," the "I am," and the "I am so-and-so." That "I am so-and-so," is that, "I am a man, I am a husband?"

KARL: Whatever. Even if you say, "I am the world," it's the same. The pure "I am" is simply space. There is no identification of "I am." It's simply the feeling of "I am," without giving any object or idea to it, simply space-like. Then going to some form—"I am the form or object," you go to the "I am so-and-so," "I am the world," whatever you make of a form. So out of formless "I am" comes form. There's a space-like "I am," and then something comes like a form into it. You become that form.

MAN: And what about the "I"?

KARL: The "I" is simply pure consciousness, formlessness. This [holds up his thumb to symbolize "I"] is the Source of formless [holds up thumb and index finger to symbolize "I am"] and form [holds up thumb, index, and middle fingers to symbolize "I am so-and-so"]. This is the formlessness which is the Source of emptiness and fullness.

MAN: And those three go together?

KARL: All this pops up like this. [holds up his thumb, index finger, and then middle finger, and then draws them back into a fist, over and over in cycles, to symbolize the coming and going of different states of aware-ness] Out of this awareness as "I" [thumb], come "I am" [thumb and index finger] and then form [thumb, index, and middle fingers]. At night, these drop together [tucks in his index and middle fingers], and this remains as deep sleep state [thumb]. But even prior to that, is this [holds up fist to symbolize Heart]. So, as this is prior to awareness, it's prior to "I am"-ness and prior to "I am so"-ness. In whatever state, this [fist] is without any state. There is statelessness.

The first notion, the first experience of light, the first *Om* or sound, is "I." Out of that "I"-thought comes "I am"-ness and "I am so"-ness. But this [fist] is always what is realizing itself as "I" [thumb] "am" [thumb and in-dex finger] "the world" [thumb, index, and middle fingers]. This [fist] you never lose; this you never left. So whether you go from this state [thumb, index, and middle fingers] to this state [thumb and index finger] to that state [thumb], it cannot make you this [fist], as you are this [fist] in any state. Simply this, Heart itself, not knowing what is Heart and what is not Heart.

This is the absolute Source [fist]; this is the Father [thumb], the Holy Spirit [thumb and index finger], the Son [thumb, index, and middle fin-ger]. "I" [thumb] "am" [thumb and index finger] "Jesus" [thumb, index, and middle finger]—or whatever you say— "I" [thumb] "am" [thumb and index finger] "man" [thumb, index, and middle finger]—comes out of this [fist]. But this [cycles fingers into and out of fist] is the realization of this [fist]. So only this [fist] is real.

But that's reality you cannot find, you cannot name, you cannot frame, you cannot do anything to it. Even to call it "reality" is too much. Because reality doesn't know reality, as Heart doesn't know Heart.

It makes no difference. There is no discrimination in the "I" or the "I am" or the "I am so-and-so." In all this, even in separation, there is no separation, in oneness there is no oneness, and in "I"-ness there is no "I"-ness. All these [thumb, index, and middle fingers] are ideas. Even the first "I," the first word or sound, is already a reflection of That.

This [fist] can never be known or not known, as you are That. That absolute knowledge you cannot leave, you cannot lose, you cannot gain, nothing is to do with it. So when Ramana says to be That which you are, he is pointing to That which is Heart itself. This you cannot forget and you cannot remember.

Simply be That which you are. But not by knowing or not knowing. In spite of knowing or not knowing, you are That which is Heart, never because. That is called "the causelessness" itself, the false state, or statelessness of existence. All names that point to That which you are.

It's enough? If something's not clear, just ask. Even that clarity comes and goes, so don't worry. You are in spite of clarity and un-clarity what you are, not because. So even that understanding may come now, or not, because even understanding comes and goes. But you may experience that absolute experience that you are in spite of understanding, not because. Here, now, you are in spite of whatever idea you have or don't have of what you are.

Whatever image you give yourself, you are in spite of that image, not because. So it may come. Okay?

[The man nods.]

TOMAS: Well, Karl, what is this knowledge that you speak about based upon?

KARL: It is based upon the experience of "I am so-and-so;" it is based upon the experience of "I am;" and it is based upon the experience of light. And as there is an experience of light or "I" or *Om*, That which is the absolute experiencer has to be prior to that. That's all. It's based upon the experience that whatever you can experience cannot be what you are. So even that primal light as the first "I," the first notion of existence, is an experience. You, as the absolute experience, have to be prior to that experience, but not by knowing it, then, simply by being prior to whatever you can experience.

So it's not like you know something. It's a total absence of knowing or not knowing.

TOMAS: But is there any difference in your knowing that, and let's say, my knowing that?

KARL: There is no *my* knowing. That's the difference. There's a total absence of one who knows or doesn't know. There was never any knower or not-knower. So there is no difference between my knowing and your knowing, because there is neither my knowing nor your knowing.

TOMAS: I know, but isn't that also knowing? It's like that thing that you say, that these are all pointers.

KARL: That's you making the difference, not me. I don't see any difference. For me, you are That which is Heart as I am—Heart itself. I speak only to That which is Heart itself anyway. But not by knowing That which is Heart, simply by being what is. It's not a form or non-form or any idea. I never speak to any idea or image. I speak to That which is. Me. Not to an idea of myself.

TOMAS: Doesn't somebody have to know that?

KARL: I don't know if you have to know that. You cannot *not* know that. That's the point. The knowledge you are, you cannot lose. So as you have not lost that knowledge, you cannot gain it back. That's all. As you are that knowledge, you cannot *not* know it.

You are the absolute knowledge of That which is Heart, because you cannot gain absolute knowledge, since you never lost it. So whatever you do to gain it back, you're stepping out of it, that's all. Simply by having the idea that you can add something to what you are—

TOMAS: Yeah, but my question is—what you just said, isn't that knowledge, and how far different is that from just knowing it intellectually, say? You say it's based upon this experience, but the ultimate thing you cannot experience, so it cannot be based upon anything.

KARL: That is the absolute experience—That which you are, you cannot experience. That absolute non-experience is an experience too. It's an absolute knowing, but without knowing or not knowing. It's a total absence of one who knows or doesn't know, so it's in spite of any coming and going. And that is the meaning of "nothing ever happened to That which you are." That which is, not an image, not an object, neither born nor not born— whatever you say, it's not—what can happen to That? Nothing every happened to That which is you, or Heart, or whatever you call it. But this is an absolute experience, to be the Absolute that is in every given moment, even prior to birth, even prior to Adam and Eve, even prior to the beginning of the universe, whatever, That which it is.

TOMAS: But there is nobody who experiences that?

KARL: There is no experiencer as a separate one, but there is an absolute experiencer as That which it is. This is not a personal experience or impersonal experience. It is simply experiencing itself, being That which is prior to whatever can be experienced, being That which is prior even to experiencing, being that Absolute— It's a pointer. I don't want to frame it by that. I simply point to That which you are, as you cannot catch it in any way. Uncatchable. "Catch me if you can."

There are differences between Tomas and Karl—all the differences of form and non-form, whatever, knowing and not knowing, but in That, there's a total stop of differences. So, for what you are, all the differences make no difference.

TOMAS: I understand all this. I just don't understand how far this understanding can be said to be based upon experience, or let's say, pointers.

KARL: It's a non-experience. It's not based upon an experience. It's based upon the absolute absence of an experiencer.

TOMAS: But you have to know that you know, otherwise, how could you talk about it? It's like a pointer, you have to know what you're pointing at.

KARL: I have to be That, and being That is absolute knowing it.

TOMAS: And how do you know that you are That?

KARL: [laughing] There is no "me" who knows or doesn't know it. That's the point. There's a total absence of a "me" who knows or doesn't know. That I cannot lose and I never gained. So this I cannot lose again because I never gained it. I don't need to know it! Knowledge needs me to know or not to know. I don't need knowledge to be what is prior to knowledge.

TOMAS: Okay, but in that sense, nobody is any different.

KARL: [laughing] Did I say anyone is different here? I said, "You make the difference, not me."

TOMAS: Well, I'm just trying to figure out the difference.

KARL: But by trying to figure out the difference, you make a difference.

TOMAS: All right.

KARL: By trying to figure out the difference between you and me, you make a difference already. I have no idea about it. There are differences, but they don't make any difference. That's all. You cannot solve this paradox.

TOMAS: Um hmm.

KARL: This *koan* you have to be. So what to do? Okay.

KAATJE: The ghost is out.

KARL: Woo-oo! The ignorant ghost is out?

KAATJE: Well, it took me a long time to understand what that means. It was never in!

KARL: That's the only way out, to see that there was never anyone in anything. So there's still no way out, but there is absolutely no need for any way out, because there never was anyone in. So what to do? Yes, this is the ghost in the bottle, eh?

KAATJE: Yes.

KARL: It's a special Dutch one, huh?

KAATJE: Yes, I was thinking and thinking—

KARL: How can that ghost come out?

[Both laugh.]

THERESE: How does the ghost get in?

KAATJE: Well, it was growing inside the bottle.

KARL: That's the point. You can imagine that it comes from wherever and it was growing inside, how to get it out of the bottle? It's like you were born in some frame, a time frame, and then you are like a little cell or "whatever creation," and then you grow in that bottle, but how can you then get out of the bottle?

[Kaatje laughs.]

So you go back to the question, "Is anyone born at all?" In this information, images, rising and growing and transforming—is there anyone at all who is born in it? It is like, "Who am I?" Who is here, now, born at all? Is that what I am?

When Ramana was lying down and questioning himself about what will happen when he dies, when the body is gone, all ideas gone, whatever can go—what happens then to That which I am?—then he had a life experience itself. That which is life itself is independent of any image or idea of being born or not born, of knowing or not knowing, whatever you can imagine, in spite of it, you are That which is life, which is Heart itself.

This is such an absolute experience, this absolute independence or absolute freedom of experience, being free of any image or idea of what you are, absolutely independent of that. This is an absolute experience, but it's not an experience of That which you are. It's experiencing that, even in the absolute absence of whatever you can experience, you still are what you are. This is all I am talking about, nothing else.

It's not an experience of something that I am. It's an experience that, in spite of what comes and goes, in spite of whatever can be known or not known, I am what I am. Never because.

When you go into the light of Arunachala, the first light of existence, of notions, the center of the universe, and you still see, Arunachala is after me, because I am not that. I am prior to that. So this is an absolute pointer that you are That which *is* Arunachala, but you are not Arunachala.

You are That which *is* light, but you are not light. You are That which is formless, but you are not formless. You are That which has form, but you have no form. Nothing is there without That which you are. But That which you are, you cannot find.

If You Wake Up, Don't Take It Personally

JAMES: I seem to recall in the past you saying that you "saw" this.

KARL: I'm seeing it now.

JAMES: Well, what is it that sees?

KARL: There is no "what." Because whatever you make out of it, it's an experience.

JAMES: Yeah. So it's the subject.

KARL: It's not even the subject. The subject you can describe, you can frame. Even the witness is witnessed by That.

JAMES: Yeah, yeah. Prior to the witness.

KARL: For whatever you say.

JAMES: So if we go back in time—

KARL: Back in time? Oh, that's hard. For that, we have to imagine "time" first.

JAMES: Okay, so if we imagine time, and we imagine a "Karl"—

KARL: Imagining "Karl," yeah, that's hard. [group laughs]

JAMES: At some point, something happened, there was some scene that happened. Not to "Karl," but within the reference of the body-mind—

KARL: You mean that at some point there was a little "Aha! Nothing ever happened to That which you are."

JAMES: In what sense? Was that seen, felt, or heard?

KARL: No. It was simply "Aha!" And then you have a coffee. Nothing special.

THERESE: I drink so much coffee lately! [group laughs]

A MAN: Aha! Coffee!

KARL: That's the whole problem with experience hunters. They always want to have a big one. "If I would, it would be a big one. Firework of existence. Existence has to celebrate me then, when I have my experience!"

MAN: Cosmic orgasm.

KARL: Yeah, the cosmic orgasm everyone is looking for.

FRANCESCO: For one minute.

MAN: That's nice.

JAMES: At the same time, with all these masters, enlightened masters of the past, there was always an event, a seeming event, that took place either in time or out of time. Ramana talks about perceiving that he was going to die, and then seeing that he wouldn't die, and other teachers have had similar experiences.

KARL: Yeah, but then absolutely pointing out that there was no before and no after, because all the ideas of time, of coming and going and happening, were totally gone. In the experience of whatever is life itself, there is no coming and going, no before and no after. So whenever this moment in time happens, there is no time anymore. Never was. So there is no special event in anything, because it is a non-event. Nothing happens! But it is so beautiful that nothing happens.

JAMES: I don't understand that. I mean, in the past I've had experiences—

KARL: You collected experiences, that's all.

JAMES: And after those experiences, my reality changed.

KARL: That's what I say. By that experience, nothing will change, because as long as there is *my* reality, and *my* reality is changing through *my* experiences—what an idea? You make a history. You even take enlightenment personally.

JAMES: Yeah, well, that's what we do, isn't it?

KARL: You cannot do otherwise. No way. I always say, if you die, don't take it personally. [group laughs] Yeah, but that's what I'm talking about. If some firework of enlightenment happens, don't take it personally. It's simply another experience of whatever you can experience, that's all. If you wake up, don't take it personally! [laughs] Every morning, you can do that—if you wake up, don't take it personally. That's all.

JAMES: I know these are just labels, but some people have the idea that there are two separate things, Self-realization and enlightenment.

KARL: Some have the idea, yes.

JAMES: You don't see that. From the absolute perspective, no, but in the relative, is there?

KARL: Is there a difference? You can make a difference, if you like. You may say enlightenment is going from the "I am so-and-so" to the "I am." *Satori*, going from identification to non-identification, you can make it "enlightenment."

You can say enlightenment is even to have an experience of the light, or an experience that you are light and everything else is illusion. Then you run around like light. "I am real, but everything else is not." So you are landing in what is called "light." And then there is an enlightened one who sees all unenlightened ones around him. So then you're in God-consciousness and you see only pigs sitting around you.

JAMES: So you can be an *avatar*, or whatever.

KARL: Whatever.

JAMES: But what about Self-realization?

KARL: I would call Self-realization the realization of That which is Self, ever-realized, and doesn't need anyone to realize anything. But this is not a realization of something, this is a non-realization. This is a realization that existence, for sure, doesn't need a pot to realize what is existence.

JAMES: And when you say that there's no advantage, you really mean that from the perspective of the Self, there's no advantage.

KARL: From where else can I talk? Should I go to the level of "the other one?" [group laughs] "Please come to my level so we can talk! Please confirm me as a level. Please confirm me as an idea, otherwise I cannot exist as an idea. Take care of me, please!"

FRANCESCO: I like this!

JAMES: Well, in a way, that's what some of us would like, I think.

KARL: Yeah, everyone likes it.

JAMES: Well, I see that you are talking from the Self—

KARL: No, I'm not talking from the Self.

JAMES: You are the Self talking to the Self, right?

KARL: I'm what Buddha said—there's preaching but no word is said to anyone.

JAMES: That's hard to believe over here.

KARL: Believe? If That is what you are, when you totally see that, nothing ever happens—this irrelevance is paradise. Everything else is bondage, being bonded to the importance of what you say, how clearly you can put it into words, and whether someone understands it or not. Oh my goodness. And maybe you can transmit by words, or by looks, what you are. "You really tune in to my receiver." In German, we say *"Du gehst mir auf den Sender"* (you're broadcasting to me).

A German WOMAN: *Wecker* (alarm clock).

KARL: You go on my clock or my watch. I would say, "I'm your alarm clock. Now I am ringing. You have to wake up!" [group laughs] So, final question.

JAMES: Final question.

KARL: Sounds promising.

JAMES: The final question—

KARL: Will you ever get it? [group laughs]

FRANCESCO: There's no way! Not today. Maybe tomorrow.

JAMES: I'm not interested in that. Why would *I* want to get it, right? Final question, for the time being anyway. In a relative sense, there seems as though there is a progression in time for a seeker. Do you agree with that? You know, that one gains more awareness or more peace.

KARL: I would say, the more you seek, the more stupid you get. [group laughs] The more you think you collect experiences in your so-called seeker life history, the more stupid you get.

The more quantity of relative knowledge you earn by seeking, the more you have to carry around, and that's stupid. So the more you seek, the more you collect experiences around your neck. Even with the final enlightenment pearl around your neck, that you want to share, then polish and nourish; the quantity of ignorance grows.

JAMES: All right. So that's quite depressing, don't you think? [group laughs]

KARL: When two hear the same thing, for one it's depressing, for the other it's totally relaxing.

JAMES: Yeah, yeah.

KARL: "Hallelujah! All that for nothing. Thank God." Or, "All that for nothing? Poor me!" You never know what comes out. [group laughs]

JAMES: So in a sense, there's no enlightenment, there's no realization, there's just giving up the search.

KARL: Who can give up the search? And who needs that advantage of giving up the search? Another stupid idea! You are adding stupidity to stupidity, ignorance to ignorance, that's all. Whatever you do, whatever you don't do—

JAMES: Is there some point where you can get so much stupidity that—

KARL: [laughing] That you explode out of that stupidity? [group laughs] Sounds clever. But it's still stupid.

JAMES: Okay, I'll shut up now.

THERESE: No!

FRANCESCO: No, please don't!

KARL: That sounds promising, but I don't believe you.

FRANCESCO: You say all the time, "yes you want, you want, you want." But is it in my hands to want?

KARL: What hands? Whose hands?

FRANCESCO: Oh, God, I understand this. Not today!

KARL: Not today? [group laughs] What is yours anyway?

FRANCESCO: I don't know.

KARL: You see? That's what I am pointing to.

FRANCESCO: Sometimes you say, "What do you want to do?" But if it's not in my hands, why do you ask what I want? I don't want anything!

KARL: I have no idea why you want.

FRANCESCO: So I go home and—no, forget it. I don't go home. [group laughs] It's too complicated.

KARL: Oh, Francesco!

FRANCESCO: Oh, I am happy. I don't know where, but this I know. [group laughs]

KARL: This sounds promising. "I am happy, I don't know where or why, but—" Yeah, that's good. So simply be That which you don't know. [laughs] That sounds quite happy. That actually is happiness that doesn't know if it's happy or not happy. You must be very happy, the happiness that doesn't know if it's happy or not happy.

FRANCESCO: I don't know anything. This is the problem.

KARL: No, that's not the problem. That there is one who wants to know even more nothing, that's the problem. Because the one who says, I know nothing—

FRANCESCO: It's so difficult to speak with you. Very difficult. So heavy. This guy comes here this morning to ask you something, and bang, bang, bang [pretends he's shooting a gun] in five seconds!

JAMES: I'm used to it by now.

KARL: I am a farmer! I have to cut at once.

FRANCESCO: You could take some time! [group laughs]

JAMES: There's a technique, Francesco. Here's how it goes. Whatever answer you want, right, you suggest the opposite thing, and then Karl tells you—

FRANCESCO: Yes, I know that. But I forget it all the time. [group laughs]

JAMES: So, if you want there to be enlightenment, you say, "Karl, there's no enlightenment, right?" Then Karl says, "Yes, there's enlightenment!" [group laughs]

FRANCESCO: He changes. From stupid, he is coming.

JAMES: Now you've got me saying these things!

KARL: I got what?

JAMES: Nothing. I never said that! [group laughs]

CHARLES: [to Karl] He's giving classes on how to understand you.

KARL: In Holland, there was one who gave pre-*satsang*.

FRANCESCO: Oh, that is a good idea.

KARL: How to behave, what to do, how to dress, how to find a soul mate in the *satsang*, and so on. [group laughs] But now he has a better position in a *tantra* temple. From pre-*satsang* to *tantra* temple. Fantastic. [to Francesco] But pre-*satsang* sounds good, no?

FRANCESCO: I think it's nice. To understand if it's possible to ask a question or not—

THERESE: And after-*satsang*.

KARL: Or, make an after-*satsang*. [laughing] How to survive *satsang*. Sounds really good.

CHARLES: Yeah, you need a hospital.

FRANCESCO: This is my *karma*. What to do?

KARL: *Karma*. Karl-ma.

FRANCESCO: Quite. In Italian, *karlma* means "quite." Karlmo.

KARL: Now, Francesco, your new name is Karlmo.

Fear Is There, but No One Fears

JAMES: Karl, would you say, in a relative sense, there's any point to what's going on here? Over and above entertainment?

KARL: Absolutely.

JAMES: Okay. Say more about that.

KARL: I would say that, without even one word I say, there would be no existence. Every word has to be said so that existence can be as absolute as existence is. Whatever aspect of existence is here, now, makes existence complete. Like if you could take one grain of sand out of the universe, it would destroy the whole universe. If you could avoid saying one word, you could destroy the whole existence.

Every idea, every word, contains the totality itself. So, in that, it makes absolute sense, but not relative sense. There is an absence of an advantage or a disadvantage, but in that absolute sense, whatever is *has* to be as it is, so that existence can be as existence is. It makes absolute sense. But who needs that sense?

JAMES: And everyone who's here has to be here?

KARL: There is no one here anyway.

JAMES: Yeah, well—

KARL: —Any idea that it *has* to be there as that form, that aspect of existence, so that existence can be the Absolute that existence is. But there is no one in existence anyway. So there is an absolute necessity, but not a relative necessity of that.

Because That which is existence is Absolute, it demands that whatever realization, whatever image, has to be as absolute as that Source. So any reflection is as absolute as That which is reflecting itself. And without one reflection, there would not even be That which you are.

There is only the absolute Heart, and the absolute realization of That which is Heart, and in that absolute realization, whatever has to be *has* to be—exactly as it is—so that That which is Heart *is* That which is Heart. So this is absolute acceptance, but there is nothing to accept. This is the total meaning of "no way out," that this word has to be spoken as it is spoken at this moment. In whatever given moment, everything has to be as it is, so that That which is *can* be as it is.

So there must be a Bush, there must be a Bin Laden, there must be all these ideas, all these dream characters—that movie has to be, so that existence can be Absolute, as it is. So there is absolutely no question that, whatever is, *has* to be, as it is. Otherwise, it wouldn't be. For some, it's quite relaxing.

JAMES: Yes, there's a certain freedom in that.

KARL: Already, it's quite peaceful. This is a peace of mind, not talking about That which is, simply by seeing that, even intellectually, even being the spirit which has a vertical understanding of that. It has to be as it is, so that it can be as it is.

TOMAS: Still, it doesn't make any difference, whether you understand.

KARL: That's the beauty of it, that it doesn't make any difference. If it would make a difference, you could control That which you are, by that. If it would make a difference, you'd really be in hell. As long as you have the idea it makes a difference, you are in hell.

But by seeing that whatever comes, even peace of mind, makes no difference for what you are, that's paradise. Then you are in spite of peace of mind or no peace of mind, not because. So, blank mind or no blank mind—who cares? In spite of a blank mind or no blank mind, you are what you are.

TOMAS: In spite of paradise or hell, you are what you are.

KARL: In spite of the idea, you are paradise.

TOMAS: But somehow knowing that also doesn't make any difference.

KARL: That's the beauty of it. Enjoy it.

TOMAS: Well—

KARL: Aw, it's very hard!

TOMAS: I can't enjoy it. Then it starts all over again.

KARL: So what?

TOMAS: No, nothing "what!"

KARL It will always start over and over again. You will never find an end to it. So what's the problem? Enjoy it! "But then it will start all over again." Still fear. Why? Why do you fear yourself?

TOMAS: I don't know.

KARL: How can you fear yourself?

TOMAS: How can I *not* fear myself?

KARL: Because there is no Self to fear.

TOMAS: Sure, that's fine to understand, but it doesn't make any difference. I mean, if I don't have a choice, how can you tell me to do something?

KARL: Who is there who doesn't have a choice?

TOMAS: I don't know.

KARL: You see? What you don't know, you fear. That you don't know, that you fear something you don't know—what an idea!

TOMAS: But whatever it is, there is not an option.

KARL: That which you don't know—not an object in time or whatever—is fearing what you don't know!

TOMAS: Right. But you just explained that it has to be this way in order for the whole thing to be as it is.

KARL: No. Every fear has to be there, that's not the problem. But there is no one who fears. As you just said, you don't know what is fearing and you don't know what you fear. There is fear. So what? It makes no difference. Ha ha ha. You just said that, "I have to fear. No, I don't enjoy it. Because then it will start again." [laughs]

JAMES: He has the sense of existing as a separate individual.

KARL: This is as far as you can go with the intellect. You go to that point of understanding, and then you see—it makes no difference. Thank God! But first, you may become very depressed. Because you did so much for that understanding, and then you see—it was all for nothing. Shit! All that seeking, all that understanding, was for nothing. Shit again! Failed again! Ha ha ha. And then I am sitting here telling you, "Oh, but that's the beauty of it!" What you are cannot be controlled by any understanding or grasping or insight. This is the beauty of freedom—that not by any understanding or insight, by any grabbing it, by any control system of ideas, can it be controlled. That's why I'm always saying that in spite of understanding, in spite of any control system, you are—never because.

ROSA: I think we need an after-*satsang*. [group laughs]

KARL: James will give a good after-*satsang*. James will share his clothes. Holy James is always sharing his clothes of knowledge.

FRANCESCO: And what should I do today?

KARL: What's that?

FRANCESCO: What can I do in the time today?

KARL: What day?

GEORG: Uh oh.

KARL: What am I doing, meanwhile?

[A woman starts to laugh uncontrollably.]

FRANCESCO: This is therapy!

[That makes her laugh more. The group joins in the laughter.]

KARL: After *satsang*, she will tell you.

[Her uncontrolled laughter continues for a few more minutes.]

KARL: *Ich warte Dir* (I'm waiting for you). "The candidate has a hundred points."

FRANCESCO: You're starting again.

ROSA: Is that called "eating up"?

KARL: Called? It's a call center. I'm a recall center.

An Australian MAN: *Total Recall*.

KARL: You've been eaten up by a total recall.

ROSA: But it's scary.

KARL: Yeah, it's a scary monster show here. All these ghosts! [group laughs] Yeah, *Rocky Horror Picture Show* all over again. But it's nice music, yeah? Ghosts can really dance. Ghost show.

ROSA: The ghost is out.

KARL: The ghost is out, but you see that it is a ghost. At the moment you see it's a ghost, the goose is out.

KAATJE: That's right.

KARL: That's why it's called "a ghost," because it "goes-st." "Go-oh-st." [group laughs]

JAMES: Is that a new one, Karl?

KARL: No, I've used that for a while. [group laughs]

JAMES: You keep a few in reserve.

Even the Idea of a *Jnani* Is Ignorance

JUAN: Karl, doesn't everybody who realizes have to get to this point of exhaustion you spoke of. "I was seeking and there was nothing to seek."
KARL: No.
JUAN: But everybody who realizes has done a lot of *sadhana* or techniques before realizing.
KARL: I tell you, there never was any realized one at all.
JUAN: But does it make a difference for a given individual to watch TV all his life or to go to *satsangs*?
KARL: No. No difference.
JUAN: Is there a possibility for the person watching TV to realize himself?
KARL: Both may. Both have the same ability, not none. Both make no difference, because by neither of them can you realize. When Ramana was asked what was the realization of Ramana, he said that there never was any Ramana who realized anything. That which is Self is ever-realized, so there is nothing to realize. But this non-event is to see that That which is existence is ever-realized and never needs any more or less realization of anyone, in the moment, that there is never anyone who is unrealized. That's all. This is a paradox. You realize there is nothing to realize. So there is no realized one left, because there was never anyone who was not realized.
JUAN: But to get to this point, it seems that, for the individual, there is a building up of energy.
KARL: This is all part of the consciousness business.
JUAN: But I never heard of anybody realizing himself in front of a TV!
KARL: Oh, there is an artist, Nam June Paik, from Korea. He' a very big artist—
FRANCESCO: Did you see this?
KARL: Yeah, he creates Buddha statues sitting in front of televisions—empty televisions. It means *Zazen*—nothing to realize.

It's hard to see that whatever you have done or not done, in spite of it, you are. You cannot do it; there is no way to it. But to see that—this is the way, to see absolutely—there is no way out of it, not by understanding—there is no before and no after—you are.

This is called, "the divine accident," but it's not an accident. It's simply called this to give it a name. It means the Self is realizing That which is, without any idea of before and after, in spite of whatever is done or not done by whatever person or object or consciousness, being in spite even of consciousness.

So, whatever you can realize, whatever is in the realm of consciousness, you are in spite of it. But whatever happens is in the realm of consciousness, of "I am"-ness, of coming and going, of Creator and creation, all that which is consciousness, which is the manifestation of existence. But to see that you are in spite of all that, in spite even of existence, there is no preparation for it. You cannot prepare yourself to be yourself. That is this absolute experience that nothing ever happened to That which you are.

This is in spite of whatever experience you had before or not. If I now would say something you could do—that because of some experience you had before, of light and this and that, that if you have this, you are what you are—you still would look for something. This looking doesn't lead to anything. But you cannot *not* do it. You have to seek. There will be looking. There will be longing. But in spite of the seeking, longing, whatever your experiences, you are.

It will happen in a split second as a side-effect of "whatever"—by the way, "Ah!"—then you can have another cup of coffee, because it is not an event. It has absolutely nothing to do with existence as you know it. So you cannot make any plan or religion of it.

All religions, all the tactics, all the tick-tack, whatever technique you use to get out of the tick-tack, is all part of the tick-tock of time. By no tactic can you get out of the tick-tack. This is like "tick"—and no more. There is not even time, there are not even ideas, nothing coming, nothing going—what to do?

But whatever you reach, by any effort, by any technique, you make a religion, and making a religion, a technique, or any understanding, you take it personally. It becomes an autobiography of an awakening. And then you may say, "my teaching is becoming clearer and clearer," or whatever. Whatever you say comes out of that "*my* understanding," "*my* realization." But it is still ignorance. So you add always ignorance to ignorance, because whatever quantity of experience you have, even this "divine" experience of love, is ignorance.

That which you are, you cannot experience in *any* sense. You are never in any sense. So even the "divine" whatever experiences of blissful blah blah blah, light, fireworks—it's nothing. Images, sensations, fleeting shadows, but not life itself.

KLARA: So somehow, you are the lucky one who got that. [group laughs]

A MAN: We start again!

Another MAN: Come on, there's an hour left!

KARL: That's what you want next life?

KLARA: I don't know, since there's no way out. I could be a businessman.

KARL: Or maybe underwear.

KLARA: Or a bird flying.

KARL: Oh, always nice things, of course. Maybe you will be immobile somewhere, not even knowing you exist, a bacteria or virus sitting in some nose!

MATTIAS: A nose full of reincarnations of *sadhus*, huh? Does one have to have a coffee after seeing that, or can I have a *lassi*? [group laughs]

KARL: Whatever. What comes next will be next. "Have another coffee" just means nothing happened and you are in spite of that. So whatever makes a difference in so-called life, the truth that you found, that you want to bring into life—my goodness, then you define what is an enlightened one and what is not, how a sage should behave, what a sage should perceive, and what is enlightenment. All this is still part of ignorance, of making frames for "whatever." Even the idea of a *jnani* is ignorance.

FRANCESCO: Oh, good day!

KARL: Good day?

FRANCESCO: Fantastic.

KARL: Fantastic, okay. But even calling that "ignorance" is ignorance. You cannot get out of ignorance. But that's beautiful. If it doesn't make any difference if you're ignorant or not, so what?

MATTIAS: It's like masochists; they also enjoy it. It's like *enjoy it* is another way to say "no way out."

KARL: No, you are in an S-M relationship. Self-masturbate—no, self-masochist? Some call it "master-bation." The master taking a bath in himself. I didn't say masturbating; I said master-bathing. Master-basting. Master-baiting. Don't take me wrong! [group laughs]

KAATJE: I didn't.

KARL: No? But it would be easy! So what was your question?

KLARA: No, it was not a question, it was just a standpoint.

KARL: I was winning in the lottery, you said?

KLARA: Yes.

A MAN: Divine lottery.

KARL: Yes, but I got nothing out of it. But that's so beautiful! You get nothing out of it. "Oh, you're the lucky one!" [group laughs] The lottery of gaining nothing. You play the lottery and then you're happy. "Oh, thank God, I gained nothing!" I have all the six numbers right, and zero in the pot.

Another MAN: Oh, they take the pot away.

KARL: You cannot smoke anymore?

MAN: No, the pot of money! [group laughs]

KARL: Okay, some serious questions now. [group laughs]

FRANCESCO: For a serious *guru.*

A Person Is One Who Hopes This Will End

KLARA: How do you recognize a real *guru?*

KARL: Don't ask me. Every seeker knows better than me. Because seekers make *gurus.* So you are the master. Ask yourself, what is a *guru* and what is not. There is always much discussion. "Oh, my *guru* is better than yours, for sure, because I have a real *guru,* you just have whatever. This one is nothing compared to that one. Just go to that one, then you will see. In the presence of that— Oh, my goodness, that one! Oy yoy yoy!" [group laughs]

CHARLES: Maybe the difference is that a false *guru* creates seekers.

KARL: You mean, false *gurus* have disciples?

CHARLES: Yeah, they make seekers. Seekers make *gurus,* but *gurus* who make seekers are a problem.

KARL: Dependency, you mean?

CHARLES: Yeah.

KARL: Still it's no problem. But there are many concepts like this. They say the *Satguru* is disappearing in front of you as you die in him. So he never makes you dependent on anything. He simply takes your whole existence away, so that you become That which is *Satguru,* that which is Self, will never try to make you dependent in any sense, for understanding or anything.

Anyone who tells you, "I can help you"—run for cover. Anyone who tells you, "I can give you something, I can transmit something, I can make you 'pfft,' give you some experience"—it's fine, it's entertainment too, but it would be not That.

So whatever makes more dependency—I don't know, it's part of the show, but if you look for That which you are, it will radically erase whatever you are not. *Der Sensenmann wird kommen* (the man with the scythe—Death—will come). Then it's *Zazen. Sense* (scythe). But this is all concepts. I have no idea.

You just ask, simply, That which is the master himself, and whatever you go to will be your master. At every moment, you are already in That which is your master. So don't worry. Whatever is life itself is here, now, and always giving you the right advice.

KLARA: I was also thinking about this, because why am I choosing to sit here? There must be a certain force—

KARL: The totality is placing that totality simply there where the totality is sitting. It's a total demand of totality that you sit there.

KLARA: And that I feel tense?

KARL: You play tennis?

KLARA: [laughing] There's a certain tension in my body.

KARL: Oh, you play too much or too little tennis? [points to a man in the group] There's a *Chi Kung* master; he can take the tension away.

It's all sensations, whatever comes to consciousness—movement, vibration—interacting. What is *your* tension? There is no "your" tension. There is simply a tension. There is energy in the vibration of that experience of feeling there's a tension. So what is with this tension?

KLARA: It's just there. It's not actually a question. I like to talk with you.

KARL: Welcome. Do you have a question?

JOAN: I feel that I'm benefiting just by being here.

KARL: Ah, yeah, me too! [group laughs] It's an absolute benefit to simply be what is. There is nothing to add to it.

JOAN: I guess I feel that my mind needs to try to think this way more and more, to practice it more and more.

KARL: We can talk about that inexhaustible need of that mind. As it is as absolute as That which is existence, what you would call "mind," which is spirit, is inexhaustible in realizing itself in whatever question. So there will always be a question, answer, question, answer, "quention," quench, quench, quench, squeeze, squeeze, squeeze, no way out.

The Holy Spirit of "I am," consciousness as "I am," always will create. It's a functioning of that totality of consciousness. This is creating every moment new, new, new, new—infinite, inexhaustible.

So there will always be a question, a longing, a seeking—this and that forms and non-forms—all this. If you really see, there will never be any end to it, because there was never any beginning to it—information, vibration, consciousness—so what? There is only a person as long as there is one who hopes this will end one day. "By *my* enlightenment, by *my* realization, I will stop that."

But if you totally see, it will never stop, because there is nothing that can stop—this is peace of mind. There is mind, but you never mind, because you see that whatever you do you cannot stop what is not there, what never started, what never will end. What to do? I can only continue to point to the Absolute you are, that in spite of mind or no-mind or any idea, you are, never because of it. What to do with that?

JOAN: It's great.

KARL: It's not so bad. But that's the thing, it's neither good nor bad. You cannot decide if it's good or bad, so it's very good. Thérèse! Still a happy failure?

THERESE: I'm waiting to see if it's going to stop. I'm like—ooh!—too good to be true?

KARL: Is there a limit to happiness?

THERESE: [laughing] I'm really waiting.

KARL: [laughing] You just keep quiet. *Steterstand* (stand steady). Maybe you?

A Finnish MAN: Me?

KARL: Yeah.

MAN: I guess whatever I say, you will cross me anyway.

KARL: Never! I'm very kind. "Don't trust him!"

MAN: This is my first time. I'm just listening. I think it's really good that you cross whatever I'm thinking because then I might gain something new. But really I don't have anything nice to say now.

KARL: No, it's good to say that. You might say something and it won't make a difference. Whatever question comes out, with or without answer, it will be "pfft."

So see that questionlessness you are, simply being That which is prior to any question and answer, it doesn't even need the fulfillment of that question as an answer. There is not the need of an answer. The question comes by itself and goes by itself, but not by an answer. So in spite of an answer, it will go again. So even the question "Who am I?" doesn't need an answer. It will be there for a while and then it will drop by itself.

MAN: Okay.

KARL: What to do?

MAN: Nothing.

KARL: Just enjoy yourself, because this will take a while. Hello! Everything fine? Do you have something? Just fishing.

The Non-doer Does the Most

ROSA: It's not a question, it's just a thought.

KARL: I always start like this, I know.

ROSA: My purpose in coming here was—I said "was"— to quiet the mind. The promise for me was that this place, Arunachala and Ramana, will help me—I know what you are going to say!—but that they will help me. [laughs] So there is really nothing to do, because there is no one who observes, there is nothing to observe the mind, the thoughts. Or the paradox that it's everything together, the observer, the observed, etc.

KARL: Whatever you say.

ROSA: I feel my purpose is not to do anything about it?

KARL: Oh, that's still a purpose.

ROSA: Yes. Therefore I say, my purpose— Okay, there is no purpose.

KARL: There is a purpose, but there is no purpose. There is time, but there is no time. There is longing, but there is no longing. What do you say then? You come and you see and then you go and you see.

ROSA: So sitting in a lotus position and meditating—

KARL: Oh, it looks very good.

ROSA: It's very fancy, yeah, but it's all—

KARL: No, it looks good. Isn't that enough?

ROSA: [laughing] It's never enough.

KARL: A rose looks very beautiful, but it never asks, "Why am I beautiful?" So you take the lotus position and it looks good. Wonderful!

ROSA: Half. I can only do half lotus. [group laughs] So, what to do? Nothing.

KARL: Even nothing is too much. Do your best.

ROSA: But that's pressure.

KARL: No. You can only do your best. You are the best you can be. The Absolute. Whatever comes out of that All-goodness, is goodness itself, it can only be good. It cannot realize itself without that. Whatever you do is the best you can do.

And it is the best. It's the absolute doing of absolute existence. Whatever doing there is, it's the absolute doing of the Absolute, doing what it can do best—simply realizing itself. Whatever is experiencing itself is the Self experiencing itself. It can only be the best.

ROSA: And the non-doer?

KARL: What non-doer? The non-doer does the most. [group laughs] The non-doer! A man from Texas said, "I am not the doer! I am the non-doer!" and then he rode a bike and forgot he was in the street—boom! [group laughs]

This is really the beauty of it. The understanding that there is nothing to do, even that understanding is fleeting. Forget it. You land on that understanding, and that understanding comes and goes. You have to nourish, you have to keep, you have to stay in the clarity—you have to abide in that understanding. But the effortlessness you are is in spite of understanding or not understanding, in spite of effort or no effort.

There is That which is effortlessness, which is your nature. You cannot reach this by any effort of doing or not doing. So simply be, what you cannot be.

Be what you cannot be. Be be! You may come to some understanding, but that will go too.

ROSA: So I'm going away empty.

KARL: That which is *you* as absolute Heart, absolutely empty of any idea of what you are and are not, even the idea of "emptiness," being empty of the idea of "emptiness," which no one can be, may come, but no one goes. As you never arrived, you cannot leave anymore. So the ghost is gone and the image, the phantom, is seen as it is.

ROSA: And there's also no bottle.

KARL: You're right. There's neither inside nor outside—but there is. If you say there is none, there's still is one.

ROSA: One?

KARL: To say, "there is no one," there's still one. If you say, "there's no inside and outside," there's still an inside and outside, because it needs one to say that there is no inside and outside, and that one is still making an inside and outside, even by saying it. There is no escape.

This is still part of that understanding. It is still ignorance. Whatever you define, it's ignorance. Any definition comes out of a definer, and that definer is a liar anyway, so whatever lie comes out of that definer himself is a lie. The first definer, "I," is already a lie, as it's an image, it's not what you are, as you are prior to that liar. Out of that lie, only lies come. The liar is *einerlei* (one something), and out of *einerlei* comes *zweierlei* (two something). German is really—, or Dutch.

KAATJE: Double Dutch.

KARL: German is double Dutch, total Dutch. [both laugh] So see, even the lie, the first image, the first mirror, the absolute mirror of what you are, already is not showing yourself. The mirror doesn't show anything, so that is what you are, It is not anything you can say, name, form, frame, "whatever." Even the first frame of the mirror is a lie. Whatever comes and shows in the mirror of awareness, as that first one, is already a lie, it becomes part of that lie. Then *es ist einerlei* (it makes no difference; it doesn't matter).

So to see the phantom, the liar, already as a lie, who then cares about what comes out of that lie? This lie cannot touch you. This lie can never change you or move you one inch.

A Polish WOMAN: The helplessness is that you see the world, but you are not in the world, but you are also the world.

KARL: Also?

WOMAN: That which you are must also be in the world.

KARL: Must be? Are you a master? Must be? Forget it.

WOMAN: Yeah.

KARL: Still trying, clack, clack, clack.

WOMAN: No.

KARL: No? Must be. Okay. Whatever you say.

FRANCESCO: It's a wonderful movie, eh?

KARL: It's not so bad.

FRANCESCO: And *sadhana* is fantastic.

KARL: [laughing] As I always tell you, in spite of *sadhana*, you are, but if you could avoid one *sadhana*, you could avoid existence. So in that sense, then, *sadhana* is fantastic. It becomes meditation without an intention that you can get something out of it. And with that *sadhana* you are already the Absolute, because there is no expectation coming out of that meditation. There is longing, but nothing to get out of the longing, so that longing is already meditation.

FRANCESCO: Yeah, but for me to understand this, I need *sadhana*.

KARL: In spite of—

FRANCESCO: In spite, in spite!

KARL: So enjoy *sadhana*. Because that is enjoying meditation, enjoying That which is meditation, because there is no expectation in it. When there is no expectation, you see nothing can be added to That which you are by doing or not doing. Then everything is meditation. You meditate about That which you are, infinitely, but not to expect any result, you can never gain the knowledge of what you are by meditation.

So you are in spite of meditation, not because. And by being in spite of meditation, there is meditation. Then you absolutely enjoy the meditation because there is no importance in it. It's not heavy, it's nothing, it's so light. Poof! It's a big poof.

KAATJE: No goal.

KARL: Even no "no goal." You have no purse anymore, because you have no purpose. You're all nothing. You have nothing to lose and nothing to gain by anything. *In Totale, habe nichts. Kann nichts, habe nichts, will nichts.* How to translate this? "Completely have nothing. Do nothing, have nothing, want nothing."

A German WOMAN: Good for nothing!

KARL: Good for nothing, worth nothing. Everything you want to avoid, you are.

An Italian MAN: I'm thinking about the meditation you are talking about. You are gone. There's simply nothing. There's no gaining. There's simply nothing, you disappear and then you are there again.

KARL: No, you never disappear.

MAN: It feels like that.

KARL: It feels like that, but that is only the sensation of an experiencer who disappears, but never you. That sensation of being and then disappearing is all part of the movie, but you never come and never go. You have to be unmovable so that movement may happen, so that appearance and disappearance may happen. What you are has to be unmovable.

The absolute experience you are never moves an inch. So India came to you; you never came to India. The body came to you, but no one ever came to the body. Simply switch. You are not a child of time, but what you call "time" is a child of you. Appearance and disappearance are fleeting shadows in what is you, as That which is experiencing itself, but you are never part of what can be experienced.

So you are not the body that is moving to whatever place, the place comes to you. All the places, all the bodies, all the sensations are in you, but you are not in any sensation. So out of the feeling that you go to sleep, sleep happens in what you are, that's all. But no one goes to sleep and no one wakes up. So you are asleep awake and awake asleep, as you are never asleep and never awake. Both are appearances and disappearances, ideas and sensations, in what you are.

MAN: It needs a click to understand it.

KARL: No, it's not an understanding. It doesn't need anything. In a split second you see it was always like this. No one ever needed any click or understanding or difference of perception. Even the difference of perception is part of the dream. So whatever you can say, whatever needs a change of anything, is part of the movie. But That which you are, which is prior to the sensational movie with appearances, ideas, and objects, will never change, by any change.

When *My* Understanding Drops, That Is Devotion

MR. IYER: I read somewhere, don't pay too much attention to the words of the master. They're not going to help you, something else is working on you. Just be as you are in *satsang.* Because in *satsang,* several people raise different types of questions. Some are relevant to me, some are not. So, I should pay attention to the things which are relevant to me and keep quiet for the other questions, or are the others also relevant to me?

KARL: *Be As You Are.*

MR. IYER: Is the influence better by hearing the words, or—?

KARL: No, the words have no influence. The words as a form have no influence. That you are here, that I am not talking to a ghost, that what is talking is no different from what is listening, it's all to see that That which is talking and That which is listening is no different, in essence.

What is called "*satsang,*" is here, now, but That which is talking does not talk to anyone. It's not what is said, not the forms, whatever ideas come as words. Every word is loaded by the absence of separation. And being loaded with the absence of separation, the listener and That which is saying something are no different. So there is the nakedness talking to the nakedness, and that counts, not the words, not the forms, not the relevant or irrelevant things. In spite of relevance or irrelevance, That which is talking and That which is listening are That which is, in essence, is Heart. So Self talks to Self, as Heart talks to Heart, as there is only That which is Heart.

So don't give so much attention to the forms and objects and words. Simply be as you are, as That which you are listening to is no different from what you are. This is always the message—there is no message, no messenger and no receiver. There is transmission and receiving, but That which is transmitting and That which is receiving are no different. So it doesn't matter what is transmitted, only that there is no transmitter and no talking to anyone who is receiving. And the absence of a transmitter and a receiver, that absolute absence of separation, of a second one, is called "*satsang.*"

That is what is meant when a master tells you to, "be as you are," and then see and show your devotion. Devotion means total respect by becoming That which is your master, by seeing that That which is speaking is no different from That which is listening, by being That which is speaking and listening, in this instant.

That is devotion. By giving up the individuality of "me," being a receiver, of *my* understanding. When this "my" drops, that is devotion, and not emotion.

So I'm asking for devotion, total devotion, by asking you to be That which is me. I don't ask you to understand or do anything. *Be As You Are* means be That which is talking, be That which is listening, but without any listener, and without seeing one who is talking. So you have to see the essence, in whatever word, in whatever comes and goes, in order to be that.

Again, these words I just said, don't count. They are totally irrelevant, being irrelevant, it's like they are erasing, annihilating, forms and objects of that understanding. It's maybe the emptiness or the absence of separation that you sit here. But no one can create this, there can be no doing for it. So what to do? Many words, huh? That's okay?

MR. IYER: Many times when you've said something, I haven't understood, but later I realize the truth in it. Right now, I don't find any difference.

KARL: The words make no difference, but if you see that words make no difference for what you are, that makes all the difference. Because then you see that, independent of understanding, independent of words, you are what you are. Be as you are in spite of the words, not because of the words. I cannot change what you are. I have nothing to give and nothing to share here. The Absolute you are doesn't need anything from me, from That which is sitting here talking. It cannot add something to what you are. I'm always pointing out that there is no teaching, no teacher, and no disciple. Whatever I say is a total pointer to that, if I am in a good position. The rest is—I don't know. So by grace, you are sitting here and I am, by grace, sitting here, and grace is all there is. And grace talks to That which is grace, telling grace, "Don't wait for grace, because grace will not come."

A WOMAN: My name is Grace! [group laughs]

FRANCESCO: Thank you for coming.

KARL: Grace just arrived!

GEORG: Have another coffee!

KARL: So don't wait for grace, because grace is already here, and grace will never come because grace is what you are. Whatever is, is grace. So you'd better not wait for it, because it will never come. It's already here. It never left you, so you cannot gain it back. You cannot lose what you are, as you are grace itself.

So don't wait for any master or anyone to bring it to you. There will never be anyone who can give it to you. And whoever tells you, "I can give it to you by initiation, by transmission," or whatever, is lying, because it cannot be given to you, as it could never be taken away from you. As you never lost what you are, you can never gain it back by anyone, not by any word, transmission, *shakti*—not by any experience you get—will you become what you are. Hallelujah!

A MAN: Is *satsang* a symptom of craziness then?

KARL: Everything is a symptom of the crazy idea that you were born. You are in a psychic hospital here, now, and I am the doctor who tells you there is only a psychic hospital, but there is no one in the hospital.

This is like telling you there is no one sick because you cannot find the patient that you are. So by not finding yourself in any place—as there is a psychic hospital, and all these ideas are part of that hospital—but by not finding anyone who is in that hospital, there is simply a hospital, so what? So you see that you are in spite of the hospital. There was never anyone in the hospital. There is craziness, but so what?

MAN: It's fun.

KARL: Oh, it's fun, it's sport, whatever you call it. Olympic game of craziness.

MAN: Who's the master?

KARL: The doctor. The craziest one is always the master. That's called "crazy wisdom." The master is always the most crazy; the peak of the craziness is the *guru*. The craziest idea that you can have is that there is a Self or *guru* at all. So on top of the craziness, there is a master of craziness. How much more crazy can one get? It's all a crazy idea, the beginning of the idea that you exist. With the crazy idea, the psychic hospital opens.

MATTIAS: Eternally open.

KARL: It never started, because this crazy idea has no beginning and no end. As there never was any beginning of the idea of "existence," it will never end. So you'd better not wait for this hospital to close, because it never opened.

THERESE: But what an imagination, eh?

KARL: What an absolute imagination you are!

THERESE: It's too much!
KARL: Too much?
THERESE: I mean, such variety, colors, smells, people—it's too much. It's so much!
KARL: And imagine, it all comes out of what you are!
THERESE: I know.
KARL: You know?
THERESE: [laughing] One first lie and boom!

Whatever You Do About Ignorance, You Make It More

PETE: It's imagination. There are no patients in the hospital; they are all imaginary. It's thoughts that arise in the mind. So, is there a corrective thought? If there are these thoughts that create imaginary people, is there a corrective thought?
KARL: You mean, is there a cure for it?
PETE: Well, I don't want to get into the trap of saying there's some understanding, some breakthrough, but is there a corrective thought that kind of backs you out?
KARL: Nisargadatta gave the ultimate medicine for the craziness, the sickness, this disease of existence. Look for the one who is there at all.
PETE: Every time my mind throws up the idea there's a person, then I have a corrective thought that reminds me, "Oh, I'm not a person. Now I remember."
KARL: But this depends on remembering. It seems to be that by understanding there is a temporary way out of the mistake, but that temporary way out is already a mistake. It's still a mistake. By understanding, you control something, you accept that you are out of impersonal consciousness, but what steps out by effort, always drops back. At the moment that effort stops, by whatever event, you're back into that. You are always depending on understanding or some effort, alertness, whatever you call it.

But I'm asking you to be the total lazy bastard you are, which has never done anything, which is in spite of doing or not doing, what it is, never because. Be That which never was in any action or non-action, what was simply, totally still in itself, without any movement ever—for that, nothing ever happened.

So even the understanding never happened, as there never was any non-understanding. There cannot be any understanding at all. So be That which is absolute knowledge but by not knowing anything. All these are words and pointers, so that you will see in a split second, that in spite of knowing or not knowing, you are what you are, not because of anything.

No one can give it to you. This is simply like when the heart is broken because you drop the love for yourself. By your interest, by your loving yourself, you are involved in these images, all the sensations—because you love yourself.

PETE: There's this imaginary person, and he came to this *satsang*, and he's talking to this imaginary person over here, and when I look at the imaginary person, he's done all these *sadhanas*, and I don't know why he's done them. I couldn't stop him from doing them; he did it, I watched. He did all these *sadhanas*, came to India, he did all these different things. I don't know why he did these crazy things.

KARL: As I said before, all the *sadhanas*, all the action, every breath you take, has to be done, as whatever is done is so unique and absolute in that action and done by that totality. Without that action, there would be no totality, there would be no Absolute. So whatever *sadhana* you have done or not done, had to be there, absolutely, and the next step you will do has to be there, because there is no way out of it.

PETE: As he's stumbling along this way, doing these *sadhanas*, this imaginary person starts reading some books about Vedanta, and he starts hearing these kind of *satsangs*, so then he starts having these corrective thoughts, what I'm calling "corrective thoughts," that make him think about himself in a different way. He starts thinking, "Oh, maybe I'm not a person, maybe this is just imaginary, maybe this is just a film that I'm watching, maybe I'm something prior to this." But again, this is all thought.

KARL: Yeah, as I said, you just add something to the ignorance that was before. Only the quantity of ignorance is expanding.

PETE: And all the words I'm hearing from the imaginary person in the chair here, the words are based upon thoughts that arise in the mind of the imaginary person.

KARL: Always adding more to the quantity of ignorance. Whatever I can say will always be ignorance. That which is—we cannot talk about anyway. I can only sit here and talk and talk and talk and add more quantity, spitting it out, and in spite of that, I am.

PETE: One person wakes up watching TV, another person does so many *sadhanas* and wakes up, but it doesn't matter. He couldn't have not done the *sadhanas*. They were done. They were there.

KARL: Yeah. He had to do the *sadhanas*. The one who was sitting in front of the television *had* to sit in front of the television, and that is meditation too. Consciousness, in whatever given moment, is meditating about That which is the Self. Whatever is consciousness is longing for that happiness, and out of that longing, there is meditation for happiness. So, if you sit in front of a television, you do it to be happy. Everything comes out of the wish to be happy all the time.

PETE: So if I go to the movie house, and I watch James Bond, and I start thinking "I am James Bond," and when he comes out the door, I start thinking, "I chose to turn right, I chose to turn left." And then later, someone says, "No, you're not James Bond. You're watching a movie, you're in a movie house, you're watching it, you didn't make those choices."

KARL: But then you are in another movie, that's all.

[The group giggles and murmurs, "Mmm," "Very interesting!", etc.]

KARL: You step from one movie to another movie.

PETE: There's some shift where I can be who I've been all along.

KARL: There's no shift. No! Never, ever.

PETE: First I thought I was James Bond; I thought I was the one who turned right—

KARL: But even as James Bond, you are who you are.

PETE: —But all along I was sitting in the movie house, watching.

KARL: But the one who tells you that you are not the movie is still in the movie. You cannot get out of the movie. You are That which is the movie, whether you like it or not, There is "no way out." You cannot go to another realm of understanding and then be out of the movie. That would be by effort again and you would be depending on it. You would still be depending on some understanding, on someone to tell you, "You are not the movie, you are not the character." So what then?

In spite of Jesus realizing the Heart, there is still existence, still seeking.

In spite of Buddha, in spite of Ramana, in spite of all the sages, there is still seeking happening and seekers sitting around listening to what cannot be told. So forget it!

AIKO: Is that called, "the ultimate joke"?

KARL: The ultimate joke is that there is not an ultimate joke. There is not even a joker. It sounds good, I know, that there will be a master and he will tell you that you are not the character you thought you were. So what then? You step from identification to non-identification. You become the "I am." "Okay, I am not in the movie," but that one who is not in the movie forgets and steps back into the movie.

You have to be—in the movie and out of the movie—what you are. If you are only in an understanding of what you are, what kind of understanding is it? What kind of existence would it be? Is that freedom?

PETE: And it's not a question of just reminding yourself, like Ramana said, do the inquiry, do the "Who am I?"

KARL: Did Ramana have a guru in the lifetime before he had that experience, who told him, "You are not the body, you are not the character?"

PETE: It's not a matter of doing, this kind of mental gymnastics of a corrective thought that reminds you that you're not?

KARL: Yeah, but it sounded like it. You're walking around saying, "I'm not the doer, I'm not the doer, I'm not the doer!" It sounds crazy. It's the same as if you walk around saying, "I'm doing it, I'm doing it, I'm doing it!" What's the difference? Corrective thought?!

Is there a "correct" thought at all? So I'm always pointing to the fact that in spite of thought, or whatever concept you can bring up, in spite of that, you are. So be That which is in spite of it and not because of any corrective thought.

PETE: Your words are pointers to the thoughts that you're having, they reflect your thoughts, and they are corrective thoughts. They are correcting me.

KARL: I am correcting no one. In spite of what I tell you, you are, not because. I have nothing to correct, as I don't see anything wrong. There was never any problem, so there is no problem to solve. I am not talking to a ghost of corrective thoughts. Who cares about these corrective thoughts and any thought of any ghost anyway? Hmm? Do you care?

JOAN: I don't know if I'm going to interpret it right, but you were saying that one who makes definitions is a liar. Immediately, this one is already a liar. So are we making an action by recognizing that it's a lie?

KARL: That is part of the lie. What an idea that you could correct a lie?! This is like the famous story of the "me" who, wants to correct the "me," and becomes a policeman himself. First, he is a thief, a liar, and he says, "Oh, I will make sure that you will become truth, from now on, I will tell you the truth. Before I was a liar, but now I will tell you the truth. This will be a 'correct' thought. With this thought, I correct you; before I was incorrect but now I am being correct! Am I fine enough for you now? Am I pleasing you now, or was I pleasing you before? Before, maybe I was annoying you, but now I will please you. From now on, I will behave. Oh my goodness, I will give you my attention now. You're very promising, my dear."

Consciousness plays both roles. "Incorrect. Correct. Now I can make you happy. Now I'm in the correct position to make you happy, to fuck you right. Now I'm a correct fucker, before I was an incorrect fucker. I'm fucking anyway!" [group "ohs" and "ah-has" and giggles]

JOAN: But how do you make it stop? Correct, incorrect—

KARL: I have no idea. For whom does it have to stop? It never started! Who needs this to stop?

JOAN: The person who is suffering.

KARL: Let it suffer. It's still the Almighty. "Oh, poor me! Poor Almighty, suffering from an idea. Oh my goodness. Being so in love with yourself, taking yourself as so important, then you suffer. Oh my Almighty, how you are suffering by taking yourself as so important! I'm very sorry about you. You feel my compassion. Hallelujah. The Almighty is suffering! Oh, I am suffering with you now." [group laughs]

JOAN: We want to be free of all this!

KARL: Because you want to be free, you are in prison—by this idea. What an idea! Freedom, wants to be free, freedom wants to be free! Hello, everyone listen! Freedom wants to be free! Everyone understand? No? Okay. What a joke! Freedom is looking for freedom. "Hey, look at me! Give me attention! I want to be free. Give me freedom!" asked Freedom. [group laughs] Ai yi yi. "Don't you see me as a person suffering?" No!

Spanish MAN: How many rehearsals this morning?

CHARLES: He's asking, how many rehearsals for this show?

KARL: *Da Capo* (from the beginning). Always *Da Capo, Da Capo, Da Capo.*

Kaputt, kaputt, kaputt (spoiled, ruined, broken to pieces).

Buddha said that the end of suffering is not finding the sufferer, that's all. So whatever you do about the suffering or the ignorance, you increase it. The more you want to avoid suffering, the more you suffer. But you cannot find the sufferer, that's all. There was never, and never will be, a sufferer.

The Self cannot suffer about the Self, because there is no second self it can suffer about. So there was never any sufferer. So what! There is suffering. Oh, my goodness. Have a drink. *Prost* (cheers for) suffering.

THERESE: One more minute.

KARL: Okay, last question.

PETE: If the corrective thought is a liar, if any thought is a liar, and you're a liar, and I'm a liar—

KARL: Isn't it wonderful? [group laughs]

MATTIAS: There's nothing reliable.

KARL: You cannot rely on anything! Everything is a lie. So you are totally "irre-lie-able." *Irrer.*

THERESE: What is *Irrer*?

KARL: *Irrer* means you are totally crazy. You are craziness itself.

PETE: But you are a funny liar, so it's fun to sit here and laugh.

KARL: That's the only thing, the humor of That which is the liar. By seeing the liar as a liar, liar, liar, it becomes all *einerlei* (one something; doesn't matter). *Einerlei* means it's all Self. So if everything's a lie, then everything is Self. But to point to truth, as long as you frame truth, you say, "Lie, lie, lie, lie, lie."

THERESE: It's like singing a song. "Lie, lie, lie, lie, lie, lie, lie!"

[Karl and others join in. "Lie, lie, lie, lie, lie, lie, lie!" Lots of laughter all around.]

THERESE: Group singing. Let's make a CD.

FRANCESCO: Look what happens after two hours with this guy!

KARL: Thank you.

[Everyone is laughing.]

"Be the unmoved Heart itself—
which was never touched or
untouched, never shaken or
changed in any sense."

January 18

The Problem Is that There Is No Problem; or, the End of Worry and Boredom

It's the Total Demand of the Totality of Existence That You Worry

KARL: Okay. Everyone knows how this works? Question and answer.

THERESE: Hey, last night I almost locked everybody in.

KARL: Yeah?

THERESE: I left the movie, and I went out to look for my shoes and some-how I locked the door from outside. And then I hear boom, boom, boom, so—

KARL: That's famous. But there must be another exit somewhere else. Was it a good movie?

THERESE: The plot was confusing and the English was too much. I under-stood nothing. The music was good.

KARL: You have to watch more movies. I learned my English from watching television in America, so I'm used to it.

THERESE: I watch English movies. I'm more used to the British English.

KARL: Mmm. I'm used to *Perry Mason*. It's so amazing, because I learned my English with *Perry Mason*.

MARY: My grandmother was addicted to watching *Perry Mason*.

KARL: Mine too. Every morning. One hour of watching *Perry Mason* and then ten minutes of *All My Children*. It was enough.

MARY: She had a box of chocolates and *Perry Mason*.

KARL: Yeah, that's paradise.

CHARLES: All right, so now that we know what paradise is, we can go.

KARL: [laughing] Sounds good. I always had an *E* in English at school.

THERESE: It's the worst note, no?

KARL: No, there's one more. In the German system, it's a *5*. If you have two *5*s, or one *6*, you're out. But if you have one *5* you can stay in the same class. So I always managed with that one *5*. In the rest of the subjects I was okay, but English—

THERESE: My English teacher had the most horrible French accent.

KARL: Ah, now we know where it comes from! Okay, then let's start—with a spiritual movie.

KLARA: Karl, I have a question. What did Ramana mean when he said to "abide in the Self"?

KARL: Self-abidance? To make a story of it . . . for me, it's like the snake of Shiva looking at his own tail. Looking at the movement you see that abidance means you bite your own tail, and by biting in your own tail you see that That which is the world is no different from what you are. For me that is "a-bite-ance."

That is compassion. You simply, totally abide in That which is. You simply go into That which is the world, what is. You identify with what is the world, and then you see there is total compassion, there is total abidance in what you are. So you bite yourself and then you see there is nothing different from what you are. Sounds good?

But Ramana meant it a bit differently, I think. Abidance in the Self is simply being That which is Heart, which is prior to the "I"-thought—to stay prior to the "I"-thought—being That from which the "I"-thought springs. To stay in the Source, as the Source you are, by seeing that "I"-thought come in the morning in whatever form of "in-form-ation," but That which you are is prior to that.

KLARA: It's actually not possible.

KARL: Nothing else is possible. You cannot *not* abide, as you are That anyway. You are That which is the Source of the "I"-thought, Heart itself, and in the Heart, the "I"-thought as an "in-form-ation" blooms. But you are not what comes as an "I"-thought, so stay in That which is permanent, absolutely permanent, as solid as it can be, the Heart itself, unmoved by the idea. That is abidance.

Be the unmoved Heart itself—which is never touched or untouched, never shaken or changed in any sense—simply by seeing the "I"-thought as a phantom thought and staying as That which is prior to it.

By being attracted to that "I"-thought, by taking it as real, you give it reality. You give it life. But you are life itself. And by your life itself you give life. Whatever you give attention to becomes reality. But if you give attention to That which is attention, that which is Heart itself, that is abidance. It's awareness of awareness. So stay in it.

But how can you stay in it? At first it's a concept, like a pointer, but the question, "Who am I?" maybe puts you into the mystery of That which is prior to it. It can annihilate the story of "me," of doership, of whatever history you can imagine, because the "I"-thought is surrounded by a cloud of history. By asking the question, there is no longer an "I" who can collect history, and more and more, the history of the "I"-thought vanishes into awareness, as the question puts you into the mystery. So it's a concept. It may erase that first concept the you are born. And, without the first concept that you are born, That which is "I" itself sinks into That which is Heart, naturally. So stay in the question. That's abidance.

But no one knows if it works or not. That's something else. But you're sitting here, by grace, and you're asking yourself the question by grace. So grace is always here, without any question. Grace leads every step you make in your whole existence anyway. The next step will be led by the totality too. So don't worry.

KLARA: But this is exactly the point. I am worrying.

KARL: You're worrying, so that is actually what totality wants you to do, to worry at that moment. Just don't doubt it. There is a total demand of the totality of existence that you worry, and that worry is exactly the next step of whatever step you take.

KLARA: I cannot follow that.

KARL: You cannot follow this, as you never followed anything. [Klara laughs] You try to follow something that you cannot follow anyway. You try to understand some mystery of existence, but you will never understand.

There will be total understanding when you *are* the mystery. Only by being the mystery, there is absolute understanding, only by the total absence of a "me" who is in the idea of "understanding." In that absence, there is absolute understanding without any doubt. But in that doubter, "me," you'll always doubt. Whatever is understanding or non-understanding, you will always doubt. This is a functioning of "me." It has to doubt. Undoubtedly. So let the doubter doubt what the doubter can doubt about. [group laughs]

KLARA: But then comes worry.

KARL: Out of doubting come worries. For sure. Out of the doubt that you exist, you worry about your existence. You become Shakespeare. Shakes by beer. "To be or not to be." You doubt.

KLARA: Yeah, I'm very much worrying about what you said yesterday, that there is no advantage.

KARL: But that there is no advantage *is* the absolute advantage. Just see it, and relax in it. Because if you see there is absolutely no advantage for what you are, with the idea of an "advantage," the idea of a "disadvantage," drops too.

Then you are free of the idea of "me," because this "me" is living out of the idea of an advantage, that's all. Without the advantage idea there is no "me" possible. But the "me" has to doubt, because in this functioning the survival system starts.

So you have to doubt that because, by the understanding, "me" will not exist. That understanding will simply annihilate you totally, taking the "me" away, because the "me" is living out of hope and advantage. So you make having no problems into a problem, because you live out of problems, that's all.

KLARA: It's true.

KARL: Yeah, it's true—or not. [group laughs] That which is "me," like an object, lives out of the doubting and worrying and advantage idea. So "whatever" tells you, "there is no problem," by that understanding, you'll always fight against it.

You will always say, "I have to meditate, I have to do something to get some understanding. I first have to understand, and then maybe I will agree. First, existence has to be tamed for me, by understanding, by controlling, then I will agree to existence!" No? Yeah, yeah, yeah.

The circus director always says that. But you are the circus, and the "I"-thought is the director who thinks he can direct the circus. But clowns do what they want, never what the director says. The clowns are the other thoughts, as well as the lions and the beasts. Hmmm? Maybe the penguins can be tamed, the penguin thoughts. Or the pigs maybe. [group laughs]

The End of Imagination

KLARA: I was thinking, hoping—the yogis are teaching that, at a certain level, you can't fall back; it's not possible; you annihilate that.

FRANCESCO: You can't?

KARL: She means the supreme Yoga where, when you annihilate the first thought of "me," of "I," the first "I"-thought is seen as a phantom, erased by being what you are, maintained in That which is Heart. After the total annihilation of the first thought, "I," then you cannot go back, because without the first thought, there's no going back. So to control the other thoughts is futile.

It all depends on the first thought. Go to the "I"-thought, directly, and simply in the question, "Who am I?" annihilate the "I"-thought, rooting it out totally by that question. The "I"-thought is the idea of being born, of existence at all. When that is really rooted out, totally up-rooted, then there is no way back. But as long as the first card is there in the card-house of your concepts, the first card will always produce another concept. The house will be built again.

You may cut some branches, but it means nothing, because the tree will grow back even further. So controlling the mind is making it grow even more.

You have to go to the root of the mind, the "I"-thought. Without rooting that out totally, it always will grow again even more, and then it will make a religion out of it. Religion comes out of spiritual experiences, but the "I"-thought is still there, and it creates a personal history of religious experiences.

There are many enlightenments and awakenings and experiences, but they are taken personally, from them comes religions, or techniques, or even a Yoga technique of cutting some branches.

Ramana was very radical, in a sense, he asked us to go directly to the root-thought. Because without that root-thought, there is no tree—there never was and never will be. That's the meaning of the supreme Yoga, which is the direct path to annihilating the first thought, the first card of your card-house of concepts. The first card of the idea even of "existence," the first notion of existence as "I," which is awareness, the "I"-awareness—which is already a phantom.

Out of awareness—as the Father, Source—always comes "I am" and "I am so-and-so." By seeing the first awareness, "I," as a mirror and not what you are, not Heart, which is prior to the "I"-thought, you stay in That which is prior, the mystery of That which is Heart. Being totally empty of any idea of what you are and what you are not, there's an absolute emptiness, which is freedom of ideas of a second, of "whatever."

So the "I"-thought may come or not, but there is no one who cares anymore, because this [holds up his fist to symbolize Heart] automatically comes as awareness [thumb], "I am"-ness [thumb and index finger], and "I am so-and-so" [thumb, index, and middle fingers]. But this [fist] is what you are absolutely. So they [thumb, index, and middle fingers] may come or not, but they never came and never will go. So they were never there. Even then, this trinity of your realization [thumb, index, and middle fingers] is Heart itself too [fist]. There is no difference anymore. This [fist] is the end of a total separation which comes with the "I"-thought. Then there may be an "I"-thought or whatever comes out of it, but all is Heart. So all there is, is Self, when this [fist] is what you are.

This is the end of imagination, because whatever you imagine then is no different from what you are, as all this [thumb, index, and middle fingers] is Heart [fist], in whatever shape and form it comes. Whatever is, is Heart. So there is no separation anymore. No second.

Whatever you want to do with the "I," "I am," and "I am so-and-so," you're simply wanting to cure something that was never. There was never any disease. But by wanting to get rid of something, you make it real. So whatever you do in "I am so-and-so" or "I am" is simply giving some reality to something that is not.

So this direct asking, "Who is that meditator I am?", going to the mystery which is Heart itself, this uproots even the idea of "existence." And then the absolute existence is there without even the idea of "existence."

It's enough supreme Yoga? Supreme. Some question about this?

MR. RAO: You understand that there is some technique, then, that you can apply to the first thought?

KARL: Ramana was offering the technique of, "Who am I?" This technique is like a concept that annihilates all the concepts of your existence, and then finally, it drops too. Say you have a concept of a disease you have to cure. Ask, "Is there anyone who is sick at all?" This is the ultimate medicine which has been offered by Nisargadatta, Ramana and others, for so long.

By the question, "Who am I?" or "Is there anyone who is sick?", you want to find yourself. But then you have to ask, "What is this finding of the Self, this seeking for That which I am?" Can it lead to a finding? Or, is it an absolute "not finding" of what you are which *is* the absolute finding? Is it by absolutely not finding what you are, that you are what you are, and not by the finding of any object or concept or whatever experience you're hunting?

So you look infinitely and then, at one point, the seeking simply drops because there is a resignation of seeing that you cannot find yourself in any place or object or experience. Then it collapses. And then you look inward for That which is, but even there, you don't find it. So there is a "not finding" on the outside and a "not finding" on the inside. So then, the total resignation comes, and you stop, full stop. Then you see you are already That which you are looking for.

So at the moment you seek, you go out. Then you have an awakening, and then you go inside to the oneness. But even in the oneness, you cannot find yourself, as you are neither the oneness nor the separation. Both are two sides of the medal, but you are always That which is the medal itself, which has many sides.

But both extreme sides—separation and oneness—are only the sides of what you are, so they are imagination. You are always That which cannot be imagined, cannot be framed by any idea. Any idea comes out of That which is the Heart itself.

So you are neither oneness nor separation. You're neither emptiness nor fullness. Whatever you say, you are not. Whatever you can imagine and frame into some concept, you are not. What you are you can never frame, you can never imagine.

So be That which you can never imagine. As That which is the eye of God can never see itself. Even the "I"-thought, which is like the experiencer waking up, is part of that experience. The "I" itself can never be experienced. Whatever you can experience is no different from what you are, but is not what you are in essence.

So abide in That which is prior to what you can imagine. And then, in that abidance, there's annihilating, or burning out, of whatever is an idea. In that awareness of awareness, there's a hellfire burning, and only that hellfire, that holocaust, can annihilate the fire of the idea of "me," which is the devil idea of "separation." So only the abidance in that awareness of awareness, which is Heart itself, can burn out the "me."

But whatever the "me" does, meditation, whatever it does, cannot lead to That. You cannot avoid it, but in spite of that, the awareness of awareness happens, but never because of any doing or not doing by the doer. So whatever you have done or not done in your so-called life history—in spite of that—awareness of the awareness will happens—not because.

Not sick anymore?

A British WOMAN: A bit better, yes.

MR. RAO: I'm wondering, if you sought inward, totally in, is there no part anymore of existence?

KARL: Nothing will change by it. You simply step out of a separate identification into the absolute identification where no one can be identified anymore. So I'm not asking you to give up anything, not even a separate identification, as all these are aspects of what you are. I simply ask you to be That which is, by identifying yourself with whatever is as That which is Heart.

But no one can do this. So whatever you do is avoiding that, because this will be the end of you. This absolute identification will simply kill you. The idea of "me" will be killed by the absolute identification, so no one can ever do that. Whatever you do is avoiding the void of "me," because whatever the "me" is doing is out of worry about its existence. So whatever comes out of the "me," the "I"-thought will be fighting against that. So even meditation or understanding will be a technique to avoid that.

You will never, by free will, hit the tree of existence. You always need a driving license to miss it. [group laughs] It is like that. That's the functioning of the separate object and the survival system which is simply running as, "I want to survive." So you want to become immortal and by wanting to become immortal, you avoid death. You meditate on immortality, what you want to become. So you will never make the final killing that is needed— the Kali head-chopping business.

That's why it's said that by grace you will chopped, whether you like it or not. But it's not by you wanting it. You can lift your head—"Oh, look, take me!" It doesn't work. It doesn't know you. When you seek grace, you will never find grace.

But when grace seeks you, you'd better watch out. That watching out is like trying to escape. Because you already feel there is something. You are already in the tiger's mouth, and in one split second it will simply click shut, but you never know when. So you are always worrying. "Maybe—Oh!—What can I do to avoid it?" And you are always doubting. "Oh! Am I in that mouth or am I not? I must be in! No, I am not in. Am I ripe enough? Am I mature enough? What can I do to get more ripe or less ripe? Do I really want it? Maybe I don't want to be a couch potato watching television all the rest of my life. No, I don't want this boredom of the absence of 'me.' No, the 'me' doesn't like that!" [group laughs]

As I would know it myself. Yeah, we all go through this. And there is nothing wrong with it. Simply see it as a functioning of that. And without one of those ideas, there would be no existence. Without even one of those worries, there would be no existence. Because whatever worry is there, whatever idea, whatever aspect of existence, it has to be exactly as it is at that moment of time—even if there is no time—absolute existence is as absolute as it is.

So nothing ever has to go for existence itself, because all this is existence. All the little worries and all the little aspects of flowers and blooming and clouds coming and going and raining and crying and tears—all this is what is. You. Not one aspect of it can you avoid. Even the avoidance you cannot avoid. So don't worry. And as you are That which is Heart itself, whatever is, is what you are. Even trying to avoid that is part of it. So what to do?

So I am sitting here to tell you, "Don't worry, be happy," because even what is worrying, the unhappiness, is part of the happiness you are. It's a "happy-ning" because, out of the absolute happiness you are, only happiness comes.

Lighting the Fire of Absolute Burn Out

PETE: If you need to worry, for the reason you are giving, what part of you doesn't worry?

KARL: The Heart never worries.

PETE: Where is the "don't worry," if you need to worry?

KARL: In That which is Heart, which is the absolute Source of whatever you can imagine, there is an imaginary "I," an imaginary "I am," and imaginary worries out of that "I am." But who cares about the functioning, the movie?

This is an absolute movie. You cannot change it because it is already shot. You cannot change one frame of it, one aspect of it. In this totality of manifestation, there is no coming and going. It is as solid as you are. There is nothing happening. There is no happening. There is no passing. So if everything is already as solid as it can be, and every frame at the moment it appears in front of you, or in you, is a total frame of that infinite movie, then you can simply enjoy the movie. You cannot change the movie, so you lie back into the absolute experiencer you are, and you enjoy the movie.

PETE: If the movie is worry—you are imagining time, and at that particular time, the movie is a movie of worry.

KARL: Yeah, enjoy the worrying.

PETE: So you can't *not* worry, because the movie *is* worry at that time.

KARL: But you shouldn't worry about the worry. [group laughs] That makes you in the movie. You care about the caretaking and that makes you step in. You become part of the movie because you care. You fall in love with the movie. So by falling in love with the images in the movie, you step into the movie. The "high love" idea may not be so nice, because you imagine the movie is different from what you are. This love even creates hate—love and hate come together, because you step into the business of polarities—by love!

But you cannot *not* step into it, because you cannot *not* fall in love with yourself. What to do? You have to be in the movie and without the movie, what you are, as you cannot avoid falling in love with what you are.

PETE: If you fall into the movie—fall in love with it—that's compassion.

KARL: No, no, no. That's not compassion. With falling in love and being in the movie, pity starts.

PETE: But you were saying earlier about the snake that bites its tail, and you used the word *compassion*. I thought that was interesting. You were saying that the more you're involved in this whole drama, the more identified—

KARL: Yeah, the only way out of the movie is to *be* the movie. That is compassion—but without one who has compassion.

PETE: Be the whole movie.

KARL: In that absolute identification with That which is the nominal existence, which never comes and never goes, there is no one identified anymore. But whatever you identify with as separate from That, you are still on some landing point of separate identification. It will swap again to something else. Even in identification with awareness, you will go back to "I am"-ness and "I am so"-ness.

This is abidance in the Heart, to be That which is Heart, which is the absolute identification with the totality of existence. In that absolute identification, there is no place, because it is so empty of "me." It is so full and so empty at the same moment. So there's a fullness of emptiness. And in that fullness of emptiness, there is no "me" anymore because there is absolutely no place for it. There is a total absence and a total presence, both together. There is no "me," never was and never will be. Then you are totally flattened by existence itself.

This is the absolute embracement of the infinite embracing itself. In that absolute embracement, that idea of "separation"—whatever idea—simply disappears, absolutely, because it was never there. There is no one who can do that. This happens out of the blue. They call it "the outburst of love," or "the outburst of existence," which is a total implosion and explosion into that absolute identification of what you are. This is the "split second," because it's not in time.

Okay?

A WOMAN: Surely.

KARL: Surely. [both laugh] So even this, whatever words I can use now, or concepts, are still only pointers to that.

PETE: That's always my problem. I am always doing it with my mind. I'm getting into that state of mind of imagining that I am everything, but then that's just another thought, another concept.

KARL: And by seeing that—

PETE: That's why I said yesterday the "corrective thought," you know?
KARL: Yeah, but that's what I told you. Even that corrective thought doesn't help you.
PETE: Right because it might not come when you need it.
KARL: But that is helping you. That is the absolute helping, to point out that That which you are never needed any help. You don't need any correction. You are absolutely correct, even in being incorrect. So the futility of me trying to help you, that is maybe helping you—to point to the helplessness you already are, which never needed any help.

Whatever imagination, whatever concept I can give you, cannot change what you are, as you already are That which is the Absolute. Whatever I can say is only a pointer to That. But you see in the mind it will never work. Then you may give up the idea that the mind can gain an advantage by understanding something. And by giving up understanding, by seeing the understanding will not deliver the goods, it drops.

The "*jnani*" idea drops and suddenly, "Oh, the *jnani* was always there. I *am* understanding, and I was looking for more understanding. What an idea! I am that absolute knowledge without any idea of knowing or not knowing. So what is living out of knowing or not knowing—the mind—cannot help me, by that seeing that the mind can do whatever the mind does, or what is consciousness can promise whatever consciousness can promise." So that devil of separation, of deliverance, can promise you something, but you see absolutely it cannot deliver that treasure you are, which is being that Absolute itself. It cannot be delivered by any idea, by any understanding, by any insight. By whatever you can imagine, it cannot come.

There is no delivery system as "oops," coming and bringing you the goods. "Oops, there it was. Oh, it is gone again." "Oops" comes, and "oops" goes. It's like enlightenment. Enlightenment comes; then, "oh!" its gone again. "Oh, shit, missed it again!" [group laughs]
PETE: "I had a glimpse of enlightenment, yesterday." [more group laughter]
KARL: "And before I could put it in my pocket it was gone. Shit. Next time I will be more alert. When it will come, I will be ready with my purse— Ah, yeah, I have it. Now, put it in my heart . Yes, I have it now. Then I can nourish it and make it shiny. Look at it! I have it. I found it. Me! I'm in the God-consciousness now. Me!" [lots of group laughter] There are many like this.

PETE: There's a very fine line between this and just spiritual burn out, you know. You just get tired of it. You get tired of the struggle and you break down—

KARL: I hope you absolutely burn out. And the question "Who am I?" is like lighting the fire of that burning out. And then it depends how many concepts there are, or how strong the "I" still is. Sometimes it is instantly gone and sometimes it burns a bit longer. But who cares how long it takes. The end will be the end of you.

And the end will be that you see there never was any beginning. And by seeing there was never any beginning of what you are, this is the end of the end, the death of death, as nothing is ever born and can die, only death can die in a split second when you see you are That which is.

No one can bear the "no ending." That which is this movie has no happy ending, as a normal movie does. You are always waiting for the end and then you can go home, but this movie has no end, I tell you. [group laughs] You are so used to going to the movies, and every movie has an end. But this movie never started and will never end. So there will be no happy ending. The happy ending is seeing that there was no beginning of the movie, but then there is no one left in that seeing who can enjoy it. So it will not be in *your* presence.

PETE: It's not a mental enjoyment. It's not in the mind, this enjoyment.

KARL: Mental? Everything before is in the mind. You step out of the imaginary joy into That which is joy itself. But in That which is joy itself, there is no enjoyer anymore. There is no one at home. In That which is home, no one can be at home. When you are That which is home, which is Heart itself, there is no one at home anymore. And there is no idea of ownership or doership left, so you are not possessed by the idea which is the heart-knot, which is always giving you the pressure of owning something.

"My heart." So you are always lonely. With the ownership idea, you step into the loneliness of existence. Because at the moment you are identified with "whatever," the lonely guy starts. The lonely movie starts, with "me" owning something. "Owner of a lonely heart." It's always there, the sadness of the one, as the "I"-thought is sadness itself. It already is separation and is false.

You can never accept the falsity and sadness. So the "no help" in that moment makes you depressed, or sad, constant sorrow is there. Then it makes you seek. Seeking that happiness in an idea you imagine you have lost, then you look for it any place, you even die for it. You will never know when, but it will, it has to happen, because whatever comes has to go, so even the idea that you imagine as a coming, will go.

But no one knows when he will burn out by that. And no one can help you. "Not even me!" So actually, as I am sitting here, I am absolutely irrelevant for what you are. I have nothing to give you, nothing to take away. I can maybe point to something but that doesn't help. It's so absolutely useless.

MR. RAO: But the pointing to it, that can help.

KARL: I have no idea. It's a paradox. I'm pointing to your absolute nature which never needed any help. So this is not a help. No one is helping anyone. This absolute, "no help," you may call it, "help," but it is not a help. You help yourself, as there is no other Self who can help you.

But the Self doesn't need Self. So there is no help. This *koan* you will never undo. What to do? I may be the most frustrated man on earth. Talking every day about the same thing, and getting no results.

AIKO: Can I just tell you one thing?

KARL: I hope not!

AIKO: It makes more quiet.

KARL: But I tell you, the quietness which comes may go again.

AIKO: But still—

KARL: Yeah, still. Enjoy it. As you see the futility of doing, if it makes you quiet, okay. By seeing it, first it comes into your spirit, into that, "I am," that understanding. And then it's resting, resting, resting more into That which is Heart itself. It's simply disappearing into the futility, into the helplessness. First it seems helpless, and then it becomes helplessness again. Because when the helplessness starts, the awareness naturally sinks into the helplessness that you are, into the absolute paradise of seeing that whatever you can see cannot give you anything, cannot deliver anything.

So it's not so bad. Putting you to sleep. I am a sleeping pill, maybe. You need a sleeping pill today, Francesco?

FRANCESCO: No, it's very sweet today. I don't believe why. What did you eat last night?

KARL: We saw a good movie last night. Very *bhakti*. "Down to the river we go." Baptism.

FRANCESCO: The title?

KARL: *Brother, Where Art Thou?*

FRANCESCO: Old movie?

KARL: No, four years.

FRANCESCO: It's not new. Is that why you're in a good mood?

KARL: I can blame it on whatever.

FRANCESCO: Sure. For you.

KARL: It can change any moment. [group laughs] As you say so. Something? Everything fine? More or less. Mexico?

ROSA: I feel that I know less than at any time before.

KARL: Yeah, that sounds good. Less and less and less and less.

ROSA: But I don't know.

KARL: Eventually, the question cannot come up, and then that awareness simply burns out. That's all. So, question by question, coming into the awareness of the helplessness or futility, it simply comes up, gets spoken out and then disappears, until you become totally empty of even the questioner.

ROSA: Sometimes I feel good, and then sometimes I feel—

KARL: Bad again.

ROSA: But not really bad or really good. More even.

KARL: It's like, before, you feel bad and then good, like heaven and hell. It's very polar. And then it comes closer and closer to the awareness line.

ROSA: Yeah, it's like that.

KARL: Then life becomes peace, like a stream or a line of peace, with fewer and fewer ups and downs, without any ticks—

FRANCESCO: This is Parkinson's. [group laughs]

KARL: Ah, no. This is like the awareness stream. Even in deep sleep, it's there. In daytime, it's waves up and down, peaks and valleys, then in sleep, you simply go down to the one-streamer. And then in the morning, it starts up and down again. More or less, with emotions, touch, movement. So less and less means you are going more and more back to the sleep state.

ROSA: Yes.

KARL: But is this being more and more detached?

ROSA: No words, no idea.

The Family Karl Never Had

ANNA: Karl, I wonder if you can, or if you could, put across all these thoughts to your parents or relatives?

KARL: If I could tell them?

ANNA: I mean, how do they react?

KARL: Oh, very nice. You think that they got a straitjacket and put me into a hospital? No.

It was nice with my mother, because before she died, I talked with her about free will and all these things. Then she had a lung operation, which took half of a cancerous lung away, and then she went into a coma for five weeks, and during that time I talked to her.

When she woke up, she said, "Karl, you're right. I cannot decide when I die, even though I really want it." She was really fed up, with the whole movie—"But as I cannot decide when I die, as this may take whatever time, who cares?" So then, after one year, one night she simply got it and then she was quiet.

But before, she was the most complaining person. I could not stand her. She was complaint itself, complaining about her whole life, all the time, "I want to die and boo hoo hoo and my mind and no one loves me." "Ah, shut up!" [group laughs]

FRANCESCO: You said this?

KARL: Yeah, I told her, "One more word and I leave. One more word and you'll never see me again."

THERESE: That's extreme.

KARL: Extreme consequence. And she knew I meant it. "One more word!" [group laughs]

THERESE: Was that after the coma?

KARL: No, it was before, but this consequence became like a borrowed energy.

FRANCESCO: Then she went into a coma, because you told her to be quiet! [group laughs]

KARL: But it was this coma that was the wonderful teaching. It taught her that she could not help herself. She really was ready to die at any moment.

"I don't want to live anymore! Totally. Absolutely. No. This pain, this whatever, no!" But then the coma came and the waking up from it, and there was a breathing out, a release, of the hope that she could decide. This idea of "free will" went. She was acceptance.

Then, for that year, she didn't complain. Everyone was so amazed. Even my father didn't tell her not to smoke anymore. Because she was still smoking, even with a hole in here [points to throat]. But no one told her to stop it. I told my father, "One word of you telling her to stop, and I will stop you." It was great. Smoking here and then the smoke coming out here. [group "ughs" and "oh mys"] But she was happy. I said, "Don't worry. One month more or less of smoking or not, who cares? My goodness. Enjoy it."
So that was like, sometimes it works.
THERESE: And your father could hear you?
KARL: No, my father was a different story. When my mother died and she was in the grave, he wanted to jump in after her, to kill himself, absolutely. "Karl, I cannot live anymore. Help me!" I said, "Okay, how can I help you? Should I get a revolver, a rope, some pills? What should I do for you? How can I kill you? How can I help you?"
[Silence.]

He became totally angry. [group laughs] "How dare you!" he said. He became so angry at me, he totally forgot that he wanted to kill himself. [more group laughter] And three months later, he had a new girlfriend. Fifteen years younger! So much for, "I don't want to live anymore!"

So, just to point out, if you are in the consequence of acceptance, of ruthlessness, this is the only way. That is compassion. Not any helping, or "how can I make you understand?"—that's all self-pity. But with the ruthlessness and the concernlessness of acceptance, in that moment you say, "Yes or no!" no other thing, do it or not. "Okay. How can I help you?" With my total acceptance of his wish, he was totally shocked out of that.

Everyone steps out of Kindergarten at that moment and grows up as the consequence of acceptance. Because this is so deadly. What to do?

That's like here. If someone comes with some consequential thing, ruthlessness alone points to the ruthlessness you are looking for. You're looking for the freedom of concernlessness, moment by moment total acceptance—in the next moment, there will be no next moment—being really in that, so whatever comes, you can say, "Yes. So what?" Everyone coming here is looking for that—freedom alone, the absolute ruthlessness and concernlessness about whatever is.

So this is a pointer, being an example of that, maybe being a running advertisement for the ruthlessness. Look, it's easy! There's nothing more easy than the ruthlessness and helplessness. Everything else is a concept of morality, or whatever helping, and comes out of the idea of "me" of self-pity. But the ruthlessness is compassion and not self-pity because there is no self who pities himself anymore.

As long as there is an idea of "me," of self, there is self-pity, and you pity yourself and you pity others. It is only with Selflessness, ruthlessness, not seeing anyone who is in any in danger, not seeing anyone who was born—you see no one gets hurt anyway, because there is no one to get hurt, as consciousness is simply transforming into "whatever." There is nothing born and nothing will die, as consciousness is infinite in itself. It simply takes another form. So what? If you are the immortality talking to the immortality that is never born, the unborn existence, what is then to happen?

Years ago, I was working sometimes for my mother in the pub, and villagers were coming, and the more drunk they became, the better I could talk to them. I really hammered into them. "Aw, come on, have some more, you're not drunken enough!" [group laughs] "I'm running the pub, so it's free beer. Come get drunk, and go to the point of concernlessness, as you are That. Be drunken by existence. Be That which is Heart, totally drunken by that nectar of concernlessness and ruthlessness and freedom. Be that. So drink. Have another one."

GEORG: Where is this pub? I want to go there. [group laughs]

KARL: You're sitting in it!

GEORG: I'll bring my glass tomorrow.

KARL: That's enough answers about my family, the family I never had. It was a nice show. Actually, it was preparation to sit here, because sitting with all the drunkenness and old men complaining about their wives—it's not so different!

MARY: Your parents owned a pub?

KARL: And a farm. Yes. So five o'clock we'd milk the cows, in the afternoon we played cards with some villagers, at night, it was beer until one and then the cows again.

MARY: They owned a farm and a pub?

KARL: Yeah. Still running. But I escaped. My sister is still there. She took over. I am so grateful. Even when she acts like a mother, I am so happy.
MARY: What do you mean?
KARL: She has to worry about the kids, so she has to be mean sometimes. It's her duty. She is a good mother. A good mother is a hassle to the rest of the world. [group laughs] She cares only about her children, what they get. But it's fine.
MARY: And you have kids?
KARL: Me? No. See, everything is a demand of the totality. If you are a mother, you have to behave like it. You have to care more about your children than others. So one side is facing love, and one side is—Grrr!—fighting. That's a mother. That's the functioning; it's totally as it has to be. So what to do? There is no one that can help it. The mother cannot *not* love the child.
MARY: Mothers are innately protective; it's biological.
KARL: That's what it is, protective. And if you are protective, sometimes you have to kill someone else. It's part of the protection. Mr. Bush, protecting Americans, has to kill Iraqis, because they need oil to run their cars. He's a mother who protects America.
MARY: Father.
KARL: Or father. It's the same. But fathers go to war, and mothers send them. [group laughs] Who is then worse? It's always the mothers sending their sons to war. Warriors. Worry about the family. "Get something for me. I want to have something on my table." It's an old tradition. What to do with it? Only we have bachelors who want to get out of it. So that's about family business.
ANNA: Yeah, it's nice to know.
KARL: Maybe then you don't have to go to the, "family constipation" seminar. [group laughs]
ANNA: Of course.
KARL: Maybe you see there is nothing coming out of any person. It's just a functioning of a functioning. So that actually takes all the guilt out of everyone. What to do then? They have to be as they are. They cannot be otherwise—as they function of whatever they are framed to in the information system, it's genetic design, or whatever you call it—of history.
FRANCESCO: Not so bad.

KARL: It doesn't make them holy.

AIKO: My mother was more advanced than me. When she was dying, I was thinking about reincarnation. That was my concept. But she said, "That's just another hope."

KARL: Yeah, you see.

AIKO: She was very good.

KARL: She knew her daughter. All these ideas are only ideas of a way out.

AIKO: That's it.

KARL: "Maybe, maybe." Always like a ship on S.O.S. "Help, I'm sinking!" "Okay, I am helping you!" [group laughs] Francesco, everything fine? Did I touch on your mother too much?

FRANCESCO: Naw. For my father, it was something very different. "You think what you want, but it is important that you work. If you work, you think what you want."

KARL: But you have to work?

FRANCESCO: Yeah.

KARL: "As long as you do what I want, you can think what you like." Same with me, no doubt! [group laughs] How is Italy?

MRS. ANGELINA: Strong story of family.

KARL: Strong family story. That's Italian. *Mamma mia!*

MRS. ANGELINA: Very heavy.

KARL: Even being an Italian mama is something.

MRS. ANGELINA: Yes, yes. Very difficult.

KARL: I tell you. What to do with it?

MRS. ANGELINA: Cooking, cooking, cooking! [group laughs]

KARL: Pasta, pasta, pasta—until *basta* (enough; stop)! And you never know when *basta* is there, but until then, there is pasta.

Between the Wisdom of Emptiness and the Fullness of Love

MATHILDA: Being of the Self, you are beyond polarity. But if you live life on earth, it cannot be.

KARL: You may say, you cannot bring it into life, because it will never be in any polarity.

MATHILDA: Yes. I mean, living on earth is all the time polarity.

KARL: This relativity is simply polarity. There are simply differences. You cannot bring the Absolute into life, because it is already there.

MATHILDA: I'm talking about in this system—

KARL: That's all there is. Even relativity is That which is Self. But Self is not relative by being relativity. It's taking the form of relativity or polarity. It is That which is polarity, but there is no polarity. It's That which is polarity, but there is no separation. It is That which is separation, and That which is separation is not separated. That "is"-ness of separateness, that "is"-ness of oneness, that "is"-ness of awareness, is always That which is existence itself, taking the shape of separation. But separation doesn't make That which is Self separated.

MATHILDA: Every time there is separation or polarity there, I cannot experience it.

KARL: It is the experience, but it cannot experience it. It takes the form of an experiencer, and it is That which is the experiencer and it is That which is experiencing and it is That which is experienced. There is no difference. But it is not the experiencer and not the experiencing and not what is experienced. But it's That which is the experiencer, That which is experiencing, and That which is experienced. That's clear! [group laughs]

When there are three different things—a subject, a function of perceiving, and what is perceived as an object—it is That which is perceiver, it is That which is perception, and it is That which is perceived—in essence, as Heart is whatever is. So That which is Heart takes the form of an experiencer, experiencing, and what is experienced. But it's not an experiencer experiencing what is experienced. But it's still That which is.

There is nothing but Heart. Whatever shape and form Heart takes doesn't make Heart separated from what is Heart. So there is separation, but there is not. There is a dream of separation, but there is no one who is separated. Clear?

So nothing has to go for That which you are. Simply be That which is, as *I Am That*. And then you are That which is the experiencer experiencing what is experienced. So you are the "I," you are the "I am," and you are the world. You are the "I," as the experiencer, as That which is the *I* of the "I."

You are the experiencing, as "I am," as space, as That which is the *I am* of the "I am." And you are That which is the world, as you are the *world* of the world. So this is a trinity of your manifestation. but you are That which is manifesting itself, so you are not manifested, even in manifestation. You are That which is manifestation, but you are still not manifested.

MATHILDA: So I can never feel it with awareness, because if I have awareness, then—

KARL: Then there is one who has awareness. You cannot own it. In all this trinity, there is no ownership. Existence cannot be owned by anyone. The owner, the owning, and what can be owned is owned by That [holds up fist] alone. So the owner [thumb], the owning [thumb and index finger], and what can be owned [thumb, index, and middle fingers], is a dream-like manifestation owned by the absolute owner which is Heart—by being That.

So the absolute owner of whatever—the ownership, the owner as relative owner of owning, and something owned—you are in essence. The absolute owner, you are, which is Heart. You cannot leave this and you cannot get it back. By any relative ownership of ideas or understanding, you cannot become the absolute owner. So whenever there is relative owning, you are not this relative owner.

As Jesus said, you can only come as naked existence. No owner can ever go through the eye of a needle. You cannot join me until you are totally naked, naked of any idea of what you are and what you are not—naked existence itself.

In that nakedness, there is paradise. Because there is no one left who can be happy or unhappy, lucky or unlucky, knowing or not knowing. All that—taking that as real, as one who does exist, as "me"—is dream-like, you make a dream real, and then you are trapped in those images and objects and you become an object. But you are That which is Heart. And you have never left it, so you cannot gain it back. By any technique or understanding, you cannot become what you are.

This understanding is not an understanding; This understanding is actually the total dropping of the one who understands. But this cannot be done by that one. It happens by itself. As it came by itself, the falling in love with that image, it drops out of love the same way, by itself, and not by any understanding or any technique or whatever the meditator has done.

MATHILDA: And what do mean by saying you are a heartbreaker?

KARL: To show you that love is not on earth, that you cannot find what you are, that whatever is the beloved you cannot own. Because this love is like you're embracing the beloved all the time, and then you are separate from what you are. You become a lover and some beloved. Heartbreaking means to show you that what you take as love is not That which is love. It cannot be controlled by you.

MATHILDA: Can you perceive it?

KARL: I would say you cannot feel it, and you cannot *not* feel it. You are absolutely it, and that absolute being it, is absolute experiencing it.

MATHILDA: Because it's beyond polarity, I cannot recognize it?

KARL: You cannot *not* recognize it. You are recognition itself. Whatever you recognize *is* what you are. What form it takes doesn't matter, it's still what it is. You cannot *not* experience what you are, as there is only That which is Heart experiencing Heart. In whatever experience, you are That which is Heart experiencing that aspect of Heart. As you cannot *not* realize yourself, whatever is realized is That which is Heart.

This is what you are. There is no difference between the real and the realization. Whatever is, is Heart, and That you cannot *not* experience, as you are That. But there is no moment without it. No experience is without Heart. So Heart is That which is the experiencer, the experiencing, and what is experienced.

You don't have to bring anything into That which is Heart because the Absolute is, even in the absolute separation, That which is, is the Absolute. There is only the absolute Heart—in separation, in oneness, and even in awareness. All is heart. Nothing has to come and go for That to be.

So you don't have to bring anything, anywhere, because it is everywhere and nowhere. This paradox you cannot dissolve. It has no place, but there is no place without it. It has no time, but there is no moment without it. That you are—between both statements.

You swing between the wisdom of emptiness and the fullness of love. In between, in that never-never land, you are. Both are sides of That which you are, emptiness and fullness, wisdom and love, and you are That which is the essence of both.

VICKI: If you are the essence of all polarities, do they become equal?

KARL: No. There is polarity, and then there is harmony in whatever this polarity brings or not. That which is polarity cannot be disturbed by whatever the polarity is or how it shows. There is no "how" anymore.

It doesn't matter where you are in the pendulum's swing—as you are the whole pendulum, you don't care where it swings. To that side, to love, to wisdom, or in the middle—you have no discrimination of any kind. Because you are the pendulum, you are the whole existence, there is no discrimination, as there is nothing separate, no second you can discriminate.

Whatever given moment of the pendulum or on the watch, you are That. So there is polarity, but there is not. There is separation, but there is no one who is separated. That's the main point. It's not the separation that is bad. It's the idea that you are "in separation." But there never was anyone that was "in separation," as you are That which is separation. You can never separate yourself from yourself, as Heart can never be separated from Heart. And Heart, That which is separation, doesn't know "separation."

MATHILDA: Slowly, slowly!

KARL: I tell you, everyday I can do that, and it's always new. Everyday, it's a new hammer—I never get tired of hammering, hammering, hammering. Day and night, until the nail is gone. And then there will be another nail, and you hammer and hammer and hammer, and another nail. For one nail you hammer down, there will be ten others. It's like words coming out of the music—always a singing heart—a hammering heart. Heart hammering.

KLARA: This is like *neti-neti.*

KARL: Yeah, but an infinite *neti-neti.* You're always drinking tea. "Nay tea, nay tea, I want coffee! [group laughs] No tea, no tea. Coffee!" So have another coffee. Nay tea. No coffee.

KLARA: I'm free to have the choice.

KARL: Oy yoy, now were stepping back. It makes you choosy? Because you have a free choice, it makes you choosy? Juicy! You will enjoy it even more when you have free will, or what?

GEORG: Karl, did anything change in your art after this event that never happened?

KARL: Yeah, it was changed. Before, there was this, "wisdom of emptiness" thing, totally, and every painting was black. There were simply black paintings and black sculptures. Everything was black. Emptiness! Black!

And then there was an outburst of this "thing." You go to the emptiness and you get totally empty of an idea and then, when you're absolutely empty, fullness comes. Totally. In that moment, total emptiness becomes

fullness. That's like what they call, "an outburst of love." When you reach
an extreme point of emptiness, of wisdom, the fullness can come. Because
the emptiness of Heart contains the fullness of existence.

Suddenly, it was fullness, and from that moment on, everything was
bright colors. So it changed from that moment on—boom!—it was really
like—poof! I was really surprised. Black and then—boom!—the board was
full of bright colors and things. But still, I make monochrome things, and
totally informal things. Total structure, out of anything. So both are there
now, both extremes, but there's nothing in between, really.

GEORG: And the painting is not just for money; it's for joy?

KARL: It's for money, I tell you. [group laughs]

GEORG: But even if the money weren't there, would you still be doing it?

KARL: Yeah, I'm stupid enough to do it without selling them. But I tell you,
I enjoy selling them, as much as I enjoy doing them. There is no difference.

VICKI: There's a waiting list, yeah?

KARL: I'm waiting for the buyers, or what?

VICKI: No, they are waiting for their paintings.

KARL: Yeah, I have to make some because they are already sold. It's a rare
situation, I tell you. [group laughs] After twenty-five years of being an artist,
this is really a rare situation. People see some, and then they say, "I want the
same style of thing."

VICKI: But in mauve. A different color.

KARL: Yeah, because my sofa is different. [group laughs] A bit different
color, please, so it matches.

MARY: There are some artists in this modern time who have the same problem where they just can't get it out fast enough.

KARL: If you become famous. But I was always more proud to not be famous, because I didn't like all the famous artists too much. I'm more into
the "infamous." I was never into Monet or any of those famous ones. Actually, they are too pretty.

MARY: Turner's pretty. You like Turner.

KARL: Sometimes, I make an exception. Oh, in his time, he was not famous, though. And I don't want to cut my ear.

GEORG: At least not your tongue! [group laughs]

KARL: Then I couldn't talk anymore. Then everyone would listen!

GEORG: We'd hear every word, Karl!

KARL: I would become Meher Baba. I would be very busy. These days, there would be a keyboard, and there would be signs here.

MARY: Just to inform you, most of the time, he was using gestures, not the alphabet board.

KARL: He had a translator besides.

MARY: Several.

KARL: But the last two weeks, he talked.

MARY: Are you serious?

KARL: I have no idea. People tell me. They said that two weeks before he died, he started to talk again.

MARY: It's so amazing, I'm starting to hear these things. For so many years, this didn't happen.

KARL: Isn't it fun to make up stories?

MARY: Now they're coming.

KARL: Who cares if it's true or not? It's like J. Krishnamurti, you know, he had stage fright. Two hours before he went on stage, he was on a psycho-therapist's couch. But then he went on stage and he was flamboyant. Every-thing was gone. But two hours before, he was in hell, he feared to go on stage. "I'm not worth it, I'm not ready, blah, blah, blah." The whole thing. That's a good story. If it's true, who cares?

MARY: Is it a story?

KARL: Ha, ha, now you are in— But who cares? It's always a nice thing to say.

The biggest teaching of Yogi Ramsuratkumar was when he was in a coma. He was attached to machines, on strings, and then when somebody came, they lifted his arm. He was like in a glass house. People could come and see him in that room, attached to machines, totally dependent. And on the auspicious day of Shivaratri, three years ago, they turned it off. Just to make it auspicious.

That's the biggest teaching you can get, helplessness itself. He was known as one of the biggest *siddhi* masters, but the teaching was the great-est I ever saw—being that total acceptance, not changing anything, on a machine, simply saying, "Okay, what comes, comes. Let be what can be. So what?"

That is the highest *siddhi* you can have. That is the almighty *siddhi*— helplessness—which makes no attempt to change anything. Total acceptance, attached to a machines, not doing anything. That I call, "teaching by example," by that total pointer. "Look, nothing can happen to what I am, on a machine with disciples around me who put the machine on and off as they like—so what?"

MARY: So Christ—

KARL: It's the same.

MARY: No, he went up to Kashmir.

KARL: That's another story. "Kashmir *wenn du kannst* ([catch me] if you can). I go to Kashmir."

VICKI: There was an artist who did that in a museum too. He had an exhibit called *Visiting Hours*, and he was in his hospital bed—in the museum!—and people could come talk to him, and he was dying, of AIDS, I think.

KARL: The whole of existence is teaching, teaching, teaching itself, all the time. Every moment. It's just to point out—it's not that he can make a promise and then keep it until he dies. Bullshit. It can change at any moment. "I promise you this now, and I drop it the next moment."

MARY: Baba always broke his promises. Always. Endlessly.

KARL: If two weeks before he died, he was speaking again—

MARY: But I don't know.

KARL: Yeah, but who cares? It would be great. That would be a teaching. Not one who keeps his promises.

MARY: You see, he did keep his promises, because he said he was going to break his silence and he did.

KARL: Anyway. Just to say, the master is all around you, every moment. That which you are is teaching yourself, infinitely, moment by moment, by whatever is. The grace is all around you. You are That which is grace, surrounded by grace. Don't worry. It's all by grace, and you are That which is grace.

So, by grace, there was Yogi Ramsuratkumar, and by grace there was Meher Baba, and by grace there is the mountain—grace is all that is. Coffee in the morning and tea at night, movies and the television, whatever, all are by grace. There are no differences in it, as That which is grace is always experiencing grace in whatever given moment. So what to do? You cannot *not* be That, so simply be That, that is grace itself, as you cannot leave what you are. As you have never left yourself, be it. That is the pointer of the mountain. Solid as solid can be. Never moving by any experience around it, by any coming or going of any seeker or non-seeker.

Total Doubt Doesn't Leave Any Doubter

KARL: Maybe you have some nice question or something? No, if everything is fine, it's fine. I'm just fishing.

A Swedish MAN: Karl, do you experience our emotions? Do you pick up emotions from us?

KARL: No. I heard of a teacher that only comes out once or twice a year because he cannot stand seekers around him. It gives him headache. I am not in that field. I know what he means, but then the back door is not really open. I know the headache coming and going, but who cares about it?

I know when there is consciousness sitting there and being in that "whatever" experience of *kundalini*, those experiences of fire coming, that inner fire, this energy in the cells, energy coming and going, what is called "*shakti*," transformation of cells and things. Every experience, whatever exists, this extreme—I feel it. But who cares? In a way, this body can take everything. It's strange. Because the concernlessness is there, it simply goes in and out, likes waves of vibration and energy. And as they are no different from what I am, who cares?

There is no, "*my* vibration" and "*your* vibration." All this is what I am. So it's not touching anything. It's simply energy penetrating energy, in a way, vibration penetrating vibration, and then all that vibration is what I am as consciousness, as totality. So what to do with it?

I don't call them emotions. There are simply vibrations of consciousness, here and now, as forms, at emotional and "whatever" levels. There are vibrations of energy, taking form or taking emotional form of energy, and they are all here, the totality, sitting here, as awareness. What to do? Enjoy the show.

It's like this filter system is simply not running anymore. There is no armor. Without a filter in front of you, there is no filter in back of you. The un-filter!

There is no one here who collects the experiences. Without that "collector" idea, or ownership idea, it comes and goes as waves. Infinite waves of experiences of what you are.

So that is maybe called, "compassion," because there is no filter system.

There is no pity. There is nothing that collects them. And without a collector, they simply come and go.

As there is this "collector" idea and you are in that "collector" idea, you collect experiences and emotions, even of others. Not only your own emotions, you collect the emotions of what you are surrounded by. "Oh, here is a black one; here is a dark one; oh, he is lusty. All these lusty people around me!" [group laughs]

A Japanese MAN: Does a *jivanmukta* know when he is a *jivanmukta*?

KARL: No.

MAN: So you cannot say you are in the same state as Ramana Maharshi or another like him?

KARL: There is no state. The statelessness, you mean? I could not say. Ramana was pointing to that statelessness, which is the absolute mystery of absolute existence, that "I am." About all the other states, there are different concepts maybe. But That, you cannot talk about, it is not a concept.

Everything else that you can name and frame, I can maybe agree or not agree with Ramana. But about That, there is no disagreement. There is no possibility of a disagreement, because That you cannot frame anyway. That statelessness which has no form or even non-form, what he was talking about, Heart itself, is what I was referring to, and there is no doubt. There is a total agreement, absolute agreement about That, to be That.

MAN: You don't have any doubts about the authority of what you're saying?

KARL: No. Even the doubting, I don't doubt. As I know everything is a lie anyway, everything I say has total doubt in it. And this total doubt doesn't leave any doubter. So in that total doubt, there is no doubter anymore.

So whatever I can say cannot bring you anything, cannot frame what is truth itself, as I can never talk about That which is truth. So whatever I say makes no difference. There's a total irrelevance of saying, of singing, of doing, whatever. This total doubting is freedom. So I totally doubt what I say. Absolutely!

Whatever can be said, what can be put in any frame of words, cannot touch That which is existence itself. For That which I am, nothing ever happened. Talking or not talking cannot change what I am. So I can doubt or not doubt. There is a total concernlessness about whatever is.

That's what Ramana was always pointing to, That which is Heart itself, which you cannot doubt. For doubting and not doubting, you have to exist prior to doubting and not doubting. But That which is prior to doubting and not doubting, you cannot doubt. The nakedness of existence, you cannot doubt. Even in doubting, you have to exist. This is Ramakrishna's basic teaching too.

It always comes back to that. In spite of knowing or not knowing, you are. In spite of doubting or not doubting, you are. Totally in spite of whatever you say or don't say, whatever you experience or don't experience, you are.

That's what I'm talking about. I'm pointing to it, but I cannot frame it into any concept. Even that is a concept. Concept, concept, concept, but it makes no difference. Even with all the differences in pointers, they all still only point to the pointlessness. They cannot make the point that they are pointing to. Inexhaustible.

The only thing I can say is, day by day I talk about it, and it's always like—you. It comes out of this inexhaustible mystery. I don't know. But That I am. It seems like I can never get enough of it. Or, it cannot get enough of what comes out of this mouth, who knows? Who cares?

Francesco, do you care? Today was nice?

FRANCESCO: I don't believe it. It was nice. I don't want to mess it up.

KARL: Normally, he complains I am too rough.

ANTONIO: Twenty more minutes, Francesco! [group laughs]

KARL: Better watch out!

A WOMAN: It's so boring somehow, if you are not the doer. There is nothing to do—

KARL: Yeah, boredom will kill you.

WOMAN: It's very boring.

KARL: I hope so. I absolutely hope that boredom will kill you. I hope what can be boredom, will kill the bored one. Because the "me" is always bored.

WOMAN: I know.

KARL: It's so boring, the "me"! It's always bored, looking for more exciting information, always wanting more. This hunger for excitement never gets satisfied. I hope it will be killed by boredom alone. Because the boring "me," is always boring.

WOMAN: Whatever I do, whatever gets done, it's not by me. So it's boring anyway.

KARL: It's not done by you? Who says so?

WOMAN: It's just done anyway.

KARL: It's not done anyway! Everything, whatever is done or not done, is because of you! You are absolutely responsible for all action and non-action, for whatever existence is and is not. It's all you.

WOMAN: I cannot influence it.

KARL: You cannot influence it? But you are the absolute Source of it. What higher influence could there be, as you are the absolute Source of whatever is and is not? Everything is by you. How much more influence would you like? Hmm? Tell me, please. Maybe I can fulfill your wish.

WOMAN: [laughing] It would still be boredom.

KARL: It would be boredom or "me," which is boredom itself, because you are boring as a "me" anyway. Any person is totally boring, the idea of "boredom." So what to do with this boring idea of "me"? Always boring, boring, boring, drilling into some object. Everyday it has to eat, everyday it has to digest, everyday it has to shit—all those personal things you have to do. The history of a person, of a "me," is boring anyway. Any history is boring.

THERESE: But there's another side too, Karl.

KARL: What side?

THERESE: Like this kind of easiness I seem to be experiencing. I find it to be boring.

KARL: Yeah, I hope so. You will be kicked out by boredom, as "Thérèse" is boring anyway.

THERESE: Nothing is coming up.

KARL: So what?

THERESE: I'd actually prefer if it were more up and down. [group laughs]

KARL: [to the rest of the group] You see, the complaining never stops! [more group laughter]

THERESE: I'm a Pisces like your mother.

KARL: She's a monkey [in Chinese astrology] and a Pisces like my mother. See, a complainer is born from that. It's never right for them anyway. That's the perfect teaching. You can do whatever you like. If you have a relationship with someone like this, you give up very soon. [group laughs]

THERESE: But maybe after the coma, something will happen!

KARL: What an idea! You're fearing yourself, because when you are yourself, you fear it's too boring. Nice excuse, I tell you. [laughs] The Almighty is saying, "Oh, maybe I better not be myself, because maybe it's too boring.

I'd better be a miserable seeker, and be in the misery, then at least I have some entertainment!"

[People in the group are gasping from laughing so hard.]

KARL: "No, it's not for me, I don't like it. I don't want to be it, because I don't like this movie. It's too boring. I'd rather be in hell and burning and being nailed and the devil comes and every thought is burning me. Yes. But this thoughtlessness, no, it's too boring for me. Me, the devil, I need some hell."

THERESE: You would be bored if you were thoughtlessness. You'd have nothing to talk about.

KARL: What is all this?

THERESE: Of course, I'm meant to complain.

KARL: The devil will always be bored by everything, even by hell, because boredom is the place of hell and that is the place of the devil—you! "Devil Thérèse," another boredom of hell.

THERESE: Walking boredom.

KARL: Walking hell. The name of boredom is "Thérèse." Whatever comes will not satisfy you. That's what you mean. So even that before, and whatever comes then, will not satisfy you.

THERESE: It's just interesting to see all this. Just watching.

KARL: [laughing] Interesting? Aw!

THERESE: [laughing] No. Everything is fine with me. [group laughs]

Be That Which Cannot Be Imagined

VICKI: But to not be the doer doesn't mean to do nothing. It means you still have to act as though you are the doer while you are on this planet.

KARL: No. Stepping out of the doership into non-doership is still doership. You simply change identification. First you identify with doing, then you identify with non-doing. It makes no difference. You are still in the hell of doing or not doing.

VICKI: Yeah, but what if you're not doing? What if you take it literally and don't do? Then you're not functioning.

KARL: But even the non-doing is doing. You're doing nothing and that's even more. You're doing nothing and that is a big one, I tell you. You cannot *not* do.

VICKI: That's what I'm saying. You have to do.

KARL: But have you done anything at all?

[Vicki sighs.]

KARL: You mean, what you think you are is the body and the body has to function as consciousness. Whatever has a form has to function as a form. And then there is doing and not-doing, and those ideas come, one by one, out of it.

VICKI: Yeah, but I don't have to take credit.

KARL: What credit? Who doesn't have to take credit? For what? Who needs this difference? And who makes a difference? Who needs the understanding and who wants to control that by that understanding? Who wants to control doing and non-doing by the understanding of a "non-doer" idea? Who needs that?

VICKI: I don't know.

KARL: "Me!" [Vicki laughs] It's the same as you wanting to step out of identification to non-identification. Who needs it? Me. You step into the oneness of non-identification for a while, then you get bored and you step back. "Oh, it's sweet, but actually, it's boring." The devil will always find a way to step back into the more hell-like but exciting separation. "Oh, I'd rather seek!" [group laughs]

BERTA: But when it's a divine accident, whatever happens to you, you cannot help it. You come into this boredom and non-boredom, and nothing is good enough.

KARL: That's what I said.

BERTA: We have this desire, this longing, to be That which you are talking about. That's why I am sitting here. I cannot get enough of what you talk about, but I also cannot stand that I cannot be anything.

KARL: Yeah, see. The paradox is there.

BERTA: But you have it easy, talking from there. [group laughs]

KARL: Come on up to the chair. Let's share the chair.

BERTA: And then whatever you say, I hear this group start to say. It's like a parrot. You say you are establishing that, so to say, and I am talking from my personal "Berta" thing, trying to get it and doing this and that, and it doesn't help.

KARL: Yeah, I hope so.

BERTA: Yeah, I hope so! [group laughs] It's actually agony, you know, to feel all the time that I still didn't get it.

KARL: I tell you again and again, because we've had this discussion for three years, [shouting] you will *never* get it!

BERTA: That is what I feel.

KARL: I hope so. Never, ever, has anyone gotten it. That's the beauty of freedom—that you cannot have it. You cannot put it in your pocket and take it home.

FRANCESCO: Are you sure? [group laughs]

KARL: What kind of freedom would it be if you could put it in your pocket and take it home? That's what makes a person. A person wants to be happy all the time.

BERTA: I can't help it.

KARL: I don't say it's wrong. That's the idea of "person," a personal advantage—having the advantage of being happy all the time.

BERTA: Yeah.

KARL: But by wanting to be happy, you are unhappy. By wanting to be excited or in amazement, you are "unamazed." Simply by wanting to be what you are, you are out of what you are.

BERTA: But you cannot help it.

KARL: No one else can be it for you.

BERTA: I know that. There's also nothing in it that I know it.

KARL: I hope so.

BERTA: So you see, it's still—

KARL: Yeah, I see, you are still enjoyed by what you are, whether you like it or not. And that's the beauty of what you are, you don't have to like yourself to be yourself.

BERTA: This morning I woke up and I was thinking, "Oh, I'm actually behind it. All these words that I say, I am behind it, as the cow in the street, as everything, I am behind it. I'm That which you've been talking about.

KARL: Prior, you mean?

BERTA: But that is a kind of parrot-like talk. So then I say, "Let's have another smoke," [group laughs] because then there's nothing. When I come to India, at first I do a whole bunch of talking, and I'm very excited—it seems so normal. And now I've come to the frame of mind of yours, and it's all empty.

KARL: Yeah, but isn't it nice, isn't it great? I can create these beautiful words, and you can feel them—ah, bah, fantastic!—and finally you see that they don't help. But that is the absolute help, that you see that—not by any understanding, not by any fine and beauty words—there will be nothing ever that can help you.

This is there because grace shows you—total resignation is grace. You resign that, by any understanding of words, by any experience, by any technique, so you can become what you are. In the absolute resignation, the absolute stopping, the total full stop, you are what you are, and it was always simply there, without any coming or going. So in a split second, nothing ever happened. Maybe it prepares you, by seeing that no beautiful words can ever satisfy you. There will be no satisfaction on earth, from anything.

BERTA: That I know by now.

KARL: You see?

BERTA: After fifty-five years, I know that.

KARL: You think you know. So grace is working. Resignation works.

It's really like a picture. By "whatever" accident, you sign up for universal seeking, longing of consciousness, meditating about what you are. And by accident, you resign from it. So you sign up in the universe, or a school, but by finding it, it cannot deliver the knowledge you're looking for, you sign out. But then, by the absolute signing out of the idea that you can get something out of the experience, suddenly there is absolute knowledge of what you are. And it was never gone.

But first you have to look—you have to listen, just to see, "Oh, it's not there, not there, not there. *Neti-neti, neti-neti.* Okay, full stop." Then it is there suddenly, so what, and then you step out again, because you cannot *not* step out. You sign in again, and then you sign out again.

That was what Ramana was referring to with the spider that wakes up, spins the network of the universe, and then out of the blue, withdraws it again. But not because of anything. In spite of whatever necessity, it does it. There is no necessity to become a spider spinning the universe, and there is no necessity to withdraw from it. It's simply out of the blue.

No one knows why. There is no "why" in anything. It's simply Self-entertainment, signing up in the universe and signing out of it. Hallelujah. Infinite. So you have to be in the universe, just as you have to be out of the universe. There is no difference for what you are, as you can never leave what you are. And you never left—even while signing up for it, being a seeker, longing—what you are.

ANNA: And to put it in other words, are we then talking about Self-realization?

KARL: Then you realize that there is nothing to realize, because whatever is Self is ever-realized, and whatever is not Self will never realize. You simply see that there never was any "no-Self." This is a paradox—you realize that there is nothing to realize.

You step into the problem that there is no problem. This is called "depression." This is called "boredom," because then you become the bored one, the bored person. Because when there is no problem, the person who was living out of problems gets bored. Don't worry.

A WOMAN: This is a big problem, everything becoming, "no problem." Then we are bored for a while—

KARL: And then you step back. Both are trying to control. You think you step into the emptiness or absence, and by that stepping into it, by your effort, you want to control again—That which is existence. You still want to put freedom in your pocket. What an idea!

THERESE: And when you see all that so clearly—that even when there's no problem, you manage to create a problem out of it—there is nothing to do about it.

KARL: What to do then? Who sees it then? It will always step back into "doership" and "non-doership" ideas, identified consciousness, non-identified consciousness—it's an infinite game. Forget it.

Consciousness cannot deliver the goods. Consciousness is as dumb as dumb can be. That's why Nisargadatta said that, prior to consciousness, you are. Consciousness is your dream. But you are the absolute dreamer. You are, with and without consciousness, what you are. Even consciousness is a dream.

BERTA: Is there never any relief?

KARL: No? Okay. [sings] "This will be the last time, this will *not* be the last time." Nisargadatta said you are prior to consciousness. So I'm not the first one, and for sure not the last one, who says consciousness is your manifestation, but you are not your manifestation. You are That which is manifesting itself, but you are not the manifestation. The manifestation is no different from what you are, so even the manifestation is imagining, but what is imagining all that can be imagined is That which cannot be imagined.

A German WOMAN: Very clear.

FRANCESCO: But this is abidance.

KARL: That is abidance—being That which cannot be imagined. So be That. But how can you not be that? It's effortlessness itself. By no effort can you become That. You become the laziest bastard you can know, but not by not knowing what a bastard is at all.

KLARA: But this is boring.

KARL: Boring? For who?

KLARA: For me.

KARL: Yeah, for you. By whatever you do, whatever meditation or technique, you want to stay in the tick-tack.

KLARA: It's terrible.

KARL: It's your functioning. That's the functioning of the Creator, Brahma. He has to create. The "I am" always has to create. The functioning of consciousness is to create, to dance with this [slaps his knees]. This Shakti, what is energy, and this Shiva, what is dancing with himself, has to dance.

What an idea that you have to stop the dance to become what you are. Then it becomes boring. Because then you stop, you have a blank mind for a while, and then you step back. You even get bored by controlling something, because the moment you control it, it's boring. "Oh, it was so nice when I didn't control my mind, there was misery." [group laughs]

If controlling or taming the bull of the mind really would stop it, there would be no world anymore. But in spite of Jesus, Buddha, Ramana, whatever sage or holy man, it runs. So the freedom of existence cannot be understood, or by whatever pointer, controlled, stopped or killed. You cannot kill something that is not even there. So in spite of all the understanding and sages and "whatever," freedom is.

That's what Ramana was pointing to. Ramana was never realized, but the Self is ever-realized. So where am I to go? What am I to do or not to do? As I am That which is Heart, and Heart cannot leave Heart, so be it. Hallelujah. It's time? Okay. Thank you very much.

GROUP: Thank you.

"There is no doership in meditation. That is the 'I am' meditating about That which is 'I am.' That's all."

January 19

Shakti hunters and Consciousness Witches; or, the End of Control Systems

You Make Yourself an Object of Desire

KARL: So okay, ready for whatever again? If some easy question comes—but those are the most dangerous ones. Sofia! Tired?

SOFIA: Of everything!

KARL: Of everything? But not retired. You ready to retire?

SOFIA: I am already.

KARL: And now you have to retire from retirement. No, it's like first you retire and then you have to retire from that too. You get tired, and then you "re-tire." Rewind. They always say that when you retire, fun starts, no? The pensioner retires and then—what then? Okay.

LOUISE: Let's get serious!

KARL: Yeah! [laughs] Whatever that means. Fresh from Santa Fe, there are new questions from America!

A Santa Fe WOMAN: I'm running out of questions. I was just sitting in the Ramanasramam bookshop, where I actually like to look, and I opened one book but then I closed it. I just saw concepts.

KARL: Well, next time. Try again. It comes back.

WOMAN: You think so?

KARL: Why not?

WOMAN: Why not!

RITA: I have a question. Why does the waking state look so much more real than the dream? When I'm in the dream then this looks real, and shortly after I wake up it just gets a different density and not so real.

KARL: But this is the same. When you drop into sleep, this is gone. Then it's the same. Maybe in the dream you ask, why is this dream so real and that dream before was not so real. Maybe there's more history in this, more contents.

RITA: Yeah, that's wonderful. Exactly.

KARL: Like day by day you can remember the days before.

RITA: I can remember the past chronologically.

KARL: But sometimes in a dream, you wake up in some whatever form, and this man or woman has a history of whatever. Then, at that moment, it is so real, that history that you speak from. No, I wouldn't say it's more or less real. Right here, now, you think this is more, maybe because you're more used to it. I don't know. But more or less reality doesn't make it more real. The quantity of more history, more whatever memory effects, you have here, now, but the memory effects don't make it more real. It's still pretty much an imagination of reality that something is there at all. Because you think that there was a moment of birth and then all the other ideas are surrounding the idea of being born and then you make a cloud of memory and history—and you take that as real. So what to do with it? If it were real, it should be there all the time.

RITA: What do you mean?

KARL: It should be there permanently. But another dream comes and another dream and even sleep and deep sleep and all the states, and in other states you don't remember the state here. There is no remembrance, there is no memory body, it's like an energy body of memories, and then you are in another form or whatever. And then there is no memory of that, because in a dream you cannot remember this dream here. Maybe you can, but it doesn't make it more real.

RITA: So it's just an infinite flower of dreams, never ending.

KARL: I would say it's an absolute dream of what you are. That total manifestation of realization is an absolute dream and imagination of That which you are. One aspect of one dream doesn't make it more or less real, because even that dream is what you are. Even to call it "a dream" is too much, I think. Even that dream is the Self. The Self, in whatever dream images, is still the Self.

But simply to say, "That's *my* dream," that's the only thing that is not fitting. The "my," the ownership idea, that's the falsity. The rest, I have no idea. But that "me" means there is me and myself, there are two selves. So whatever you come to, whatever this world is or not, it's like *myself, my world*—all depends on "my," the idea of "me" owning something else. This is separation.

From the "me," from the root "I"-thought, come all these ideas of ownership and doership. Whatever dream comes out of it always starts with the dreamer, "I." So the separate dreamer is already part of the dream.

So be prior to the dreamer, be the absolute dreamer which is never in any relative idea of "me" and "my." No ownership idea or doership idea is possible because you are prior to all the dreams or no dreams or whatever, you cannot define it.

Whatever you can imagine, even the imagination of the first dreamer, is imagination. You imagine yourself, and the imagined self is already the "I"-thought, and the dream starts. But seeing that you can experience the "I"-thought means you cannot be it. It's already the imagination of some second self. The mistake is then to take the second self as real. Then you step into separation. Then there's "me" and "myself," and even out of that, other selves come.

RITA: So from your point of view, so to speak, there's nobody else here as a second.

KARL: No, there are infinite forms and shapes of Self.

RITA: But not separate.

KARL: There is not even the idea of "oneness." For the Self, there is neither oneness nor the idea of "Self." There is simply That which is Heart, and Heart is all there is, as That is life itself. There is nothing else alive.

So every other idea of being alive, whatever life means, any definition, is a reflection of That, but it is not That. So Heart is all there is, as That is life itself. The rest is fiction anyway. It needs one who calls something a fiction or illusion, so it needs an illusion to call something else an illusion.

Heart doesn't know anything. By not knowing what is Heart and what is not Heart, you are That which is Heart. So the total absence of an idea of what you are and what you are not, and not by any definition, is what you are. Whatever you say, or define, is separation. It's simply a pointer to call it "the emptiness of heart," the emptiness of ideas of what is Heart and what is not heart, to call it "the essence of existence" or "the nakedness of existence."

And the rest is to figure out if the dream is more real, and why this and that is all part of consciousness contemplating about what consciousness is. It's all part of Self-inquiry, but Self-inquiry of consciousness will not lead you to what you are. You will not become what you are by Self-inquiry.

RITA: So what to do? Nothing?

KARL: You meditate. Because your nature is meditation as consciousness, and that meditation means you have no expectation of a result. So you are as you are. You are the meditation, which is meditation in nature, action without intention.

Simply see, there is no result coming out of whatever is done or not done. You cannot become what you are by understanding. In spite of knowing or not knowing—you are. So if you are totally, in spite of whatever, you can know or not know, then there is meditation because you cannot *not* realize yourself.

And realizing yourself is meditating about That which you are. Out of the meditation, the whole dream starts. This dream is meditating about what you are as consciousness. This is a manifestation of what you are. That is meditation without intention. At the moment intention is part of the meditation, it becomes a personal "me," because there is an advantage idea. "By meditating, I can become what I am looking for, what I am longing for." You make yourself an object of desire, of a goal. Then you are in the control business. You become, "the meditator." You are *doing* meditation.

But you have to *be* meditation. There is no doership in meditation. That is the "I am" meditating about That which is "I am." That's all.

LOUISE: [laughing] That's all!

KARL: Very simple. So what? Out of the meditation, the totality of manifestation is there. At the moment there is *my* meditation, with some kind of goal, then there is no meditation. There is a control system of "me" running on the idea that there is something to control and something to gain. That is called "seeking" and "longing." But by no seeking and by no finding, you will become what is a seeker. So in spite of seeking, you are That which is the seeker, not because.

If seeking would help you, if seeking were your nature, it would always be there. But in deep sleep, there is no seeker and no seeking. It simply starts when you wake up, and then you take Stone Age behavior of collecting some food for the winter, even in that looking for what you are. Then you collect experiences of whatever kind of *shakti*, because "maybe the darkness, the winter will come, and I will need all those experiences of light so that I can survive in the darkness of existence!" [group laughs]

That makes you a *shakti* hunter, hunting presences of gurus, experiences, just to be warm in winter. This is the genetic design, for whatever reason. With the Stone Age behavior, you have to control your surroundings because, otherwise, you die. But to put this control system onto That, to use it to look for what you are, that makes you miserable. That is suffering. It becomes a psychological idea, that by whatever you do, you can add something to what you are.

So what to do? What does Hungaria say to all of that?

Hungarian WOMAN: I don't have something original.

KARL: You don't have an original idea about it? No help?

WOMAN: You know, when you are looking at me, I get red.

KARL: You become shy?

WOMAN: [giggling] Like in my childhood, if I did something and someone looked at me.

KARL: I feel it too. I catch you pretending.

WOMAN: Pretending what?

KARL: Whatever. It's like if you have a child who has done something naughty, and then, "Oh, I know what you have done!" I knew that you pretend.

WOMAN: I have no idea what I did, though. [group laughs]

KARL: You have no idea? *That* you know. [group laughs] Okay, I look somewhere else. Yes?

Life Itself Cannot Get More Naked

RITA: Is there any aspect of the Self that is just contemplating itself?

KARL: No, there's not an aspect who is contemplating. It's the Self. Nothing is without the Self.

RITA: So there is no bad, no good?
KARL: There is, but there is not. You cannot say there is not, because if you say there is not, there is still, "there is not." You have to say something like, "In the dream, it is; in reality, it is not." So in the realization, it is; but in reality, not. So all there is, is the dream, but there is no dream. This paradox you cannot solve. This *koan* you cannot understand.
RITA: It drives you mad.
KARL: Yeah, but by being totally mad, totally confused, and then in the experience of total confusion, you see that total confusion cannot touch what you are. So what then? You simply see that you are never in any senses, that no senses of confusion, or experience of confusion, can touch what you are. Because That which you are can never be confused. So even in the total confusion of not knowing or "whatever," being in total chaos, you still are what you are.

But this is actually the experience of Ramana, when he was lying down and had his death experience, whatever could die, he let die. But life itself was still untouched by it. So life itself cannot be touched by any object or idea which can drop, which comes and goes. So if you let all the dream ideas and concepts, simply drop away, in the substratum which is left over— the total leftover of existence, the total nakedness, what cannot get any more naked—you will see that life itself is ever unborn and never dies and you can never leave it.

Simply see that, what you can experience, you cannot be. So by seeing whatever experience, you drop, you go more and more back to what is the absolute experiencer, as you see the experiencer as part of the experience. It again becomes That which is life itself, which is never coming and never going, which is not part of the phenomena of fleeting shadows of experiences, experiencers, and whatever. That's why it's called, "dream-like." It's not a dream, but it's dream-like.
RITA: There seems to be a gap between what you're talking about and what I'm experiencing.
KARL: No, no. It seems to be. But I tell you, That which is here, now, is That which is the absolute experiencer sitting there in the camera position of what you are, just looking out of. There is perception, pure perception. The pure perception, that which is awareness, is like a canvas. It was there as a baby and even before, untouched by any sensation of being born or

sensation of whatever this dream meant to be.

I'm talking only to the nakedness which was never changed, never moved, nothing ever happened to it. As I'm not talking to a ghost, not to any idea, I'm always talking to That which I am, That which is untouched by anything, and can never be touched by any idea, so it cannot be made or unmade by anything. So be That which is a baby even before innocence. In no sense.

RITA: Innocent.

KARL: Not in no cent. You are in no sense. It doesn't pay.

LOUISE: And who needs to know that?

KARL: You. Who else? That which is asking needs to know.

LOUISE: Why?

KARL: Why not?

LOUISE: Okay, why not?

KARL: Why?! Otherwise you would not sit here. Would you? "Could you, would you?"

LOUISE: That nakedness is sitting here.

KARL: Yeah. Facing itself in front of nakedness so that it can be made just an idea, reminded to be the nakedness. That's all. But it's nothing new. It's simply, "Aha! Oh, yes." So in this sense, I cannot help you, I just point to That—That which cannot be helped at all, not even reminded, because it has never forgotten itself, so even a reminder is too much.

LOUISE: And stubbornness still comes up, I am still stubborn, again and again.

KARL: It's fun. That's why she gets red, because she is so stubborn and she never listens to what is told to her. [group laughs]

LOUISE: It's because you are so handsome, that's why she doesn't listen. [more group laughter]

Hungarian WOMAN: Serious!

KARL: The ideas!

WOMAN: Now you are red!

KARL: I know when she gets red. That's compassion! [group laughs] No, if I'm honest, whoever comes with whatever emotional or energetic thing, it's here. There is no difference.

Another WOMAN: If you're honest for her—

KARL: Otherwise I am lying too. But even if I'm honest, I'm lying, you

know. [group laughs] Especially when I say that I am honest. It's a special
lie. It's like, "How often did I tell you!"
Hungarian WOMAN: This is my mind!
KARL: Hammering into you. "How often do I tell you again that this is not!"
LOUISE: It's a flowering, the blushing is a flowering.
KARL: A flowering.
LOUISE: Of the flesh. Blush of the flower of nakedness.
KARL: Yeah, I said, if the energy is touched, if this bump becomes awake,
it's like an energy flesh. It's like the elephant wakes up. Ramana would say,
when asked why he shook so much, "What to do when an elephant wakes up
in a hut?" It is unavoidable, because it's like falling in love.
Hungarian WOMAN: [laughing] I know.
KARL: So I'm pointing out, when this happens, it's a good pointer for helplessness, as you cannot avoid falling in love, you cannot avoid what comes
out of the blue, out of That which is life itself—life energy starts and it's
uncontrollable.
A British WOMAN: It makes you blind.
KARL: That is the beauty of it, you experience complete controllessness,
because you cannot control it. Everything you have, even thoughts, you can
control—maybe—by meditation techniques. You can control your acceptance, your tolerance limits, but when controllessness happens you cannot
control it, it's simply, "Ah, shit! Again!," everything is for nothing.
    So falling in love is the same, as the controllessness simply shows itself.
Especially when you want to avoid it, you are then even more in it. You cannot *not* fall in love.
LOUISE: And then you fall out again.
KARL: Even falling out, you cannot avoid. So it's the same for both extreme
situations—you fall in love and you cannot avoid it—this helplessness—and
then it drops out, as you can only drop out when you drop out, and not by
wanting to get out. You want to make a split in a relationship, but you hang
on like there's no way out. You suffer, you continue to do everything, and
then in a split second there is a total resignation of "whatever," as it breaks
your heart, and you drop out. But it's not one moment before. And from
that moment on, it's like, "How could I have ever been in love with that
one?" [group laughs]
    But until that moment, you cannot help yourself. You are *klingt* (rung).

Bam. Isn't it amazing? But everything is like this. Smoking, every addiction, is like this.

LOUISE: So first you have that going on with the nakedness, and after you fall out of it again, do you just become Joe Blow and go to work, eight to five, or what happens then?

KARL: When, what?

LOUISE: Well, you're falling in love with the nakedness, and then you fall out again, right?

KARL: No, no. Falling in love with the nakedness you cannot do.

LOUISE: You cannot?

KARL: Nakedness cannot fall in love with nakedness. Nakedness cannot avoid falling in love with an image. That's different. But nakedness cannot fall in love with nakedness. In nakedness, there's no idea of separation, there's no falling in anything.

But out of that nakedness—with whatever image—you fall in love. And as you fall in love with an idea, you fall into your own trap. You imagine something, because you cannot *not* imagine yourself. You cannot avoid awakening to the "I"-awareness, and then "I am" comes and you cannot avoid it.

Then you fall in love with the image around you, and you cannot avoid this either. Finally, you fall out again—which is also unavoidable. So all the way, there is helplessness.

I always point to the Absolute you are, which is total helplessness. All the way, in no sense, was there ever any control. You can never control yourself as there is no second one to control. So in whatever circumstance or state, there is neither control nor no control. Helplessness is all there is. So whatever is, is as it is, but never because you control it or do something or have something.

So in that, everything is a totality of controllessness and freedom. Whatever is, is freedom itself. In whatever circumstance, there's freedom. And that freedom you cannot lose and you cannot gain, as you are that freedom of totality of existence which cannot help itself. Total helplessness itself— that is freedom.

Now you have a dream of control, you have a dream of free will, and all this is just a dream, because there was never anything like this.

That Helplessness Is the Almighty

LOUISE: I just get caught in this duality again when you say "helplessness," because if there is helplessness, there is help.

KARL: No, no! Helplessness is prior to help and no help. You misunderstand helplessness. You take it as personal helplessness, but in helplessness, there is no person left. Without any idea of help and no help, there is no one left. When there is help and no help, it is a personal help and no help. But in helplessness there is no separation.

LOUISE: Give me a practical example.

KARL: Wishlessness.

LOUISE: Give me a practical example; I'm just a simple-minded person.

KARL: Oh, she is always lying. What a liar! [group laughs]

LOUISE: Give me an example about the helplessness. What does it look like?

KARL: I just gave you an example. If you fall in love with someone, you cannot help it. You cannot decide when to wake up in the morning. Very practical.

LOUISE: I do!

KARL: You never do!

LOUISE: I stay another hour in bed or something like this.

KARL: You stay, but you are awake.

LOUISE: Dream-like awake.

KARL: What "dream-like awake"?

LOUISE: [giggles] Oh, I don't know.

KARL: Listen to her! She's a Tai Chi type. She Tai, Tai Chi. "I am in control!" [group laughs] Energy master. There are many energy masters. She is Tai and Tai Chi, and then comes She Gong She Gong and Gong She! You once told me, "With my energy, I can control everything." No? Didn't you?

LOUISE: [laughing] I told you that?

KARL: I remember.

LOUISE: Look at all these people here. They're coming.

KARL: All because of you.

LOUISE: No, because of you!

KARL: Me? No, I'm sure not because of me.

LOUISE: Twelve thousand miles and here we are.

KARL: Helplessness is the almighty power.

LOUISE: Uh, huh. So that's your practical example now? You're not satisfying me.

KARL: Satisfied? You will never be satisfied. You cannot be satisfied. How can you be satisfied? What an idea, that an idea can be satisfied?! And who wants you to be satisfied?

LOUISE: You.

KARL: No, no, no. I'm not here to please you or make you satisfied. Who cares about your satisfaction? No, no, no. That's everywoman, "Please make me satisfied! Give me something!" [group laughs] No, no, no. "Try harder, now. Give me some practical advice!" That's the old technique. [more group laughter]

LOUISE: [laughing] You're not falling for that! Now you're old enough.

KARL: "Oh, you can do better now. More practice. You promised to satisfy me!" [group laughs] Michael?

LOUISE: Leave him alone! [group laughs]

KARL: "Don't talk to him!" Otherwise, head off for Michael. [group laughs] So what is your practical—?

LOUISE: Okay, never mind!

KARL: Never mind?

LOUISE: Enough abuse for one day. [group laughs]

KARL: Abuse? Oh, she gets really psychological now. [group laughs] She is really clever. Smarty, psychological—

LOUISE: [laughing] With a stupid mind.

KARL: With a stupid mind? Oh, I tell you!

LOUISE: Oh, you make me laugh and cry at the same time!

KARL: That sounds good, first a headache and then laughing and crying.

LOUISE: Two for one!

KARL: Bam, bam. It's a good example. Okay. Some questions about this, some more practical advice?

RITA: [laughing] So basically, everything is a paradox, you cannot experience—you cannot figure out anything, so all this searching is completely futile.

KARL: Yeah, thank God. Imagine if you could control existence by your seeking and your understanding? What an idea!

RITA: So better stay home, if you can.

KARL: No one can stay home. There is no one at home! First find home. You will never find home. My goodness. There is no one at home. It's an idea.

"Stay home." "Abide in yourself!" [group laughs] If that would work, then after Jesus, Buddha, and all these great sages, the Self would never go out again. Hmm? But look at it. It doesn't stop. Even after all these holy ones, the dream runs and runs and runs. So that's the beauty of existence, freedom—you cannot control it by understanding or by any insight of any kind or by any practical advice. "How can I control myself?" No.

You can talk about the Almighty you are. What is the meaning of being almighty? Almighty means there is no second you can control, and you cannot be controlled by any second, by anything else. That is being almighty. But that also means there is no second to control and no second who can control you, you cannot even control yourself.

So controllessness is your nature. Controllessness is absolute acceptance, but there is nothing to accept, because there is only the Self. That is absolute acceptance, and not any relative acceptance of practical advice or of anything by control.

Whenever a person accepts, it's controlling. So whatever you do as practicing acceptance, you want to control your surroundings by accepting them. You want to be detached from whatever. Your control system is running. So you even want to get enlightened, because you want control. Even with enlightenment, you take it personally, and you become "the enlightened one." Then you are in God-consciousness, and everything else is a pig stall.

RITA: Pig stall!

KARL: It has to be. Whoever is looking for something, it's because of that. "I control, because I see separation. There are separate worlds, separate others, and out of all that, I have to control myself." Then you even want to control freedom. My goodness. Put it in your pocket and take it home, as you want to stay home. No?

RITA: [laughing] Not particularly.

KARL: This absolute "no way out," this absolute helplessness, that is paradise. That is being almighty, because the helplessness means there is no control from inside or outside. For That which you are, nothing ever happened, and no one else can control what you are.

And no circumstance can change you, or do anything to you, as all the circumstances are because of you, but you are not because of anything. You are causelessness itself. Whatever has a cause is not what you are. So objective and sensational life, or no life, can ever touch the eternal life you are. So be it. There is no practical advice to become that.

LOUISE: It's like an infant. You become like an infant.

KARL: You don't become anything.

LOUISE: It is like this! The helplessness is like an infant—

KARL: That is helpless. There is an infant who is helpless, but the infant is not helplessness. You cannot make an object helplessness. In helplessness, there is no object and subject anymore; there is no second. There is a total helplessness. If you call it an infant who is helpless, it's not the helplessness I mean.

MATHILDA: It's more like an animal?

KARL: No. Even that is helpless, but not helplessness. Helplessness means a total absence of an idea of control, of a controller. But even an animal you would say has control, maybe. By "control," you define it. You cannot define it as that.

MATHILDA: An animal does not want control, does not think about control.

KARL: An animal is hungry, and for hunger it kills. As your mind gets hungry for ideas, you kill for them.

MATHILDA: It's not thinking about it.

KARL: But what is the mind? It's like a stomach that gets hungry. It's an infinite hungry stomach that wants to get more experiences. What's the difference between your stomach and your brain? Both want to work.

MATHILDA: It's instinct, I guess.

KARL: Instinct?

LOUISE: It stinks. [group laughs]

KARL: It stinks! You think you smell and after the smell, you go. You have "in-stinked." Because it stinks. But you are the tastelessness. You can never smell yourself. So whatever you go for by instinct, it's not what you are. What you are never stinks. So there is no "in-stinked."

You're Never Prepared for the Infinite You Are

MATHILDA: I have another question. If I cannot influence my future by wish or by will, then how does it happen? When I have a thought or an idea, it becomes true, sometimes very quickly. For example, sometimes when I'm thinking, "Oh, I want to meet this friend of mine," even though he is living in another country, when I go out on the street, I meet him!

KARL: But isn't it so logical? In order for you to meet a friend in the future, you first have to think about meeting him. First you have to make an idea, or an idea comes, "I want to meet this person" and then you make an effort to meet him.

Because you have to make an effort, so that the future can be as the future can be. It's an interrelation of future and past. It's very easy to understand. First you have to want to drink before you drink.

MATHILDA: Yeah, but, normally—

KARL: Normally?

MATHILDA: This example is very simple, I should give you a more complicated one. [group laughs] Really, this friend, he cannot be there. I live in Germany, and he lives in Italy, and one day I think, "Oh, I want to meet him," and then I go on the street to have a cup of coffee and there he is standing in front of me.

KARL: Do you really think consciousness doesn't know what comes next? Where do the ideas come from?

MATHILDA: Sometimes—

KARL: What sometimes? There is no sometimes. Consciousness is the Source of the ever-functioning of consciousness. There is no limit between yesterday, tomorrow, and now. There is That which is consciousness all throughout manifestation. Why shouldn't consciousness know the next moment already? Whatever consciousness is concentrating on, it can become—the future, whatever. Sometimes it is called, "psychic."

MATHILDA: So I can—

KARL: If you put all your concentration on becoming a witch, you will become a witch who can look into the future. Consciousness can do whatever. If it's meant to be, it will happen. So there is no limit in consciousness.

MATHILDA: So it's the consciousness which creates—

KARL: Yes, it's a witch. A bitch and a witch. The consciousness witch. [group laughs]

MATHILDA: So it's the consciousness that creates my thoughts and ideas, it's not my mind?

KARL: There was never any mind that created anything. Mind is created by That. Consciousness, as formless consciousness, takes information of the mind as the "I"-thought, and then a cloud of thoughts surround it. But all that is an "in-form-ation" of consciousness. There was never any such mind that created anything.

MATHILDA: But it seems to me that meditation and doing *sadhana* makes a difference. In former times—

KARL: In former times?

MATHILDA: Before I did *sadhana*, it was not so much like now, that I have a thought or an idea and it happens suddenly.

KARL: Oh, you have caused this oneness, or what? Cause of miracles?

MATHILDA: No, I didn't say this well.

KARL: But it sounds like it. It's like an *avatar* seminar or something. You always want to have a parking place when you need one. [group laughs]

AIKO: There's your practical example!

KARL: That's your special trick, yeah. All the witches start with that. Nice control system.

MATHILDA: I still don't understand. Yesterday, I was told that I cannot influence my thoughts or wishes.

KARL: You cannot want what you want, because That which is wanting it already wanted it. The movie is already shot. So that there can be wanting, out of the wanting, something will happen, because this is part of the movie. It's a cause and effect. There is an action-reaction chain, and everything is interrelated, but no one is there who can want it. Even the wanting, you cannot want. You cannot think before you think. You cannot want before you want.

MATHILDA: I thought that these visions come out of my mind.

KARL: Even that you cannot think. You cannot decide what you think next. You cannot pre-think.

MATHILDA: I thought this was the construction, because I have this aim in my mind.

KARL: Oh, you cannot aim, but you aim. Just simply see it. You cannot want what you want. You cannot pre-think. You have to think. Then you think, because of the thinking, you think.

BERTA: And it looks like you do it your own way.

KARL: It looks like that, but that's why I say it's a dream.

BERTA: Like, I think I'll go to Karl.

KARL: Yeah, but where does that thought come from?

BERTA: Ah, yeah. [group laughs]

KARL: Oy yoy! It's like dominoes. Your brain is like a domino play. First one domino has to fall, and then all the others go together. It's like an action-reaction chain. But first, the first domino has to drop. And who makes the first domino drop? That's the whole question. After the first on drops, you think, "Oh, that was because of what was before," but what was before the before the before the before? Who made the first domino drop?

BERTA: What came first, the chicken or the egg?

KARL: Is there any chicken or any egg? You come later! [group laughs]

MATHILDA: And there are many thoughts and visions which are not fulfilled.

KARL: I hope so. Imagine that the weather is like it is because there are so many wishing for it. Imagine if every wish were fulfilled! [group laughs]

A MAN: What a mess!

KARL: First you're here and then—boom—you're in New York! Only by imagination, you're there. But imagine the flip flop, nothing would be there anymore, if every wish would poof, poof, poof!

FRANCESCO: One day you try!

KARL: Wishful thinking!

MATHILDA: So do you think everything is fixed? My whole future is fixed by karma?

KARL: No. Just find the one who has a future, who has a past, and then we'll talk about what is fixed and not fixed. First find one who cares about it and who needs to know it. "Me!" The first, "any me" you have to find. And any "me" is an enemy. Especially that, "me" that wants to know, "what is 'me'?" It's an enemy. So first try to find that enemy, and then we can talk about the future or past of that enemy.

AIKO: That's a trick that everyone uses.

KARL: Yeah, a trick.

A MAN: It's mean.

KARL: It's me.

AIKO: Then there's nobody to ask anymore.

A WOMAN: She got it!

KARL: She got it. Thank God, she "God" it.

AIKO: I read it.

KARL: "I read it"! [group laughs] There's a famous saying from Wittgenstein, but Einstein said it too, that he could only bear humanity by seeing that humanity cannot want what humanity wants. So there is no guilt or sin in anything, doing or not doing from humanity, as humanity cannot decide what humanity wants to want. That means everything comes out of the absolute Source of existence, That totality demands whatever has to be done and not done. There is no separate "me" who can decide whatever.

This is already freedom. So what comes next is already decided, in the sense that you cannot decide what comes next from what is "me." The totality, the total circumstance, is dictating every next movement. Even the next breath or a finger which moves, comes out of the totality.

MATHILDA: So then I will become very lazy.

KARL: Lazy? You have never done anything. How can you become lazy? You have never done anything at all. How can you *become* lazy? My goodness!

MATHILDA: Sometimes, it's stressful.

KARL: Stress? Where?

MATHILDA: Work, relationships.

KARL: Just to be alive is stress.

MATHILDA: So, if it doesn't matter, I will not work anymore.

KARL: You think *you* can decide? You think now, by whatever understanding, you can decide what comes next?

MATHILDA: I don't want to fight for something anymore.

KARL: Aw! When there will be fighting, there will be fighting, whether you like it or not.

MATHILDA: I can decide.

KARL: You can decide? Oh, the witch again. "I can decide! You cannot take my free will away! It's the last thing I will give away."

MATHILDA: I can give up, you know.

KARL: You cannot give up. What can you give up? What is yours anyway?

MATHILDA: Things I'm forced to do.

KARL: You're forced?

MATHILDA: By my own discipline.

KARL: By your own discipline? Oh, my goodness. Now we are really getting into some trouble!

BERTA: But Karl, it's very confusing because we are living in a world where the body is taken for what you are. So, when you say "you," the "you" that you talk about, the "me" that is sitting here—I don't know how to say it—but it's very confusing.

KARL: Yeah, I hope so.

BERTA: And this whole thing of free will—

KARL: I am sitting here to make confused what can get confused, and for you to see in a split second, that That which you are was never and will never be confused, in whatever circumstance. And what can be confused is simply an idea, an object that can be touched, moved and jiggled. That which you are, simply being the absolute awareness, or That which is perception itself, the absolute perceiver, Self itself, was never touched by any sensation, and was never confused or not confused by anything.

So this makes confused what can get confused. That which is here, now, is here so you totally go to the helplessness or hopelessness or whatever, and you see that That which you are never needed any hope or help, in any sense. What needs help and has any hope was never there, because it's a dream figure. It's simply appearing and disappearing, and you never depend on the dream figure. So then you may become That again, that which is concernlessness, which never cared about anything.

BERTA: But you are linked to this dream figure for—I'm already fifty-five years—

KARL: Ah, no! [group laughs]

BERTA: So I start to call it "I" instead of a number. What can you do?

KARL: Yeah, for fifty-five numbers. You are such a number.

BERTA: Every morning I wake up with the same dream figure. "Oh, I'm there again."

KARL: Hello, again.

BERTA: I know.

KARL: So what? At night you say goodbye, and in the morning, you say hello.

BERTA: And it goes on and on and on.

KARL: And it will never stop. It will never disappear, because there is nothing to disappear. It will go on and on and on and on.

LOUISE: "A sweet song."

KARL: *Hari Om!* Carry On! Yeah, you have to face your infinite nature, and your infinite nature means there is no coming and going even in the realization of what you are. The dream will never stop, as it never started. The dream-like realization is what you are, and the realization of what is you is as infinite as you are.

And no person can bear that. If you look into the infinite, you will be gone. No one can take it. No one ever could take the infinite. That was the meaning when U. G. Krishnamurti came to Ramana and asked, "Can you give me what you have?" And Ramana said, "I can give it to you, but can you take it?"

That's all, this question—can you take it? And there will never be anyone prepared or ready to take it, to be the infinite, That which has no coming and going, which is never born and never dies. Whoever is born, cannot face That. Facing the never-ending, eternal life, you as Berta would be gone in an instant and was never there in the first place. But Berta cannot take it.

That's why I never talk to Berta. I always talk to That which is the Absolute already and never that which left what it is. Only the Absolute can take it, only the Absolute can be That infinite, never-born and undying, immortal existence. Whatever the idea of "mortality" is, being mortal, cannot take immortality, never ever. Because in the infinite embracement of being That which is infinite, you will be annihilated as an idea of a separate life, of being born and dying—in that instant.

Whatever is before, the understanding, of "me" and any control system, doesn't count anyway. You can never, by understanding, control That. By becoming a sorcerer or *bruha* (witch) or whatever, you can never control existence. You can never come to a point of being prepared for the infinite you are.

I can talk total nonsense about whatever is, wishs and no wishs, who comes in this form and why is this like this—it's all irrelevant, absolutely irrelevant, because it cannot touch what you are. It cannot make you what you are. So understanding or not understanding, who cares? I have nothing to give you, not even understanding. Because not by any understanding, or by any control system, will you control existence or become what you are.

That's the beauty of existence, that not by any control system can it be controlled. It's all ideas, all concepts, of one who would like to be in control. But even I couldn't decide to get out of the womb at that moment! The first domino came out. Then the domino becomes a, "domina," a controller. Domination. Dictation. [group laughs]

Simply out of the idea of being born, of that, "me-steak" being born, the first domino falls. And then you think, after whatever came, it's because the domino before it there, but it was all out of the "me-steak." Meanwhile, you can't decide whether to come out or not. But I am here to tell you, you never came out of any womb as you are, you are always that, "child of a barren woman."

RITA: So there is actually no "me-steak"?

KARL: There is, but there is not. But to take yourself as that "me-steak," if you identify with that steak, this is a "me"-steak, the first mistake, and you become an object in time.

RITA: But it cannot be avoided either.

KARL: No. This first domino, popping up as "I"-thought, coming out of the Heart, you cannot avoid. You cannot avoid waking up to "I"-awareness, and out of the "I"-awareness comes "I am" and "I am so-and-so." Unavoidable. But I am here, maybe so you can see, That which is Heart—which is what you are as "I," "I am," and world—you never lost your nature. You are here, now, the absolute existence, the nakedness.

You never lost the nakedness, so whatever dress you put on, whatever idea you take as a concept, it is merely a concept, and one day it will be gone, as the last shirt has no pockets. Even the enlightenment you may have and whatever body experiences you have, you cannot take with you to whatever.

RITA: So there is no sense of any personal history anyway.

KARL: Yeah, this saying, "The last shirt has no pockets," means that, at that moment, you are naked. Then you get dressed again. But you can be naked here and now. Be the nakedness which is simply dressed by an idea, and be it simply by seeing the dress as an idea, the body as an idea. You are the nakedness, dressed. You don't have to undress to become that nakedness. You simply see that it's all dressing. Then you can make a salad out of it. [group laughs]

What Needs Some Help Is Simply a Dream Character

LOUISE: Can you talk about why it's not in everybody's nature, why are there only a few, a handful of people, having this desire?
KARL: I tell you, there's even none.
LOUISE: Say it again.
KARL: "A few" would be saying too much. There is no one who has any desire. Desire is there, but there is no one who has desire. So there is even none. Even less than you thought.
LOUISE: He is such a fuck! [group laughs] He has this innocent approach, you know—
KARL: [laughing] Innocent? Innocent approach?! It's like someone comes to Jesus, saying, "I have a nail and a hammer. It's just an innocent approach. [group laughs] Very innocent. Don't worry. I just have a hammer and a nail. I just want to nail you on existence. Why are there only so few? Jesus, tell me."
LOUISE: Okay.
KARL: Okay?
LOUISE: Okay.
KARL: Then you go "from Pontius to Pilatus" and ask the same question. "Tell me, why?"
LOUISE: No, this time I said "how." I didn't say "why."
KARL: Ah, "how." It's the same.
LOUISE: No really, how come?
KARL: You are in America too long. You've become a red-skinned Indian. "How! How is it? How can we get out of it?" How? "Beat me up before you go." So what, how?
LOUISE: Okay, never mind!
KARL: No, you have to see, any sausage saleswoman who cuts sausage wants to be happy. That's the approach of happiness. Whatever is done by consciousness is the longing for happiness, it comes out of the meditation about That which is happiness itself, unconditioned happiness. Whatever you do as a person is out of wanting to be happy all the time. This is the meaning of "person." Whatever the person is doing, in whatever circumstance—

LOUISE: Yeah, we want peace, we want happiness, we want joy.

KARL: And you will even murder, you will kill for happiness, for peace. So what is an approach? There are six billion approaches.

LOUISE: So six billion would approach this place here.

KARL: But for them, it is maybe the, "Mercedes Arunachala." They think, "If I would drive a Mercedes, I would be Arunachala," because Arunachala is simply unconditional happiness—Heart. "If I drive a Mercedes, I would be happy forever."

But at the moment you turn the key and drive, there is always a bigger car to drive, and you're still in a shit hole. There's always something better.

And then the idea of "enlightenment" comes. "First there will be realization and then there will be realization of the realization of the—." Oh my goodness. so it is even with enlightenment. "Oh, there is enlightenment, but that is only the first step." [group laughs] Is that like it? So then there is, "Oh, once there was enlightenment, but that was only the first step, and then I realized, really! And I had my first *satori* at fifteen. Oh yes. But then later on, it was 'Ah!' Then I didn't know, but now I know!" [group laughs]

What a bushel of ideas come—always getting more and more of what you cannot get anyway. Then, there are even levels of enlightenment. Imagine! "Are you more or less enlightened?"

It's like the question, "Are you more or less pregnant?," "I feel a little pregnant." [group laughs] "I feel a little dead, already." [lots of group laughter and background noise]

LOUISE: [laughing] Did you say "twirls"?

KARL: Girls? Turtles?

LOUISE: Does it hurt? Are you hurting?

KARL: Are you heard? Shepherd. Sheep, sheep. There's a popular expression, "deep sharing." It's like a sheep shearing. Being together, being totally honest with each other. It's like shaving, with a not-so-sharp knife. [group laughs]

LOUISE: Yeah, they put the sheep between the legs—

KARL: I know.

LOUISE: —squeeze the butt, and that fixes it.

KARL: Okay.

LOUISE: Now you say "okay"!

KARL: Why not? I'm always surprised.

LOUISE: Really.

KARL: What to do? Okay. Back to the experience. You can have the experience of free will, but there is still no one who has free will. It's a dream-like experience. I don't deny it. You can make that "whatever." It's okay. But to call it, "*my* experience" and "*my* doing," it becomes a history.

You have the experience of free will, but so what? With a history, with "me" being born and remaining in the history of *my* so-called life, every moment, you collect it around, *my* neck, and then want to have an enlightenment experience, or whatever *avatar* experience there is. You put all the bullshit behind so that no one can see it anymore, and you only wear the one shining in front of you, you nourish it and show it to everyone—that's a person. What to do with it? It has to be like it is, because it's meant like this. Otherwise, it wouldn't be like this. So enjoy the show.

But the happiness you look for and long for, whatever you want to be, you cannot become through anything we have just talked about. No sensation, no experience, no understanding, whatever comes and goes, can make you That which you are. But that you have to see by yourself. No one else can give it to you. It cannot be transmitted. It cannot be given by understanding, by anything.

So if I say, I hope I was as irrelevant as always, I point to the hopelessness that I cannot give you anything as hope or help, since what you are is already the Almighty and for sure doesn't need any help. What needs some help is simply the dream character in what you are. The idea that needs help—so what?—it may need help and get help or not, but who cares about the phantom who gets some help or not. It's the phantom who has the idea of having free will. Hallelujah. My goodness. Being a bitch or witch.

Hungarian WOMAN: Stubborn.

KARL: Stubborn.

MATHILDA: If there's nothing to do and nothing to think, isn't it most comfortable to do nothing?

KARL: Try. Yeah, try. Try not to digest. [group laughs] Very simple. I just ask you very simply, try not to digest. It's the same as if I asked you not to think. "Wouldn't it then be the most easy thing that I just stop thinking?"

MATHILDA: No. I mean, to do nothing.

KARL: It's the same.

MATHILDA: I know I cannot *not* think.

KARL: But what's the difference? This is like the digestion of existence, making you do something. Lifting your finger is a digestion of existence. It's really like this idea that you have done anything at all, it's an idea. All the doing, what was done and will be done, is coming out of existence itself, out of energy itself which is consciousness, always creating the next action out of what is the chain reaction of karmic consciousness. There was never any personal doing or not doing. So you cannot *not* do anything. And the "nothing" you want to do is much too big for you. Imagine if you could do nothing. No way.

[Karl drinks his lemonade.]

FRANCESCO: Nice drink with sugar?

KARL: Urine with vitamins. I'm in a therapy. [group laughs]

A WOMAN: Really?

KARL: Yeah, I have inner therapy. All the time. It's called "digestion." [group laughs]

FRANCESCO: It's good?

KARL: Fantastic!

Raped by Existence

ANTONIO: I have a little question.

FRANCESCO: Oh, God! I don't believe it. Be careful! [group laughs]

ANTONIO: Not because, but—

FRANCESCO: Not because!

ANTONIO: In spite, in spite! Whatever language you use. You say that the Self has no taste—

KARL: No, I did not say, "no taste." The Self is tastelessness.

ANTONIO: Okay, tastelessness.

KARL: The tastelessness cannot be tasted.

ANTONIO: Yeah, so the question is—

KARL: I didn't say it doesn't have any taste!

ANTONIO: Okay, okay! Whatever you say! [group laughs] That is not the point. The question is, when Ramana realized— Oh! [group laughs]

FRANCESCO: Don't say it like that!

ANTONIO: Okay. There was an experience of dropping everything, but he was not giving *satsang*. Somebody put him in this position to give *satsang*. So who says "the tastelessness" without saying this?

KARL: Don't make me sit here, or what?

ANTONIO: You or Ramana or Buddha. Because there is no Buddha himself, no Ramana himself, no you yourself sitting here. You have no choice.

KARL: You have to say, "I am sitting by myself here." Not by anything else.

SOFIA: Because there is the aspiration of That.

KARL: There is a freedom of decision, and the freedom of decision itself is existence, the freedom of decision decided to sit here.

ANTONIO: So this is also meant in Buddha's case?

KARL: In whatever case. Buddha said that there was never any Buddha on earth and never will be. You see a person sitting somewhere, Buddha might say that there is a figure, but there is no one sitting there. And Buddha, That which is the nature of what you are, is never a part of anything. This dream, this manifestation, is as it is. There are objects and things, dream objects, but there is, in no sense, any decision.

Freedom is all there is—helplessness—That absolute absence of an idea of "*my* will" or "not *my* will" or "*my* freedom" or "not freedom"—sitting here or not sitting here—concernlessness, is freedom. Because, you see, you cannot *not* sit here, because the moment you sit here, there is simply a total demand.

ANTONIO: So in this case, existence put you just there?

KARL: No, no one is put anywhere. It's part of the dream.

ANTONIO: In the dream.

KARL: But no one puts anyone anywhere. There is simply a dream of existence. No one is put or asked to do anything.

You are still in the point of view of a person, it seems like you are being forced to sit here. By seeing that you cannot decide to sit here, but there is still someone sitting, you think you are being raped when you sit here. You become a helpless person. You're seeing existence as raping you, every minute, because it does with you what existence wants. Huh?

ANTONIO: No idea.

KARL: If you sit here as you are, thinking that existence is demanding that you sit here—that's what I mean when I say that you feel raped by existence.

You are sitting here against your will. There is still an idea that by thinking, "it is not *my* will to sit here" that existence forces you to sit here and you're being raped by existence.

FRANCESCO: I lost you. I lost everything.

KARL: *Alla* understood?

FRANCESCO: No, I mean *a la dent.* [group laughs] I tell you. I know.

KARL: I just want to point out, with understanding, when you see existence in total control, you are still there as a "me," you are raped. This is misery, once again, because you think you are raped by existence and existence is against you. You even make existence your enemy. No?

FRANCESCO: She needs to lie down. Let's make room for her.

[Mrs. Angelina lies down and rests. She is not well. She and Francesco talk to each other quietly in Italian while the *satsang* continues.]

A WOMAN: That's true. This is again helplessness.

KARL: No, it's helpless. It's not the helplessness. When you are That which is the helplessness, there is no existence who does anything to you. Then you are That which is existence, and there is no one who does anything with anyone. But if, by whatever understanding, you come to see that existence is doing everything, you're still separate from existence, and then you are raped by existence. "Oh, poor me again!" All this is self-pity. All these ideas of "self" are always self-pity. There is still separation, and separation is hell.

CHARLES: Because you think you have a choice.

KARL: Yeah, but even if you think you have no choice, you are still in that misery of having no choice. First you think you are the doer, and then you become the non-doer by understanding "I am not doing anything," but you are still in the misery. It makes no difference. So the understanding, that you are the non-doer and existence does everything, doesn't help either, because you even make that, *my* understanding and then there is no freedom in understanding. There is no freedom in the idea of "freedom," and there is no understanding in understanding.

MARY: "I-me-my" is the only problem.

KARL: Even that is not a problem.

MARY: Yeah, but I mean, you know.

KARL: Yeah, I mean! You know what I mean, you know! [group laughs]

MARY: To see that is—

KARL: It means nothing. Again and again, I point out that, no moment of understanding, by whatever insight, by the highest knowledge, can you get it, by whatever!—Forget it.

It is like, in the *Mahabharata*, when Yudhistara went with Krishna to hell. It is hell for the mind to see that there is no way out. And then there is the question from Krishna, "Can you take it, can you be in the misery, for whatever you imagine of time, for eternity? Is there any wish of avoidance left in what you are?"

And then there was simply a total resignation of that which cares. "Whatever. Let it be, as it is." Then suddenly, there was no hell, no Krishna, no Yudhistara—there was nothing left. There was simply the Absolute itself, without any avoidance, as absolute blankness of ideas of what it is and what it is not. This is a direct pointer to the absolute acceptance, that which cannot be done.

Emptiness of Heart is suddenly there, it is not by any doing or not doing, nor by understanding, or by anyone who understood or not. It's a total absence of understanding, a total absence of freedom. It is the total absence or emptiness of Heart which can contain That which is absolute existence. You are naked here and now, and you don't have to undress for it. You are totally empty. Whatever ideas come in the morning, they were not there before. So you're prior to these ideas, which come as a dressing. You are, in spite of ideas and concepts, never because. So whatever comes with the idea of "me" in the morning, whatever understanding or not understanding, is fleeting. It cannot add something to what you are.

You dress in the morning and undress at night. It's Infinite. But you are still the nakedness itself that was never dressed by anything. So simply be the nakedness. It's very simple. Stay in the nakedness. In the morning, when you get dressed you say, "Okay. Hello and Goodbye." Absolute goodbye and absolute hello. Every night you say, "If I don't see you tomorrow morning, it was very nice to meet you." And then the next morning you say, "Ah, hello, it's you again. Okay."
[Silence. A few giggles.]
KARL: That's hell.
Hungarian WOMAN: What is it?
KARL: When That which is life becomes aware of the Absolute which it is, hell starts. Because when awareness is there, the holocaust starts. In the holocaust or hellfire of awareness—only in the awareness of awareness, which

is hellfire itself—the devil burns out.

WOMAN: [laughing] You think I have any idea of what you are talking about?

[The group explodes with laughter.]

KARL: Makes no difference. I'm not talking to any idea anyway!

WOMAN: I know, I feel you are not talking to me.

KARL: No, see!

WOMAN: Maybe that's why I'm not getting it.

KARL: I always say I don't talk to ghosts.

WOMAN: I know. I feel it's ghosts—

KARL: Ghosts. Way behind. Everyone always says, "If you look at me and you talk to me, I don't understand anything."

WOMAN: Yeah!

KARL: "You have to talk to someone else. Then maybe I will understand the words."

WOMAN: No, even if I just sit here. Before, I thought I understood something, but now there's no way to keep any—

KARL: That sounds good. It's like there is nothing anymore that this knowing or not knowing can hang onto. It always simply drops again.

WOMAN: Yeah, it feels like sleeping.

KARL: But you're still awake.

WOMAN: [laughing] I'm awake. I'm driving, but I'm not sleeping.

KARL: Hmm. Aw, it's not so bad.

WOMAN: No.

You Can Never Shut Up

KARL: Maybe something there? No? If something is there, just out with it. I may bite, but it's not so tragic. Everything fine? There's always life's little questions, it always starts like this, and then it becomes very big. Berta, on your birthday, do you have 55 questions.

BERTA: I'm collecting them. [group laughs]

KARL: Saving them for later.

BERTA: But knowing this doesn't help. Like sitting with you, I get a kind of very sharp mind and a direction, but it doesn't help.

KARL: That's why it's so sharp. Because it doesn't help.

BERTA: It's not meant to help, I know.

KARL: Yeah, by this paradox, you even see that a sharp mind, intellectual understanding, or beautiful words cannot touch you. They are there, and for a while it may be relaxing or not, or whatever it is, but so what? And then?

BERTA: Yeah, "and then?"

KARL: That's what I mean—"and then?"

BERTA: That is what I am now into.

KARL: And I was pointing to "and then?"

BERTA: [sarcastically] Yeah, "and then?"! [group laughs]

THERESE: Sixty-five times, "and then?" "and then?"!

A MAN: Have a cup of tea.

KARL: Have a cup of tea because if nothing helps—wah—hallelujah!

BERTA: Yeah, nothing helps.

KARL: Yeah, wonderful.

BERTA: [exasperated] Yeah, wonderful! [group laughs]

KARL: That's peace. Only the idea that you hope that someday there will be some help for you, there will be someone or something that helps you, there will be some event of whatever understanding and then you will be happy ever after—makes war. But if you see there will be no moment like this that helps you, that can get you out of what you are—this is peace. You are in war only because you hope to win something, to gain something. But if you really see there is nothing for you to gain by anything, you are already in peace of mind, because there is no, "so what?" There is always that, "so what?" "And then?"

BERTA: What you just said, that's what I say to myself. So there are two again, talking, and one self says to the other, "Oh, you are That already."

KARL: Isn't it fun? One self says, "Hello again." The other self says, "Oh, yes, I am here. Nice to meet you again." "Long time, no see." "Ah, last night. Oh, yes." "Last night?" "Ah, yeah, interesting." "Very interesting." [group laughs]

BERTA: There is this eternal—

KARL: Conversation.

BERTA: Reporter.
KARL: The eternal conservation.
BERTA: All the time reporting, blah blah blah, you know. It's all the time.
KARL: But if you're not conserving it anymore, there's a conversation but not a conservation. If you don't put it in a tin of history, there's a conversation running, but so what? Now you talk with yourself. Infinite talking, infinite universe. But if there is no history in it, no yesterday, no tomorrow, no moment before, it's simply now speaking, talking to yourself, without any previous thought. It's always new and fresh. [stands up, shifting from side to side to take alternate roles] "Hello!" "Ah! Do I know you?" [group laughs] "Ah, nice to meet you." "It seems I know you, but I don't know."
THERESE: It's good to stand up?
KARL: [sitting back down] Oh! It's a circus. Soon I will be—
MARY: Juggling.
KARL: Juggling! Berta, there is no problem.
A MAN: "There has to be a problem, there has to be!"
KARL: You always talk with yourself. What's the matter? You see by all the talking, it's only fun because nothing comes out of it. You're shutting all the time. Shutting around. But you cannot shut up. Talking never started and will never stop. You can never shut up. The more you try to shut up and control yourself, the more you are involved in talking, and you make it serious, important. You become more and more heavy, and then you become a person who takes himself so fucking important. "Whatever I say is so fucking important! I'm a fucking important speaker!" [group laughs]
FRANCESCO: I've had enough of that!
KARL: "I am really fucked by myself! But it's fucking important!" [more group laughter]
MARY: This is as good as words, the body language.
KARL: Body language. Sandwich walking. *Ein Witz zwischen zwei Ohren* (a joke between two ears). Walking. "Hello!" That's called, "me."
BERTA: Already it's a long time. There's no use in that.
THERESE: She sees you as a joke, no?
KARL: Yeah, but what about herself? That's the problem.
A WOMAN: But others do.
KARL: Others do?
BERTA: No, for myself—

KARL: For yourself? Oh, show me yourself.

[Silence.]

KARL: What does Berta's self look like?

BERTA: I only can parrot you.

KARL: Ah, parrot me. Become a parrot. Parroting. [birds are squawking in the background] Hmm. Something today? Israel?

An Israeli MAN: It's a secret. I can ask myself.

KARL: [laughing] "I don't need you anymore!" Yeah, that's the best thing! Who needs you? Enjoy!

MAN: Enjoy, back!

KARL: It's so simple you can even ask yourself. Ha! Beautiful. I can go home. Ha! As if you didn't always ask yourself this. But the Self doesn't know more than yourself. Is there any, "me-self" in, "your-self"? What to do?

BERTA: But you never have—you talk yourself. You say, "I cannot help anybody, so my talking is useless, so what the fuck am I doing here, let's stay at home." That kind of talk.

KARL: That's what you would say if you would sit here, I think. [group laughs]

BERTA: If whatever you say doesn't help—

KARL: Yeah!

BERTA: So you just talk and talk and talk.

KARL: I'm always saying, I should be the most frustrated man on earth. But it makes me so happy. This is freedom, that no one gets it anyway. I can say and sing, I can make nonsense, whatever. It makes no difference. That it doesn't make any difference, that's freedom. I can make so much nonsense, because everything is so much nonsense anyway. It never will make any sense, because it doesn't need any sense! This is beautiful!

Imagine if I could be helpful. That would be hell! I would be the devil. Whoever tells you, "I can help you" for sure is the devil himself. And the devil himself needs self-help. [group laughs]

RITA: You could just sing songs or something.

KARL: No, I couldn't. Every word has to come out just as it is now. When there is singing, there is singing; when there is talking, there is talking. It cannot be anything other than what I am doing right now. It's all fairy tales, comparison to whatever. "Ramana didn't saying anything for twenty years, and then he spoke. Why are you speaking?" Comparison, blah, blah, blah.

"Jesus walked on water. Ha, he couldn't swim. Ha ha ha." [group laughs]
MARY: This is true. The *avatar* doesn't swim. No, serious! Meher Baba says— [group laughs]
KARL: Thank God I'm not the *avatar*. I can swim.

You Cannot *Not* Enjoy Yourself

SOFIA: I can understand about the nonsense, but I cannot drop homesickness.
KARL: I can tell you the joke again.
SOFIA: I cannot drop that. It's not a joke for me. That's it.
KARL: But I tell you, it's a joke. For That which is home itself, being homesick is a joke, whether you like it or not. Your sickness is a joke.
AIKO: So that's the good news. Where is the bad news?
KARL: Any news is bad news, because nothing is new anyway. And when nothing is new, nothing is old. That's the beauty of it.
LOUISE: "No news is good news." It's a saying.
KARL: But it's still news.
MARY: It's still "in-form-ation." [group laughs]
FRANCESCO: This is a present for you.
KARL: Everyday birthday, or what?
FRANCESCO: Yeah. For you.
KARL: Congratulations! Da da da da da!
LOUISE: Now you are singing!
KARL: Every morning, before I wake up, it's like *"Junge, komm bald wieder"* (boy, come back soon). [group laughs] My ship will come. "Relation-ship" will come. The *Titanic* will sink anyway. If you are a Titan, you become a Titanic, a sinking ship. The ship was called, *Titanic* because it was the biggest of its time. But all the giants of understanding, they have to sink.
RITA: Better to keep a small profile.
KARL: A postcard from nowhere?
RITA: No, better to keep a low profile.
KARL: A low profile? Where?

RITA: [laughing] I don't know.

KARL: You don't know? Some will say that you have to make yourself visible so that it can hit you. But it doesn't work. Every seeker says, "Ah, the guillotine! Enlightenment! Please cut my head first. Please, please!" But then sad existence comes, and says, "No!" [group laughs]

FRANCESCO: This is very depressing.

KARL: That is his position all the time. "Take me! Take me!"

MARY: That was a good film, *The Titanic.*

KARL: I haven't seen it.

MARY: You haven't seen it? You've seen all the films, I thought.

KARL: I don't watch romance. Bah! Disgusting. "Relation-shit." [group laughs]

A MAN: There was one point—the special effects guys are all hanging on—

KARL: Well, maybe one minute of the movie is okay. There's a happy ending, I know.

MAN: No, it sinks.

KARL: But that's a happy ending for me, when everyone dies! [group laughs]

MARY: Did you see *Liar, Liar?*

KARL: No.

THERESE: You need to see it.

MARY: It's out there.

KARL: Out there?

MARY: I think you would like it.

KARL: I like everything. That's not the issue.

A WOMAN: Except *Titanic.*

KARL: Except *Titanic.*

MARY: What about *About Schmidt?*

THERESE: *As Good As It Gets.* That's a good one for you.

MARY: Yeah. If you like—

KARL: What, I have not seen, I don't like. [group laughs] It's very easy. What I have seen, I like. She wants to make a movie menu. "Ah, this is nice, that is nice." It can't be, because I have not seen it.

ANTONIO: It means the first one was enough. You liked what you have seen, so the first film was enough.

KARL: What film?

ANTONIO: This film.

KARL: The first horror, coming out of the womb, I tell you, was enough! The movie of coming out of darkness—Ahhh! It's enough. It's enough horror to be alive. It's a moment-by-moment horror movie.

MARY: Unless you know it's a dream.

KARL: Who knows it's a dream? It's still part of the horror movie. "Unless"! What an idea, "unless"?!

MARY: Those are just words.

KARL: Yeah, again! "You know what I mean!"

MARY: Let's get another word for *mean*.

KARL: It's a very nice word. With, "you know what I mean. . ." it's like you are mean enough.

There was a very mean person who came to a talk in Berlin. Very mean. He said, "Oh, you're wearing a watch, you must be disturbed."

THERESE: Why?

KARL: Because whoever wears a watch is disturbed. Why? I have no idea. Ask him.

He was a teacher, "whatever," spiritual teacher, he came with three or four of his disciples and wanted to make some noise. "I'll show you who is better!" Whatever. I said, "Okay." Then I talked and he stared and shouted, "I know!" I said, "You know? Oh, welcome. Please tell us what you know." He answered, "I know!" He then became enraged. I then said, "Please tell us. Everyone is waiting for you. Everyone is curious to know what you know." He again answered, "I know!" Then he became really angry, and at the peak of his rage he said, "If you know, you would know that I know!" [group laughs]

MARY: He's really red.

KARL: [laughing] I'm not joking. But that was really the meanest thing. As you say, "You know what I mean." It's like, "If you would know, you would know what I mean."

MARY: It's a good word.

KARL: Yeah, it's a good word.

MARY: But to sneak by, it's not a good word with you.

KARL: To sneak by? To sneak by the snake? It's not so good with me?

MARY: Never mind.

KARL: You're really confronted with many faces, I tell you. Many faces of being mean. "I mean." "If you know what I mean." "Very meaningful." The last question now.

ROSA: Last call.

KARL: The last Karl for today.

LOUISE: [giggling] The cup is full. No, the tape is full.

KARL: No, no. There's two hours more. Don't worry.

LOUISE: It's on overload.

KARL: Because you are talking on it.

LOUISE: Who is talking?

KARL: I have no idea.

FRANCESCO: That's a big question for the last question.

KARL: Look who is talking. *Look Who's Talking.*

MARY: Karl? So the framing, just for the beauty of it. Just for the beauty of it?

KARL: For what beauty?

MARY: The framing, not to get anything, but just for the beauty of it.

KARL: No, the framing is there because you make it into a picture, and when you have a picture you like to frame it. That's all.

MARY: I get it.

KARL: Especially when you have a good picture, you want to frame it. You want to keep it.

MARY: It's nice. Not to get anything from it. But just—ooh.

KARL: What "ooh"? That framing it, you make a history of framing something, of framing the moment.

MARY: To remember.

KARL: What can you not remember? To say you can't remember it, you have to remember it.

MARY: I'm not saying that this is truth.

KARL: What's true? What's a lie?

MARY: I like framing.

KARL: Then you like to frame it. Then you are stuck in framing.

MARY: I'm not stuck!

KARL: Of course you are stuck in framing.

MARY: I'm not stuck!

KARL: [sternly] You are stuck in framing! [group laughs]

MARY: I like framing.

KARL: She even frames divine love. She's framing everything. She's a framer. It's her job. She's selling frames.

MARY: [laughing] No, I'm not! I'm not making any money.

KARL: The one who says, "No, I'm not!" I know for sure is one. "I am not, I am not. No, I have not done it! No, no, not me! No, I'm not like this. No!"

MARY: Should I do anything with this liking to frame?

KARL: I have no idea what you should do. I have no idea.

MARY: Neither do I.

KARL: Enjoy it.

MARY: I do enjoy it.

KARL: Yeah? Okay. As you cannot *not* enjoy yourself. As if anyone could sit here and not enjoy himself. Whatever is sitting here is the Self enjoying itself. Infinitely. Even not enjoying is enjoying itself. You cannot step out of enjoyment, as you are enjoyment itself. You entertain yourself infinitely. You cannot step out of the entertainment you are. Part of the entertainment is talking and not talking. And you cannot *not* entertain yourself, as that is all that you are—entertainment. My goodness. Hallelujah! Thank you very much. [group laughs]

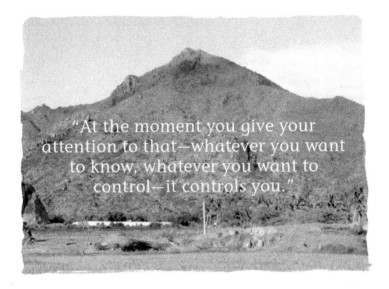

"At the moment you give your attention to that—whatever you want to know, whatever you want to control—it controls you."

January 20

In Spite of My Saying Anything Relevant, You Sit There; or, the End of All Means

You Are Here for Total Relaxation

CHARLES: Tomorrow everybody will be in straight-jackets, I think.

JAMES: We already are!

KARL: You get straightened up. By *Jin-shin-jitsu*. It's a material art for straightening up people.

THERESE: A martial art?

KARL: Material. It straightens up matter. Makes me very strong. Ready?

ANTONIO: Ready. I don't know for what, but ready.

KARL: Sofia?

SOFIA: Just one thing. Where I can find some peyote? [group laughs]

KARL: Is it for you?

SOFIA: Yeah, why not? At this point! [more group laughter]

KARL: "I'm ready for peyote."

FRANCESCO: I'm ready for something.

KARL: Let's see if peyote is ready for you.

FRANCESCO: Maybe it's good news.

KARL: Okay. Whatever. [background noises] Another one died, or what? The drums. Yeah, they go to the burning place with music.

GEORG: Do you know where the burning *ghats* are?

LIZ: Varanasi.

GEORG: No, around here.

KARL: Liz is happy again.

LIZ: Oh, yeah. I'm home. And I can be cut up into pieces again. I love it!

KARL: Ready for becoming mincemeat again! If there is no serious questions, I will just joke around.

ANTONIO: Go on. Continue.

A WOMAN: Keep going!

ANTONIO: It doesn't matter. It's fine.

KARL: For me too. If someone wants to have a more serious talk, you can always trigger a serious question.

ANTONIO: That's true. More than two hours can be taken up with serious questions.

KARL: With an easy question!

ANTONIO: Yeah, with an easy question too.

KARL: Just a simple, easy question today!

THERESE: Hey, Karl. You know what comes up, I meet all these friends from the past? So many from Lucknow [where Papaji lived] are wondering, "Why do you need to sit with someone again?" I've been thinking it over, and I don't feel I need to sit again.

KARL: I hope so.

THERESE: It's just a pleasure. It's just fun. And then a question pokes out of the blue. "Yeah," it says, "why do you have to sit with someone?"

KARL: Because they got rid of their addiction they say, "Why are you still addicted?" They think they have gotten rid their addiction. It's like a smoker who stops smoking, and then says, "You still smoking? You didn't make it? Look at me!"

LIZ: I'm thinking about that myself. But to me it seems like, if I sit here, it goes deeper somehow. Maybe I need to hear it over and over again, but it goes deeper. It helps me get quieter. I don't know if it's an addiction. I don't care. It works.

KARL: Well, I always say, when you accept that the addiction will never go away, so what, then? Do you enjoy the addiction?

LIZ: Yes.

KARL: And you are not proud about it. You will never get over the addiction of Self-inquiry. Self-inquiry is the nature of consciousness. There is nothing to get rid of. So then it's fun, just to ask, "Who am I?," but don't expect any insight or answer or whatever. This is "Who am I?" This is actually going on here. "Who am I?" without the expectation of a result. This is fun. It becomes really light, relaxed and peaceful. Because peace is already there—then peace is not like an idea. So what?

MONIKA: We could do it alone.

KARL: You are never alone, my dear.

MONIKA: By the self.

KARL: By what self? [group laughs] Me and myself can do it alone. Me and me and me. We can do it alone. In Germany, there's a t-shirt—on the front it says "I'm schizophrenic," and on the back it says "Me too." "I could do it alone. Just me." You are alone here. Who is here?

MONIKA: Yeah.

KARL: Anybody at home here? [group laughs]

MONIKA: I feel like a school failure.

KARL: I hope so.

MONIKA: I've heard it for twenty years.

KARL: *Sitzenbleibe, hängenbleibe* (held back in school, stuck in a jam).

MONIKA: Yeah, *genau* (exactly)!

THERESE: I don't see the difference. Like, for example, my friends hang out on the mountain all the time, and for them, the mountain is not a problem, but to sit with somebody, they say, "How can you still do that?" But I don't see the difference. You are the mountain.

KARL: I have no idea. Let them sit and sit again. As you will sit and sit and sit. It's a sit-in. You have to sit it out. But you can never sit it out; it's a sit-in.

MARY: It's a happening.

KARL: "How many years do I have to sit in, being an inmate in a prison, before I get released out of prison?" But people first have to feel like an inmate, and then they can step out and say, "Oh, I am free now out of the prison!" But the outside is as much a prison as the inside. You cannot escape what you are. There's one idea of being an inmate, and then another idea of being an "outmate." It's a psychic hospital anyway. There's an inner and an outer. The universe is a psychic hospital, whether you like it or not. And you are the only patient. [group laughs]

LIZ: That's too hard, too rough.

KARL: Too rough. [outside, a workman hammers] Oh, today we have sounds here. It's not only me hammering? Some co-workers! [group laughs]

LIZ: The outer reflects the inner.

KARL: Yeah? All because of you!

LIZ: Because I believe that? Ah, problem.

KARL: Problem. Fine. What to do?

[The hammering stops.]

LIZ: You see I stopped? I stopped the hammering.

KARL: Ah, you! Thank you.

LIZ: In one minute, they'll start again. [hammering starts again; group laughs]

FRANCESCO: Take them away.

KARL: Or get used to it. Everything's fine?

KAATJE: Maybe you can elaborate about time?

KARL: Oh, that's hard. First we have to find time and then we can talk about it.

KAATJE: Because sometimes we say "time flies" or "there is no time."

KARL: It seems to be there is no time, and then again there is a flow of time. Slow motion and speed. So what's the question about?

KAATJE: I don't get it sometimes. Some people can say what is going to happen, and then it happens. Sometimes I experience things and I say, "I've been there before. I have experienced this before." How can I know?

KARL: If you concentrate on that, maybe you'll get an answer from it. I have no idea. If you're interested in it, you can concentrate on it, and then you may find an answer. Because for That there will be an answer. But are you wondering if there is destiny or not?

KAATJE: Sometimes I'm sure, sometimes I'm not sure. Sometimes I just know, sometimes I don't know at all. It's confusing.

KARL: Yeah, I hope so.

KAATJE: It is. It is!

KARL: The question would be, who gets confused, who needs to know and who wants control by knowing that?

KAATJE: That's it. I want to control.

KARL: For sure. You want to have it as you like it. That's a person. That's the functioning of a person who wants to control the future, because there was a past and now all this. There's differences and then the differences have to be known, because what you know is your friend and what you don't know is your enemy. So you want to know everything because you want to make friends with everything. Because if you have your friends around you, then

you can relax. Then the war will be over. "When I totally know what is, by knowing it and controlling it, I will be in charge, in self-control, I will be the king of the universe." This is the *avatar* training they offer somewhere.
KAATJE: I'm not in control at all.
KARL: I'm sitting here for you to see that being the controllessness is paradise. Whatever idea you have of control is controlling you. So, as you want to control time, time controls you. At the moment you give your attention to that—whatever you want to know, whatever you want to control—it controls you.
KAATJE: That's right.
KARL: So even by knowledge—if you put all your concentration on the Self, what you want to control is the Self—you are controlled by the wanting to know yourself. That is misery. This is like—whew!—I'm stuffed into wanting it.
KAATJE: Wanting.
KARL: But what to do? How can you not want that? Because you're longing so much for that, to be That which you're longing for. So out of the longing you try to control That. But you do it so often, you have so much experience of trying to control it, that in the end it's always misery.
KAATJE: Yeah.
KARL: Because the moment you want to control yourself, you are separated from what you are. You make whatever you want to control the object of your control. So you make yourself an object of knowledge, an object of time, and an object of "whatever"—and this is suffering. So how to stop suffering?
KAATJE: How to stop that suffering? Even this morning, we were doing this. [laughs] Ridiculous! I can see it's crazy and still I do it.
KARL: She asked, "Why am I still sitting here?" If there is no "because," no goal, it's fun. It's just relaxing and peaceful, doing it without any expectation, life becomes meditation itself.
FRANCESCO: Relaxed?
KARL: Luxury.
FRANCESCO: You told her to relax?
KARL: The luxury of being relaxed.
FRANCESCO: This is not in my vocabulary! [group laughs]
KARL: Put it down.

FRANCESCO: I didn't know I came here to relax.

KARL: You are here for total relaxation.

FRANCESCO: Are you sure?

KARL: Yeah!

FRANCESCO: You tell me this now?

KARL: Two months later, I tell him why he is sitting here.

FRANCESCO: Normally, I am depressed. Now I relax.

KARL: But you have to go through the eye of the needle to go to total relaxation. Before it was depression. You have to become very small.

FRANCESCO: Now I have become relaxed. Now I know.

GROUP: Aw!

FRANCESCO: Yes, I like this. [group laughs]

KARL: "I'm loving my depression."

FRANCESCO: For me, it's nice. [group laughs]

KARL: Compassion.

FRANCESCO: Yeah. You tell me!

KARL: Flowering of compassion.

FRANCESCO: Yes. I know.

KARL: You will be reduced to the max. And when you are reduced to the max, you are emptiness and fullness. There is a total absence of an idea of what you are and what you are not. And when you are reduced to that nakedness of existence, there is no eye of the needle anymore, there is nothing. There is no second anymore, no idea of you and others anymore, and that is a total relaxation. For that, you are sitting here.

FRANCESCO: So it means you help me.

KARL: No, I am not helping you.

FRANCESCO: Who does this? Why do I come here?

KARL: For That, you come here, but not to be helped. You come to get rid of some idea of "help."

FRANCESCO: But inside is help. Maybe.

KARL: Maybe? He always wants to offend me. He tells me, "You help me." [group laughs] I tell you again and again.

FRANCESCO: Oh, "again and again" starts!

KARL: Again and again and again. There is nothing to gain. [group laughs] Sounds good, eh? I tell you again and again and again, there is nothing to gain. *Gähnen* in German means "to yawn." *Zum Gähnen* (leads to yawning)—

again and again and again. Nothing to gain.

FRANCESCO: Will you repeat it? I don't understand something. [group laughs] I lost the last piece.

KARL: The last piece you lost.

FRANCESCO: I will write it down.

KARL: You write it down, and then you will have to repeat it a thousand times today.

FRANCESCO: Oh, yeah, this is *sadhana*! [group laughs]

KARL: That would make you happy. "Ah, he gave me something to do! He likes me! I can do something."

FRANCESCO: You give me too much free time.

KARL: That's okay?

KAATJE: It's okay.

KARL: It's time now. [both laugh] Now in slow motion. Aaah-gggainnnn—Okay.

Nothing Has to Go for You to Be That Which Is

JAMES: I have a question about what you were just saying, about nothing to gain. I can see from your perspective of the Self that there is nothing to gain or lose, but if we were to take the perspective of an individual, then there is something to lose, isn't there?

KARL: Yeah, to be an individual.

JAMES: Exactly.

KARL: But you think that has to go for That which you are.

JAMES: No, it doesn't have to go for That which you are. But for the sense of individuality, it has to go for there to be peace.

KARL: No, it has to be. The idea that individuality has to go enables individuality to stay. As long as you are in the idea that individuality has to go, as an individual, you can stay. It's a survival system.

JAMES: I understand that.

KARL: It's the thief again who becomes the policeman.

JAMES: Same old thing.

KARL: Whatever it does it wants to survive. Every technique you do, every *tapas, sadhana,* whatever you do is a technique of survival. As a ghost. you say, "I have to be relevant. Without being relevant, I don't exist. So I make myself relevant and make a technique relevant to get rid of myself.
JAMES: Yeah.
KARL: Fantastic.
JAMES: It's great.
KARL: Really great.
JAMES: So this teaching is that there's nothing to get, nowhere to go, nothing to do—
KARL: —In that sense, for what you are. But in every other sense—if you want to be a millionaire, for example, you have to work really hard.
JAMES: But I think a lot of people take the teaching of "there's nothing to get, nowhere to go, nothing to do" from the perspective of the individual.
KARL: They want to bring it into daily life.
JAMES: They have an intellectual understanding of that and then believe they are there.
KARL: No problem.
JAMES: It's no problem. Well, I know that. There are no problems.
KARL: There's problems, but they don't make a problem. There are differences, but they don't make any difference. So in the dream-like individual existence, there are all kinds of problems and understandings and concepts, they all come out of the first concept of "me." And they will always be there.

As you see, since Jesus, Buddha, and all these enlightened ones, the world still runs. With all the individual ideas of dream characters doing their daily life or not, with time and non-time—all that goes on and on and on. There are pundits and teachers and disciples and it all goes on and on and on. It will never stop, because it never started.

The beauty of all this is nothing has to stop, nothing has to come, nothing has to be changed for you to be That which is, what is you. That's why we are talking here and now about That which is. Nothing has to go, not even the "me," or whatever idea you have of waking up in the morning. There is no danger for That. Simply relax. No one wants anything from you, even as an individual. You can absolutely be the individual; nothing has to go. The one who says something has to go is the little devil inside who is always telling you that you have to do something.

JAMES: Okay, my understanding has been, prior to this conversation, that there really isn't an individual here, or anywhere, but there seems to be, and that there is nothing this sense of individuality can do to lose that sense of individuality, yet the sense of individuality can actually drop, if that is destined. Now what I heard you say, what I thought I heard, is that the sense of individuality doesn't have to drop at all for there to be, whatever, freedom.

KARL: Exactly.

JAMES: Now that's not something I knew prior to a few minutes ago, and that seems worth exploring a bit more.

KARL: It's simply when you see that whatever is, is what you are, you are That which is the Absolute. There's a sense of individuality, but also there is no one. It's a paradox. There's an absolute sense of individuality, but no one has it, there's no ownership in That, in *my* sense of individuality. There's simply one aspect of existence, as what I am, as the Self, expressing itself as a sense of individuality. But even that is totally Heart.

Whatever is, is Self, or Heart. Whatever you name or frame, you cannot get rid of That. You cannot get rid of what you are. And the sense of individuality is part of your infinite nature. There's nothing wrong or right with it. It's simply one experience, one Self-experience, you have with yourself. There is nothing to do with it or not to do with it.

Even the sense, that the individuality has to go as a concept, has to be there. This is another part of Self-experience. It goes on and on and on, like a chain reaction of consciousness, one concept creating another concept creating another concept or experience, whatever you may say. It's all experiences of That which is Self, experiencing itself, realizing itself in infinite possibilities. It is sometimes individual, sometimes personal, sometimes impersonal, sometimes even as "whatever."

And the only thing that I point to is that there is no way out. You cannot escape one single aspect of your infinite nature. One aspect of the absolute nature you are *is* that sense of individuality. This Absolute is everything, as the Absolute is all there is. So even the aspects are as absolute as That which they come from.

Even the reflection is an absolute reflection of the absolute, infinite sun you are—the Self. And for the sun, I tell you, nothing has to go, because the sun doesn't know any shadow, any reflection, nothing. It's simply there as it is. Solid and fixed, as unmovable as That which is sun.

And the shadow keeps having the idea the shadow has to go. "Shadow has to go, shadow has to go!" It's an infinite dance of shadows. But find the one who needs that to drop.

By not finding yourself in all these movie-like experiences, you become the absolute experiencer, where the separate experiencer is simply part of the experience. So for the absolute experiencer, nothing ever changes at all. There is nothing that ever happened to That.

And for the shadow-like experiencer, the shadows will always change, the ideas, the points of view, whatever you think, every minute there is a change in it. One day you think, "Oh, I have to go," the next day, "Maybe I can stay." It is always changing. But in spite of the change, in spite of personal or impersonal, you are. This is part of the change. Going from identification to non-identification, and even to awareness, it's all part of the shadowland. It's all the dreamland.

JAMES: It's still the shadow.

KARL: Even the light of awareness is shadow. Even the experience of the light is shadow. For That which is Heart, there is no experience as light, because That which is light doesn't know itself as light.

So the first experience of light is a mirror. It's a reflection of the Absolute. But the Absolute may be in total darkness, because in total darkness you cannot experience yourself. It's an absolute non-experience, a non-event.

So whatever the first event as awareness is, is a reflection of the absolute non-event. Whatever happens out of the Father, Holy Spirit, and Son, all these reflections—they never change. Or they change, but because they change, they don't change. That which we are talking about is always in spite, never because. To say that something has to change for you to be what you are is all part of a conceptual framework.

JAMES: But I'm saying for there to be freedom in the individual.

KARL: Imagine if freedom would need you to drop in order to be freedom! What kind of freedom would that be?

JAMES: Yeah, well, obviously.

KARL: What kind of freedom are you looking for? Relative freedom you put in your pocket, and because of "you" dropping, you will be free?

JAMES: I think that's what we're all looking for.

KARL: But as you are That which is freedom, by looking for freedom, you are looking for an idea of "freedom," and you make yourself an object of desire, of freedom. And then you are in the longing business.

JAMES: That's what we're all in, isn't it?

KARL: But imagine if you found freedom? Then you could put it in some concept of yours. It could be *your* freedom. What kind of freedom would it be? It would be owned by James.

JAMES: No, no, okay. There's an understanding that freedom can't be obtained by anyone, but in spite of that, in certain individuals, as far as we can say that—

KARL: Never, ever!

JAMES: —there is an experience of freedom—

KARL: You cannot experience freedom. It's not an experience. It's an absolute absence of an experiencer experiencing what can be experienced. It's a total absence of an absence of an experience.

JAMES: Right. So in certain individuals—

KARL: What?

JAMES: [laughing] What you just said— [group laughs]

KARL: It never happened. It never happened to anyone.

JAMES: Yeah, I get that.

KARL: You get that? [more group laughter]

JAMES: Kind of.

KARL: Kind of? Those are Buddha's words and Ramana's words. They all say the same thing—it never happened to anyone. As the Self is ever-realized, what is not the Self, as a reflection, can never realize That which is the Self.

JAMES: And we're all being the Self.

KARL: You are not the Self. You cannot *be* the Self. Even the idea of "being" is too much. That absolute existence has the absolute absence of any idea of existence or non-existence, even of the notion of existence. So your "being" is still too much. Even the impersonal being is too much, because there is still separation from personal being. You're still separate.

Whatever you define, whatever "*my* being" and "*I* drop" and "bop bop," whatever you do, is separation. Whatever you do for That which you are, is separation. But you cannot separate yourself from yourself.

As you never lost yourself and you cannot lose yourself, there is never any way out of what you are. So do it. It's fun. That's why I say it's totally irrelevant to talk about it, but it's fun. It's entertainment. But nothing will come out of it.

And that is the beauty of entertainment. You can enjoy it because there's no heaviness, no importance in it, because it's totally irrelevant. It cannot bring you anything.

This is relaxing. The next moment cannot add something to what I am. So as I cannot gain something, I cannot lose something. By whatever. So be it, or not. Who cares?

You Will Never Be Free from Freedom

TOMAS: But Karl, when you say that, it seems to me at least, that it's based on something else than if I would say it.

KARL: Maybe.

TOMAS: I could say the same thing, but there seems to be a difference.

KARL: Because you talk out of experience.

TOMAS: Well, I'm not saying that. But whatever you are talking out of is obviously not the same thing that I talk out of.

KARL: We can talk about where I am talking from.

TOMAS: So where are you talking from?

KARL: I have no idea. [group laughs]

TOMAS: That's a cop out. It's not fair.

KARL: No, that's actually what's there. It's a total absence of any idea of where it comes from or where it doesn't come from.

TOMAS: But even that is based upon something. I don't have that.

KARL: It's based on the non-knowing but not on any experience. It's based on the non-event, on the non-happening.

TOMAS: I could say that too.

KARL: Yeah, say it!

TOMAS: But it is not the same. I mean, there must be something there, whether you say it happened or it didn't happen, that makes a difference— even if maybe there is no difference.

KARL: There's an absolute difference that, for That which I am, nothing makes a difference. You're sitting "there" because you think it will make a difference. But "there" is an Absolute "here" for which, never, ever, anything made a difference. But you are still in the idea that it will make a difference when this is "there."

TOMAS: But if I am still in the idea, it implies that sometime in the future, I will not be in the idea.

KARL: Maybe you will not be in the idea. Yes. Why not?

TOMAS: But that wouldn't make any difference.

KARL: Again, it will not make any difference. As I see you, as I am That which is you, there is no difference. There is freedom all over. There is nothing to come, nothing to go, for That which you are.

TOMAS: But somehow there must be a difference because I don't see that in you.

KARL: I don't see anything in you because I don't know you. I don't speak to ghosts.

TOMAS: Right. But I do.

KARL: Yeah, you are in ghostland. You give attention to the ghostland and I give attention only to That which is.

TOMAS: So is that a difference or not?

KARL: It is a difference, but it doesn't make a difference.

TOMAS: Well, I do understand that but—

KARL: Isn't it beautiful? There are all these differences, you look out of the difference of "me" and "others," and I look out of the absolute absence of that. But it makes no difference.

TOMAS: To you! [group laughs]

KARL: No, for the existence I am speaking about, that freedom, it makes no difference. From the individual point of view, it makes a hell of a difference, for sure. But it still makes no difference.

FRANCESCO: Yes, what you say is very clear—very, very [kisses fingertips]. But—

KARL: What?

FRANCESCO: It's for you. For me, it's only masturbation. Big masturbation. All the time. [group laughs]

KARL: As I always say—

FRANCESCO: I come only for that.

KARL: He comes for masturbation. He's a *Brahmachari*.

FRANCESCO: Maybe. Some people tell me.

SOFIA: There's something I don't understand. You said there can be a sense of individuality with no one there.

KARL: Why not?

SOFIA: How can you have a sense of individuality, while no one is there?

KARL: Since it was before, why should something change? Nisargadatta said in the last ten days of his life—there's a little booklet—even one hour before he died, he said that the last traces of individuality were leaving him. What would you say about that?

SOFIA: Is this no one?

KARL: More or less sense of individuality—why not?

SOFIA: But in this case, there is someone.

KARL: Yes, of course, there is an absolute one!

SOFIA: No, you said there is no one.

KARL: What "no one"? There is no *person*. But there is still the Absolute. As you are, there is no difference. You are still the Absolute who thinks there is a little absolute, little self. But it's still the Absolute. It makes no difference. What?

FRANCESCO: I know nothing! I don't know anything. You know. I don't know. What is the difference? I don't know. For me, it's the same. [group laughs]

KARL: Why should it go? For whom should it go? Who needs something to go?

SOFIA: But you always say that no one has to be there!

KARL: Yeah, but there is still one there. Even if there is no one there, still one is there.

SOFIA: In the absolute point of view, yes.

KARL: No. There is an absolute Self, but not knowing the Self. In that sense, there is no one there.

SOFIA: But then there is no individuality!

KARL: In that sense, there is no one there. But there is still a reflection of That which is. As long as this body is there, there is a sense of individuality.

LIZ: And what you're saying is that's part of the Self, that sense.

SOFIA: And then you say that nobody is there. You're saying, "I don't see anybody."

KARL: There is, because I see there are shadow-like shapes, but the essence of those shapes is what I am. It makes no difference.

SOFIA: Oh, okay.

KARL: What okay?

SOFIA: What can I say? Nothing.

LIZ: What I'm hearing is that you're saying that, within the individuality, that's part of the Self.

KARL: There are no parts of the Self.

LIZ: It's a shadow of the Self. It will be there anyway, whether you know the Self or not. [silence] No?

KARL: I simply point out that knowledge about it will make no difference, as there is no advantage in knowing yourself.

LIZ: Okay.

KARL: But in the absence of an advantage is an absence of a disadvantage. In knowing and not knowing, you are what you are. I'm talking about the absolute freedom from dependency on knowing or not knowing. I'm not talking about some knowledge of myself, because that would still be dependency. In spite of knowing and not knowing, I am what I am, not because.

LIZ: Okay.

KARL: I'm always talking about that. In spite of individuality, of personal and impersonal experiences, I am what I am.

LIZ: And in spite of attachment, in spite of desire, I am what I am. Regardless.

KARL: That's what God was saying when he was asked who he is. "I am that I am." In spite of whatever. So who needs this drop of individuality?

LIZ: It's there, but it doesn't matter, because I am what I am.

KARL: As I say, there's all these differences, moment by moment, differences of experiences, but they make no difference. So enjoy the differences, because they don't make any difference!

Only because you think the next moment makes a difference for what you are, you make it important. You become self-important. Then you become very heavy and very important.

LIZ: The garden or the *satsang*. Doesn't matter. You are what you are. That's it.

KARL: It's entertainment. Enjoy it!

LIZ: Enjoy gardening. Enjoy *satsang*.

KARL: You cannot *not* enjoy it.

SOFIA: Enjoy the separateness and so on.

KARL: Because even in the separateness, you cannot be separate, that's all. You cannot separate from what you are.

SOFIA: But if this is just a matter of comprehension then—

KARL: What? It always starts with the understanding, the understanding of the Holy Spirit, "I am." It can start with a vertical understanding, in spite of any horizontal understanding of coming and going, of experiences. It always starts with the vertical understanding of spirit.

SOFIA: Between the vertical and horizontal, there is a meeting.

KARL: A meeting. It's always now. A meeting now.

SOFIA: So that's in space and time—now, now, now.

KARL: No. There is a vertical now and a horizontal eternity. In the middle is the Heart of the now and eternity, which is an eternal now. This eternal now you are, in essence. This eternal now is what you are, which is the Heart of existence, nakedness. And out of nakedness, there is a horizontal eternity and a vertical now. And you cannot step out of it. [silence] Sofia now gets angry.

SOFIA: No, no. Not anger. Something else.

KARL: What is it?

SOFIA: I don't know.

KARL: Fed up?

SOFIA: I don't know.

JAMES: Karl, would you say that you were speaking very clearly about something that we can't understand.

KARL: I hope not.

JAMES: All right. Would you say that you were speaking unclearly about something we can't understand.

KARL: I hope not. [group laughs]

JAMES: You hope not.

KARL: I don't speak at all about what I cannot speak about.

JAMES: Can we understand what you say?

KARL: No.

JAMES: No. Thank you.

FRANCESCO: This is funny.

THERESE: What's wrong if we do?

KARL: Nothing. But you still don't understand.

JAMES: You can't understand.

KARL: But that's the beauty again, really, if you absolutely see, in spite of understanding or not understanding, you are. No understanding can make you what you are, and no not understanding can unmake you. What the hell are you looking for?

FRANCESCO: Why are you telling me this?!

KARL: Why not?

FRANCESCO: Yes, why? If I have this, why do you come here? Why do you spend your time here, and why do I spend my time in this boring sitting?

KARL: I'm sitting here because there is a, "why not" sitting here. You are sitting there because there is a, "why" sitting. It's a "why" meeting a "why not."

FRANCESCO: Yeah, but why do I need this all the time? Why do I need you to tell me, "you are, you are." You are who? You are—

KARL: [barking like a dog] Row row row!

FRANCESCO: —the stupid self! This is a very stupid self. [group laughs] No, this morning, I don't believe what I tell you.

KARL: No, the Self is not stupid.

FRANCESCO: I am very stupid.

KARL: Consciousness is stupid.

THERESE: This morning, he was cross with the Self! [group laughs]

FRANCESCO: I blow everything. You stupid boy!

LIZ: "Stupid" is a concept.

FRANCESCO: I don't believe it. Who needs this junk? Who needs this play? Who?!

KARL: You.

FRANCESCO: Who?

KARL: You.

FRANCESCO: I don't believe. I keep doing my *sadhana*, and it's no good to do *sadhana*, because *sadhana* is not what I am. But at the same time, I don't know what I am. But I do know, because I am. [group laughs] You tell me I need nothing, but at the same time, I need to come here for you to tell me I don't need anything!

KARL: But that's freedom!

FRANCESCO: But I don't know who is free. "But I'm free!" [sarcastically] Oh, fantastic. [group laughs]

KARL: But that's the beauty of freedom.

FRANCESCO: This is very useful information.

KARL: I always tell you. Self-satisfaction.

FRANCESCO: No, no. It's only masturbation. "But you don't write." Oh God, I want to write, but no. All the time!

KARL: After the cosmic orgasm, he will be happier, masturbating all the time. [group laughs]

FRANCESCO: But at the same time, I don't want to stop it.

KARL: I know.

FRANCESCO: This is very crazy. [group laughs]

LIZ: And I must say, I love the way you speak, for my own frustration. Thank you.

FRANCESCO: Ah, this is only the beginning. [big group laughter] Every time that you tell me, "you are free," [makes a choking sound] this is terrible.

KARL: I never tell you *you* are free.

FRANCESCO: Oh, or something. Who is free? This is too much.

KARL: You will never be free.

FRANCESCO: Okay. Thank you, because I couldn't decide. [group laughs]

KARL: I always tell you there is no way out. How can freedom be free—from what? You will never be free from freedom.

FRANCESCO: [offering his chest] More. You get me more. Please! [group laughs; Karl pretends to shoot him] Oh God.

KARL: Yeah. It's a joke, totally. Like freedom is there looking for freedom. It's the joke of the universe. All the time.

SOFIA: You are the only one who sees that.

KARL: Come on!

FRANCESCO: Come on what? What do you mean, come on?

KARL: You are simply so much in love with your self-importance that you cannot see it. You are so in love with yourself.

FRANCESCO: You know this?

KARL: Yeah, I see it.

FRANCESCO: I don't know.

KARL: Well, I just told you.

FRANCESCO: You told me what?! You don't know what you say! When I ask you, you tell me, "I don't know."

KARL: But this I know.

There Is Not Even One Who Can Control a Second

JAMES: Karl, are you in love with yourself?

KARL: I have no idea about love, no idea about love, hate or anything. I'm talking about That which is prior to love and hate and all this. There is no idea. There is a total absence of love or hating or all the polarity of concepts about myself. It all belongs to the dream.

That dream figure, Karl, maybe he is in love or not in love. For That which is Karl, what is in spite of Karl and never because of Karl, there is no concept of love or no love or anything. There's a conceptlessness about everything.

JAMES: The place where you come from, where the sense of something comes from—

KARL: What is Heart. That is called "Heart," which is the absolute Source that has no source.

JAMES: Whereas the sense of identification that most people have is with this personal sense of self.

KARL: Because they are glued by love to their image.

JAMES: They are glued by love to that sense?

KARL: They are glued by falling in love with an image of themselves. The Self is glued to the Self because it takes an image of itself as a second self, as real. It starts the lover and the beloved, and that is the beginning of separation, then there is "me" and the other. So even with an image of divine truth, divine love, or whatever, separates you from That. However you define yourself, whatever you fall in love with, it's separation. Because for love, it needs two.

For That which is called "peace," there is no second, there is no action or non-action. Love is an idea of the lover and the beloved. But with peace, immense peace, absolute peace, you cannot make a concept of it, of some high peace or low peace, for example. There is only peace.

JAMES: Sometimes the glue seems to be less gluey and there's peace.

KARL: That's why it's called "a split second." You drop, in a split second, out of love, and then the glue is gone.

JAMES: For me, sometimes, there's this thing in time, for maybe days or weeks, a sense of peace, a sense of knowing.

KARL: You simply step into the oneness—from the separation into the one-ness. Then you step out of the hate, because during separation, you hate separation. You can never accept separation. Then you step into oneness, what you may call, "love." And then you are in that love—that "ah, love!"

JAMES: But it's just experience.

KARL: What you can step into, you can step out of again. This is like the ping pong everyone knows. Heaven and hell. Hell is separation and heaven is oneness, and both are because the other is.

JAMES: They are just polarities.

KARL: They are simply representing the polarity of heaven and hell. Heaven is creating hell and hell is creating heaven. Both are co-dependent, total-ly depending on each other. Without the idea of "heaven," there is no hell; without the idea of "hell," there is no heaven. Both need each other totally. So "hate" and "love" come together as concepts too, as polarity. When you make the oneness "supreme love" and separation "hell," you stretch out the extremes of heaven and hell.

JAMES: So there is no advantage to either?

KARL: No. You realize yourself in oneness, in what is love, and you realize yourself in separation, which is hate. Both come out of the same Source, out of the absence of both, out of That which is awareness, That which is the Father, the Source [Karl holds up his thumb].

But with any source, there is always the question, "What is the Source of that source?" So then the concept of "the absolute Heart" is created [holds up fist], which is prior to the "I"-thought as the first "I," That which is prior to the "I" of awareness. With the notion of existence [thumb], already, out of the light, comes "heaven" and "hell" [index and middle fingers], the ideas, as polarity.

Then it is called "enlightenment" when you experience the awareness that is prior to heaven and hell [thumb]. But even from the awareness you can always go back. So then it said that you have to have "awareness of awareness." That even the awareness of, "I" has to sink into That which is prior to it [fist].

So finally you come to the absolute experience that you are in spite of the light [thumb], in spite of "I am"-ness [index finger], in spite of "I am so"-ness [middle finger]. This [fist] is absolute being, in spite of the realization that, in a split second, for That which you are, nothing has come or gone. There is absolutely no need or necessity for anything to be or not to be, as you are not any idea or non-idea of any existence.

That first notion of existence depends on you, but you are not dependent on it. That's freedom, that's *moksha*, but you cannot reach that *moksha*, not by awareness, not by "I am"-ness, not by *samadhi*, or any understanding.

This is understanding [thumb and index finger]. Then you can go to super, super understanding of awareness [thumb]. But even the awareness of super, super understanding is fleeting. This [thumb] is already the root of heaven of heaven and hell. So to get a total root channel treatment— what is there to do? That's why I'm always hammering on that "in spite."

JAMES: I think I understand something here, now.

KARL: They're jealous.

JAMES: Don't worry, it's not an ultimate understanding. [group laughs] Basically, there's nothing one can do for that [fist]. But *sadhana* can lead to that [thumb].

KARL: *Sadhana* ends there [thumb]. And what comes as everything before, is by grace.

JAMES: I think there's a lot of confusion. A lot of people think "this" is it [thumb], and *sadhana* can get one to "this," so let's do *sadhana*, lots of *sadhana.*

KARL: Yeah. It's not bad. Why not?

JAMES: But it doesn't lead to this [fist].

KARL: No.

JAMES: Nothing can lead to this [fist]. So then there's this thing, okay, *sadhana* is pointless, a waste of time. That is an idea out there.

KARL: I know.

JAMES: I'm not sure whether you've said that.

KARL: No. You cannot *not* do *sadhana. Sadhana* will happen, like a dreamlike experience. You cannot avoid what you are. And *sadhana, tapas,* whatever technique, is part of your realization. But simply see there is no one who is doing it or not doing it.

JAMES: Yeah.

KARL: There is absolutely no way out.

JAMES: You can't get to there [thumb] unless you know that [index finger].

KARL: But from there [thumb] you always go back.

JAMES: Many teachers have said that there is no point in doing *sadhana*. Papaji, for instance, said this. Yet he did years and years of incredible *sadhana*.
KARL: Yeah. "Krishna, Krishna, Krishna!"
MONIKA: He said that he wasted his time. It didn't get him anywhere.
LIZ: That's what he said.
KARL: I'm sure he would say, "I could not avoid doing it, but not by doing, I am. I am, in spite of it. But still, I could not avoid it."
JAMES: When he came to Ramana, Ramana said that *sadhana* had brought him there, and then Papaji had the experience. You see what I'm saying?
KARL: One thing leads to the other thing.
JAMES: Right. So why would anyone say it's pointless?
KARL: There is a point in the dream-like realization, but it makes no difference for what you are anyway.
JAMES: No.
KARL: But you come to the point you cannot go to.
CHARLES: It makes a difference for the dream, but not for the Self?
KARL: Even for the dream, it makes no difference because, in spite of the understanding, the next moment will be as the next moment is, but life will continue as it is, never because of understanding. Everything, whatever is, is in spite of any understanding or not understanding.

You cannot control the uncontrollable because there is nothing to control. There is no one who can control a second. So in the absence of a second, there is a total controllessness. And even in time, what you would call "time," this dream is uncontrollable, because there is not a dream you can control.
FRANCESCO: So?
KARL: What "so"? So la la.
FRANCESCO: All the time, this!
KARL: Now you hate yourself because you made yourself do so much.
FRANCESCO: Oh.
CHARLES: Before you used the analogy of electricity that flows through a light or a blender or anything else—that is like the life force.
KARL: But electricity, energy, or consciousness is the same.
CHARLES: Right. And the mistake is to believe that this is independent of the life force or the electricity.
KARL: No. That which is electricity takes the form of information, but it's

still electricity. That formless energy, as consciousness, takes the form of information, it makes no difference.

So there is a personal and an impersonal consciousness. But even the impersonal consciousness, what is awareness as pure consciousness, takes the form of impersonal, cosmic consciousness and personal, individual consciousness. But it makes no difference.

CHARLES: To the electricity?

KARL: For consciousness, it makes no difference.

CHARLES: Right.

KARL: So whatever shape and form it takes, it makes no difference. It's still That which it is.

CHARLES: It would seem to make a difference to the personal consciousness, as an experiencer.

KARL: Yeah, but there is still no difference.

CHARLES: Still no difference. Even though it seems to make a difference for us.

KARL: There's simply a different point of view, of information, or whatever, but it makes no difference. There are different points of view. So what?

CHARLES: It's only a point of view, which isn't real.

KARL: Yeah, and that point of view is changing all the time. Changing, changing, changing. Not for one minute are you the same person. Your point of view changes every moment. You add something to that point, or you take another position. One day you are pro-war and the next day you are anti-war.

CHARLES: One day we want to sit with somebody, and the next day we think we don't need to.

KARL: One day, "He's the greatest master I ever met," and the next day, "Oh, shit." [group laughs]

LIZ: Just another German.

KARL: Yeah. You bow down to him, and then the next day, just another German. But I like it.

Whatever You Make an Advantage Puts You at a Disadvantage

JAMES: Karl, can you just go back to the point you were making about the movie—there's nothing anyone can do to control the movie—can you say some more on that?

KARL: The movie is already shot.

JAMES: That analogy is quite helpful.

KARL: The next frame of the movie is already done. You cannot change That which is already there. The absolute realization of That which is Heart happens at once, and even then, nothing ever happened, because it is infinite, without beginning and end, as That which is the Absolute itself. So the next moment is already there because there is nothing new, as well as nothing old.

There is the infinite now—absolute, infinite time, you may say, with all infinite forms. All the aspects are there, whatever can possibly be an aspect of what existence is. The vertical now, as formlessness, is always here. With a "moment," you simply cut through that, you take one aspect, one moment, out of the infinite manifestation of what you are. So the next moment is already part of that manifestation.

You cannot change manifestation. It's called, "mani-fest-ation." It's many *faltig* (folded, wrinkled), many aspects, but it's *fest* (firm, solid). There is no moving, no coming, no going, nothing happens in it.

All dream-like happenings, the comings and goings, are you, experiencing moment by moment, what you are from the infinite perception and points of view. So you are the absolute perceiver, perceiving itself out of the individual perception, or from whatever point or space-like camera position, looking into That which one is. So we take dream-like positions, looking into That which we are, as consciousness.

But absolutely, you change your point of view every moment. So absolute perception is never part of sensation, but all sensations are in that. You are the absolute Source, in time, in all the ideas and movie projections, but you are never part of it. No matter what your perception, point of view, or camera position, you are still not apart of it. You may still have the "experience" of being in it, but you are never in it.

CHARLES: So what I perceive as "me" is just a point of view? But I try and maintain it, somehow.

KARL: You want to fix it.

CHARLES: To fix it, to have continuity.

KARL: You want to make this person real by fixing the point of view.

CHARLES: Right.

KARL: You make *my* experiences, into a history. By the little idea, "my," this ownership idea, by falling in love with this image, you're trapped in it.

CHARLES: So small.

KARL: But it's okay too.

TOMAS: So Karl, within the image of the movie, how does "the split second" that you sometimes refer to fit in there? I mean, what is that within the movie?

KARL: Even that is part of the movie.

TOMAS: So it does happen?

KARL: It does happen, but nothing happens.

JAMES: It only happens in the movie!

TOMAS: It only happens to the movie?

MONIKA: It's an explosion.

MATTIAS: An implosion.

KARL: It's just a word, just an expression, for something you cannot name, you cannot frame, you can't do anything with it.

TOMAS: What is the "split second" or "divine accident" or whatever it is?

KARL: It's here, now.

TOMAS: What are you pointing to when you say that?

KARL: I'm pointing to That which you are.

TOMAS: And the split second?

KARL: You are the split second.

TOMAS: Wow. Can you say more about that?

KARL: I always point to That which is perception itself, wherein all the ideas of time and non-time and all the experiences appear, but it is never an appearance. I'm always pointing to That which is neither in time nor in non-time, which is in absolutely no idea, which is always, in spite. I am pointing to the absolute Source you are—which is an infinite accident! An infinite split second!

TOMAS: So the whole movie is the split second?

KARL: Yeah, in a second, in one awakening, in one realization, everything is there. So the split second is here, now. With this [claps once], you create the manifestation. Boom! Every moment the manifestation—boom—boom—boom!

TOMAS: And then within a split second, the movie continues, but somehow it also stops.

KARL: It's a full stop. By seeing that it is a movie—

TOMAS: What is puzzling to me is, it seems so obvious, so simple and clear, and yet somehow, it doesn't happen.

KARL: No, if it's not meant to be, then it's not meant to be.

TOMAS: Who needs it to be?

KARL: I don't know. Who wants to control it?

TOMAS: I don't know.

KARL: You see? I don't either. Who needs the control, and who needs to know?

CHARLES: And when deep sleep happens? It's like the electricity is no longer going through that form?

KARL: In that, you are like a pot in which electricity bubbles. And then in deep sleep—

CHARLES: There's no bubbling?

KARL: There is no attention, so there's no energy, because the attention puts you down.

CHARLES: But the electricity is still there, the same?

KARL: But it's a flat line. And then you wake up and bing bing bing again. But it's still the same energy. Between deep sleep, as a flat line, and in the morning, bing bing bing—it makes no difference. There is consciousness in a flat liner and consciousness in a bing bing bing—individual bing bing bing or impersonal bing bing bing or flat line as awareness.

MONIKA: Why don't we stay in flat line? I mean, why is the bubble always coming back?

KARL: Look, some masters may go to drink from the *samadhi* of awareness, and then after a thousand years, they come out again and are thirsty.

SOFIA: But deep sleep is not *samadhi*.

KARL: But deep sleep and awareness are the same. So they go to the deep sleep state of awareness, and they stay there by concentration, by *siddhis*, by whatever they do. They want to control the awareness state of deep sleep and then stay in it. With all the *sadhanas* and techniques you do, all the attention you give to that, you can stay there. But one moment without the effort and—boom—you are out again. It needs someone to have an advantage, and whatever you make as an advantage, even the awareness state, whatever *samadhi* you make into an advantage, you are in a disadvantage that you need one.

SOFIA: Well, it feels peaceful.

KARL: For a while.

That's why I wanted to show everyone the *Samsara* movie, because it's really clear. For three years, three months, three weeks, three days, three hours, a Tibetan teacher was in *samadhi*, in the awareness, nails like this, hair like this [shows long fingernails and hair], everything was fine, everyone was happy. "Oh, he made it!" All the friends said, "Wah!"

Then they woke him up. Since they were in Tibet, they woke him up with rituals, *pujas*, life energy, some electricity. Out of the flat line, ooh, slowly, "whoo," he was in the form again. Ah! Everyone was happy. They made *puja* . . . Tibet . . . Blare, blare, blare [makes trumpet sounds]. "He made it! One Lama!" Tra la la.

The very first night, his friend, who was full of bliss, looked at him, "My friend made it. Ah! Light! Three years. He made it!" And then he looked, and slowly in the blanket arose a little tent. A "tent-dency," a tendency! Oh! And then slowly a white circle surrounded that tendency. [group laughs]

MONIKA: Oh dear.

KARL: And his friend said, "Ah no! Lost it again!!" [group laughs]

You Are the Choicelessness

FRANCESCO: But not every case is like this.

KARL: What is every case? Not in your case? You're still hoping that in your case, it will not happen?

FRANCESCO: But it's not in every case.

KARL: What case?

FRANCESCO: Ramana or Nisargadatta or—
KARL: Did you go to Ramana at night? [group laughs]
FRANCESCO: Not this! Boy, boy, boy, not this!
KARL: That's what I'm pointing to. It doesn't matter. I just said that *sama-dhi*, whatever you can reach, is nothing.
LIZ: If you keep coming in and out.
KARL: You will always keep coming in and out. You have no choice. You are the choicelessness. You cannot choose to stay in "whatever."
FRANCESCO: But Nisargadatta—
KARL: My goodness. Bullshit. There never was any Nisargadatta, Ramana. My goodness! Shut up with this!
FRANCESCO: Shut him up. Nisargadatta spoke all the time to visitors, "You stay, you stay. That is so important. You stay to understand it."
KARL: I tell you, how can you *not* stay?
FRANCESCO: For me, it's the same. You and he are only two different voices speaking. One told me this is true; the other told me this isn't true!
KARL: Both are bullshit.
FRANCESCO: Maybe this is more true because—
KARL: He's more famous. [group laughs]
FRANCESCO: No, it's the same. It's only two different voices. And he told me different. One told me, "That is nothing. That is not you." Oh, I understand, it's not me, but—
KARL: Isn't it wonderful?
FRANCESCO: Oh, it's not wonderful! What are you doing, if you are coming? He told me, "Don't make this!" This is boring. Please don't come. I don't want to stay in this *samadhi*, please.
KARL: Who doesn't want to stay there?
FRANCESCO: If you tell me one thing, I don't want it. If you tell me the other thing, this is boring. This is nothing for you. This is not what you are.
KARL: That puts you into the *neti-neti.* So it is not even that. *Neti-neti*, whatever you can experience.
FRANCESCO: I understand that in these two hours you want to speak only of the Self, but what I am is not simple to understand, and at the same time, I am this boy.
KARL: Yeah, you will never understand it, thank God, you will never understand.

FRANCESCO: I don't know why I come here. [group laughs]

KARL: To see the beauty of freedom, that you can never understand and control freedom.

FRANCESCO: But this is only what you tell me now. If I don't believe or if I believe, for me it's the same.

KARL: Yes.

FRANCESCO: Because it's all in my mind, maybe, this hour, or after one hour, I won't believe anything.

KARL: Thank God there was never any mind. Who cares about what was never there?

FRANCESCO: This is just another idea.

KARL: So what?

FRANCESCO: Okay.

KARL: For who? Me, me, me.

FRANCESCO: Yeah. Me, me, me.

KARL: Love yourself.

FRANCESCO: I don't know! It's the same for me. It doesn't change anything.

KARL: I hope so.

FRANCESCO: This is very heavy.

KARL: What's heavy?

FRANCESCO: "I hope so." [group laughs]

KARL: I absolutely hope so. That's the absolute hope, that nothing will change by what I say. Imagine if something would change by my saying something?! I could control existence. Oh my goodness.

FRANCESCO: "I want to control everything!" [group laughs] This control, control, control! Yeah, why not?

KARL: Yeah, why not? Try hard, Francesco.

FRANCESCO: In reality, I don't know why I like you. [group laughs] But sometimes, some words from you, from your voice, from this—sorry—this stupid consciousness, it tells me all the time what I am, that I am free, and want to control, and am out of this control, oh my goodness! I like my father now. [big group laughter] My father was in control. I think, maybe I should go home. "My father, you are my *guru*, and I didn't understand anything in my life!" [group laughs]

KARL: Don't you see? I am working for your father, [group laughs] [to group] He is the son of a manufacturer in Italy and his father wants him to take over the factory and he said, "No, I want to do *sadhana*."

FRANCESCO: I want to go to Tiruvannamalai! And you think this is a stupid idea. I can't believe I stay here in this flat, in the stupid flat with the water that doesn't—Aaah! [group laughs] For what? For nothing!

KARL: Then I tell him, "That's freedom, my dear!"

FRANCESCO: This is stupid consciousness.

KARL: That's freedom, because you have no choice. The choicelessness is freedom. Wonderful.

FRANCESCO: Don't touch the rose. You put this down!

VICKI: That's really controlling! [group laughs]

FRANCESCO: From now on, I want to control everything. [group laughs] I will go home and make a lot of money. I want to control the world.

KARL: So now I can go to your father and get my salary? [group laughs]

FRANCESCO: When I worked inside the factory, he looked at me and said, "Oh, my son! You are very nice."

KARL: "I love you."

FRANCESCO: This, no.

KARL: No?

FRANCESCO: This, no. That's too much.

KARL: It is always saved for one's last words. "Son, I never told you, but I loved you. Ugh." "I worked so hard—for that. All was for nothing. He loved me all the time, and I always worked for that love. Why didn't you tell me earlier?"

MONIKA: See, that's why the Americans always say, "I love you" all the time. [group laughs] They don't want to miss the opportunity.

KARL: No moment without. Just to fill "that" with that.

FRANCESCO: I'm sorry.

KARL: The Italian. Drama!

FRANCESCO: No, maybe people understand everything. Maybe people understand what is "free."

KARL: Don't worry.

FRANCESCO: No, no. I don't worry. I'm happy for them.

KARL: [laughing] No one believes you.

FRANCESCO: I don't believe one person.

KARL: Okay, that's good.

FRANCESCO: But not from you. From this stupid consciousness.

Wanting to Take a Little Control of
Your Life, You Become a Little Controller

EMMA: I have a question. Again about the "split second." It's somewhat frightening for me. Is it that the split second takes care of itself?
KARL: No. The split second never cares one bit. There's a total concernlessness in the split second.
EMMA: By this I meant, actually, that I don't have any influence?
KARL: No, it doesn't take care. It's simply That, to be That which is, that "I" experiencing what is, in spite of whatever, is experienced, That never changes one inch, by whatever experience of the sensational world or dream world or whatever comes and goes, that changes. That's all.

That is here, now, That which it was as a baby and prior to being a baby—in the split second, through the whole of eternal time, from Adam and Eve, to the beginning of experiencing, and since then, it has never changed one inch. The unborn, never-changing perception itself, which is the eye of God, the eye of Buddha, your Buddha-nature, cannot see itself, but whatever it sees, it cannot be. So it never changes by any experience, and never changes by any circumstances.

So for That, nothing ever happened. In the split second you see that— That which is perception itself, nothing ever happened. These separate experiences, the person, is simply part of circumstance, but That which is perception itself was never a part of any circumstance.

It's never in the world nor not in the world. All the ideas, knowing and not knowing, all that you can name and not name, you are, in spite of—everything is appearance-like, sensation-like—That which is prior to all ideas of sensing and sensation and what can be sensed, cannot be touched. So it's a non-event, because there is a total absence of any event, because nothing ever happened.
EMMA: And why are you winning the lottery and not me?
KARL: What lottery? As I said, consciousness doesn't know separation, and

consciousness doesn't care who wins the lottery, who gets the pot. It takes six billion possibilities, and maybe one out of six billion, or maybe two, or maybe one out of one billion. But who cares? There is noone who gets it.

If consciousness as this [points to his body] gets it, the whole of totality gets it. The Self, which is the totality of consciousness, doesn't care about who gets it. It doesn't know anyone! It has so many possibilities of trying and sitting and *sadhanas*—whatever—and it may drop for one form, but it's anyway in all forms, so it doesn't care in what form it happens.

EMMA: [sighing] Yeah, yeah.

KARL: That non-happening happens now. There is always the non-happening. The split second is here, now. There is nothing to come. It happens for no one. It didn't happen for Karl, I tell you. It never happens to anybody. It never happens to any concept of spirit. It never happens to consciousness. When the inner sun rises—Self-awareness—when awareness becomes aware of the awareness, which is awareness, it's in no one's hands.

That's why it's called, "an accident." By accident you step into the dream, and by accident you step out. You fall in love by accident and, by "whatever" resignation of love, you step out. That is the "split second." In a split second, you fall in love; in a split second, you drop out.

So love is the glue. You're glued by love to what you are. You are in a total relationship with yourself and any relationships you hate, because it makes you suffer.

MRS. ANGELINA: How do you remember all of these things?

KARL: Nothing has to be remembered. As you have never forgotten anything, there is nothing to remember.

EMMA: So love is actually my enemy?

KARL: No. Not an enemy.

EMMA: Isn't that what you said?

KARL: You're simply the choicelessness. Freedom cannot choose *not* to fall in love. So love is one aspect of your nature. There is nothing wrong with it. But I tell you, the love that you make as an icon, the big one, is nothing special. You cannot *not* love yourself. But not by love, you are. In spite of loving or not loving, you are what you are, never because. This is freedom. In spite of loving, in spite of oneness, in spite of whatever idea, you are, never because. My goodness.

You are the Almighty. You are absolutely in control, but you have no control. You are That which is control, but you have no control. So by wanting to create a "little" control of your life, you become the little controller. But you are already the Almighty. Because of you, everything is. What is more control, more power? You are power itself, but you have no power—there is no ownership in it. There is no, *my* control, there is only the idea of "*my* control," you step into the little controllership.

FRANCESCO: No, no, big. Not small. I don't want small.

KARL: [sweetly] Francesco!

FRANCESCO: All or nothing.

KARL: Yeah, so totally see, by no experience, by no coming and going of any sensation, will you become That, what is That. So be That! And by being That, you are the Almighty, but not by becoming it, by any sensation, by any second-hand experience.

FRANCESCO: So this is *samadhi*.

KARL: No. There is no *samadhi*. What Ramana pointed to, is That which is your nature, your absolute nature, which is statelessness, there is no idea of *samadhi*. There is no state of *samadhi*.

FRANCESCO: Yeah, yeah. but I tell you many times.

KARL: What?

FRANCESCO: I'm not interested in the Self. At all.

KARL: Oh.

FRANCESCO: Yeah.

KARL: I know. You are interested in control.

FRANCESCO: No I am not interested in the Self because I don't want to understand something, because it is not possible to understand anything about the Self. So I think—sorry—but I think it's very boring, this talk on the Self. Why do I spend my time looking into understanding, when it is not possible to understand?

KARL: Who wastes his time here? What is *your* time?

FRANCESCO: Stupid waste of time.

KARL: It's very stupid to say, "I waste my time." You will be wasted, whether you like it or not.

FRANCESCO: This is a problem. A very big problem.

KARL: You will be enjoyed, whether you like it or not.

FRANCESCO: It's another problem.

KARL: [laughing] It's another problem! As I always say, God loves you anyway. By the love of God you are, and by the hate of God you will disappear, or what?

FRANCESCO: Yeah, but, sometimes, it's difficult not to understand, because I don't want to understand, it's too much for me to understand—maybe—is there another word in English for not understanding, but near?

KARL: Close? Getting close to understanding?

FRANCESCO: Many times you tell us, "You're it, you're it," but when you read Nisargadatta or someone else—

MARY: "Apperceive." Nisargadatta Maharaj speaks about apperception.

FRANCESCO: I feel it. And I believe that. At the same time, I'm right here, this boy, right in this place, and in front of me is you, and I repeat, I don't know why I believe you. You tell me, "No, that is not true." I understand I am the Self, I don't need *sadhana*, but at the same time, to understand what I am, what do I do? So I do it.

KARL: Whatever you do, don't worry.

FRANCESCO: In spite of, eh?

KARL: No I tell you, absolute consciousness knows best, so don't worry. The next step is perfectly the next step.

Doubt Whatever You Can Understand

MARY: There's a little bit of a smell of faith here.

KARL: Faith?

MARY: Well, you were saying, "Don't worry, don't worry." So talk about faith.

KARL: I'm talking to the Absolute that can worry or not worry. In spite of worrying or not worrying it is the Absolute, so don't worry.

MARY: What is faith?

KARL: I have no idea. Who needs it? I have no idea.

MARY: It's a step.

KARL: Yeah. It's a step, a stepping stone.

MRS. ANGELINA: It's a movie.

FRANCESCO: *Samsara.* Stupid movie. Not the movie, my movie is stupid!

MRS. ANGELINA: Delicate smell of roses. Just joking.

KARL: Pure love!

FRANCESCO: Yeah, this is the problem with this.

MARY: In faith, there is listening.

KARL: Faith makes you an addict. So fate is part of love, part of addiction.

MARY: No, faith.

KARL: Yeah, face to face with fate. I'm fading away. Face to faith with fate, I'm fading away! [group laughs]

MARY: Yeah, that's good. I really think a book should be made of all these little Karlisms. Right? Really awesome. It'd really sell. You could make a lot of money.

KARL: Thank God I don't know where they come from.

MONIKA: Now I know why we sit here!

KARL: Karl-ower. It's Karl Hour!

FRANCESCO: It keeps changing, maybe, but if you say this, no—

KARL: Say what?

VICKI: He's saying that you wouldn't make a lot of money.

KARL: No. That's my destiny. I won't make a lot of money by my blah blah blah. Because I don't promise—

MARY: We'll see. The day is young.

KARL: He says.

FRANCESCO: I don't know.

KARL: But I tell you, the beauty of it is that I can say whatever bullshit I want and you will sit here or not.

MONIKA: Worse!

KARL: Yeah, I tell you. Everyone is sitting here with concernlessness. In spite of my saying something stupid, intelligent, or anything relevant, you still sit here. What to do?

But that's freedom. Again and again, I put say that this is freedom. In spite of whatever bullshit or nonsense one says, you have to sit there. You martyr your brain. "He says something, but I cannot find any sense in it. But I'm sitting here. There must be something! Why am I sitting here? I'm not sitting here for nothing! There must be something. Then again, no, no, no, blah, blah, blah."

MARY: I've never been so relaxed.

KARL: You see this nonsense is so relaxing. For some, but not for him [points to Francesco].

MARY: He's just pretending. He's an actor. The Italian actor.

KARL: He wants to intrigue us with something. He's a total mischievous consciousness. He's like a bitch. Consciousness is a bitch.

FRANCESCO: I know, I know. I tell you!

KARL: But you are that bitch.

FRANCESCO: I know. That's the problem.

KARL: You bite yourself. That's called "Self-abidance." You bite yourself. Then you become the dog who bites his own tail and gets hungry for his own blood. It's a famous story, a bliss story of biting your own tail and then getting hungry for your own blood.

SOFIA: I know.

KARL: You remember that story, Sofia? Pundit, here, you read everything! [Sofia laughs]

It's from one of the Upanishads, the Self biting its own tail and getting the taste of the blood of bliss, and simply thinking it's something else, like that bliss of gods, blissful states of oneness or something. Then it bites again and again, sucking and sucking on the bliss of biting its own tail. "It hurts but, oh, I cannot get enough of it, that nectar of existence!"

This is like being addicted to the bliss or the oneness of heaven. It's like the Self becoming a dog. God becomes a dog who bites his own tail and sucks his own blood out of the bliss, because he thinks, "This is something different which gives me something." In a split second he sees his own tail, "Oh, I'm biting my own tail! I am the blood itself. I am That which is the dog." Then it's God again. But in that idea, you become a dog. Then it really becomes a dog's life. Very dogmatic. [group laughs]

That's where it comes from. You become a dog and you become dog-matic. Then you write "dog-uments" about it. [more group laughter] It all comes from that. Dog dreams, "dog-tors"—

MARY: I never go to "dog-tors"!

KARL: Now you see it's a joke. Ha, ha, ha.

LIZ: I'm going to sit here dogmatically, until the dogma of it—

KARL: Yeah, it's another dogma!

LIZ: I'm going to abide in it until I understand it. I'm going to come back and back!

KARL: "I'm going to sit here until I get it!" [group laughs]

LIZ: Until the dogma is set.

KARL: Dog, sit! Bow wow!

FRANCESCO: What is nice, is that after, I don't remember anything. Not only this, but in my life.

THERESE: That's why you come back in the morning! [group laughs]

KARL: It's the grace of forgetfulness. Bow wow wow! Sofia soon comes barking.

MARY: Francesco, me too.

SOFIA: Perhaps not only you. Perhaps many others! [group laughs]

FRANCESCO: Can I touch your feet? [big group laughter]

ANTONIO: Please allow some *sadhana* for him.

FRANCESCO: I want to control—

KARL: He wants to control me.

FRANCESCO: No, not that. I want to control, but maybe I made a mistake.

A German MAN: Maybe there will be a miracle from touching your feet.

KARL: A miracle? Yeah, yeah. *Ein Mirakel wird von oben* (a miracle will come from above). Miracle Whip. [group laughs] So some questions about the dog?

MONIKA: It's God spelled backwards.

KARL: It's the opposite only, the reverse. God reversed is dog. First you become a dog by, "I am who?" getting into the dogma of concepts, and then with the question, "Who am I?" the dog becomes God again. But the whole way, there was God, as a dog or as God, it makes no difference.

In the ancient scriptures, they characterize consciousness as a bitch. And you never know when consciousness will bite you. So you can behave well for a while, and it's very kind to you.

FRANCESCO: No, no.

KARL: But one day—it bites you. Out of the blue, it bites you, so that's why it's called "a bitch." You never know when, it's totally unpredictable. That which is this, that which is consciousness, the manifestation of "whatever," is unpredictable. You can never predict what comes next.

You try so hard to control the next moment, living out of the past into the future, you want to control the future by wanting to control the past, by clearing the past, by unlocking the knots of *karma*, even then you want to control the next *karmic* step. In that control system, you are as a dog. But to see the unpredictable nature of existence—to be That, is unpredictable— pow!

MARY: That's really cool.

KARL: It's really cool! Or hot. It's very hot. Can you take the heat you are?

FRANCESCO: No, no.

KARL: No one can take it, but for what you are, it's nothing. You can never take it, as you cannot own it—simply by being it, nothing is more simple than that. It's simplicity itself . . . by being it, but not by becoming it. Hmm?

ROSA: I'm speechless. It seems so simple.

KARL: Because it's so simple, it's impossible to do.

ROSA: The mind doesn't like simplicity.

KARL: The mind? What mind?

ROSA: [pointing to her head] That one.

KARL: That one? That one which is not. The one which is not doesn't like what is not neither. That sounds good.

ROSA: It's a nice phantom.

KARL: Phantom likes to be confused.

ROSA: You know, today I had the idea, "I understand, so this must be wrong, because it's beyond understanding." [laughs] So I felt guilty that I understood.

KARL: Oh, that's good. Doubting whatever you can understand. Totally doubt it. Become the total doubting. Because whatever is new, cannot be it. You are still, in spite of whatever understanding, however beautiful it can be. Whatever makes sense or not, in spite of it, you are. It will go again. So don't hang on to it. Because the trip is that you always hang on to whatever blissful experience you take as understanding, as deep. "And I was never as close as then, to what I am." What an idea?!

ROSA: Then it's gone. It was just a moment.

KARL: You simply make a document out of an experience. You take it personally, you make it into a history, you even want to make a personal history out of Self-experience. But there is no history in the Self, there never will be.

ROSA: So I must doubt myself?

KARL: If this happens here, now, that you doubt even the understanding which comes—if you doubt it totally and say, "no, no, no, no"—then stay in the no-no, and just simply see what comes out of it. Nothing will come out of it. So when nothing rising out of that no-no, which is Heart, this non-happening, this non-event, this no-no, will become what you are, the emptiness of a non-event. This is the emptiness of Heart, peace. The emptiness of Heart which contains the fullness of existence.

With the slightest idea, "I understand," there is one who understands, and that one who understands occupies the whole of whatever is Heart at the moment. So whatever you define, whatever understanding is yours, this "me," this "mine," this ownership, is a heart-knot, and with this knot, you're always in the pressure.

ROSA: It's great!

KARL: It's great! So the no-no—

MARY: Absolute *neti-neti*—

KARL: Yeah, the absolute "no-no" is an absolute "yes"—to be That which is, but without saying it—being quiet. Whatever comes is an absolute no-no to what comes and goes. That is an absolute yes, but a quiet yes, a silent yes, without anyone who says it. But the "no-no" depends on consciousness, so consciousness has to go to the "no-no." That which is silence itself, which is an absolute yes to existence, is simply what it is. Sounds good, no? But it's another document in time.

MRS. ANGELINA: Karl, perhaps I don't understand what you say. Are you saying that out of this nothing, something comes?

KARL: No. Because there is nothing, there can be something. So out of nothing, something has to be. Because as long as there is nothing, there has to be something.

MRS. ANGELINA: It's not clear.

KARL: Yeah, I hope so! If you understand that, there is no one who understands anymore.

MRS. ANGELINA: Good.

KARL: Good? So you'd better take care about your non-understanding, because that keeps you as you are.

MRS. ANGELINA: Yes, but non-understanding, forgetting, another movie, another movie. What's the use?

[Mrs. Angelina is serious and upset. The boisterous room becomes silent.]

KARL: Don't ask me.

MRS. ANGELINA: You can't use anything. Nothing is real then.

KARL: But is that relevant?

MRS. ANGELINA: It seems relevant.

KARL: But to talk, to make that a statement, is that relevant?

MRS. ANGELINA: Just put together any kind of words, you know? Just put together any kind of action, it doesn't matter what, blah, blah, making another movie, another time, another timeless you—

KARL: No, now you are talking out of the person who wants to make everything the same. This is boring personal history.

MRS. ANGELINA: It's not boring. It's relevant.

KARL: But the relevance for the person makes it a boring story, because it's an idea.

MRS. ANGELINA: So what's the use of learning anything?

KARL: Why not?

MRS. ANGELINA: To unlearn?

KARL: What "unlearn"?

MRS. ANGELINA: To unlearn what we already know and shouldn't know.

KARL: For what?

MRS. ANGELINA: For no reason.

KARL: So learning for no reason and unlearning for no reason. Both—

MRS. ANGELINA: Both are irrelevant.

KARL: Both are irrelevant. So what? It's fun.

MRS. ANGELINA: It's confusing.

KARL: So what?

MRS. ANGELINA: So what!

KARL: You are That which is confusion. Who cares? Huh?

MRS. ANGELINA: Out of nothing, nothing rises. Nothing rises out of nothing!

KARL: I tell you!

MRS. ANGELINA: You start like this—

KARL: No, I'm not starting. As long as there is the idea of "nothing," there is something. Nothing is too much.

MRS. ANGELINA: It's already too much. Something—

KARL: As long as there is nothing, there is something. Out of emptiness, comes form. So even the idea of "emptiness" creates form. You cannot avoid that.

Nothing is the same. Or, you can create another concept that everything is unique, every moment is as unique as it can be. The Self is always absolutely unique in its expression, then whatever comes is never the same.

There is no boredom.

There is only boredom the moment there is a history of experiences and you want to compare them. At the moment you are a dog, you are boredom itself. Because you write everything down in the history of *your* thing, and you want to make it relevant or irrelevant, and whatever comes out of that traps you in that loneliness. That's boring. "Owner of a lonely heart." Francesco! Enjoying himself.

FRANCESCO: Oh, I don't know.

MRS. ANGELINA: *Neti-neti* is not like this.

KARL: Yeah, but who cares?

MRS. ANGELINA: Nobody cares.

KARL: But you care that you don't care?

MRS. ANGELINA: Nobody don't care.

KARL: No?

MRS. ANGELINA: No problem. Everything I can hear or see, I cannot say to anyone.

KARL: Aw.

MRS. ANGELINA: No problem.

KARL: Sounds good.

MRS. ANGELINA: Maybe—

KARL: Maybe.

MRS. ANGELINA: It's not a definition that you can say, "Oh, this is maybe another concept, another loneliness, another boredom, another teacher, frame, definition of something." After one second, it's different. Then, I could say, "Yes, maybe it's like this, so I can keep this good thing tomorrow." But this time, it's not like this anymore.

KARL: Don't ask me.

MRS. ANGELINA: Who do I have to ask?

KARL: I have no idea. I'm not a pastor who gives confirmation.

MRS. ANGELINA: If I want confirmation, I wouldn't come here.

KARL: You see?

MRS. ANGELINA: Maybe I should go to some other possibility.

KARL: Many possibilities. Confirmed.

[Silence.]

EMMA: I'm very much amazed you talk every day for two hours about what you can't talk about. It's a miracle.

KARL: Yeah, if "I" could only do that. That's amazing, incredible, like *Incredible India*. It's a bluff.

EMMA: [laughing] It's a bluff?

KARL: Yeah, it's a bluff.

[Silence.]

KARL: [rubbing hands and clapping] No question? Then we are through? Okay. Thank you.

GROUP: Thank you.

FRANCESCO: So can I touch your feet? [group laughs]

"Silence is all there is. Nothing happens in That. Never anything comes or goes in That which you are."

January 21

Always in Spite, Never Because; or, the End of "Acceptance"

Consciousness Is Inexhaustible

KARL: Still two minutes to go. We can have some fun. Everything fine?

SOFIA: It's better not to ask.

KARL: Oh, I like to ask. Okay, then. Same procedure as everyday—no procedure. If you're new, it is question, answer. Simply informal. Whoever has a question, it may be answered.

FRANCESCO: And "may be" it's true!

KARL: Francesco!

FRANCESCO: You told me only ten percent.

KARL: I give you nil.

FRANCESCO: I talk—oh no!—I started up. [group laughs]

KARL: You promised you wouldn't talk.

SOFIA: He said, "I will not ask him anything today!"

FRANCESCO: We start now, no? [group laughs]

LOUISE: So it appears that, if there are clear instructions, one to ten, or if there is a belief—you can select "whatever"—it appears that things can be easy, if there is a structure. So if you were to give us one-to-ten instructions—

KARL: Instructions?

LOUISE: Why does it appear so easy in life when you follow certain instructional rules? Like you purchase a machine, right, and you read the instructions and it tells you how to plug it in and—boom—it functions.

KARL: Manual. You need a "man-u-el." Manuel. [group laughs]

LOUISE: So, Karl, the confusion only begins if there is no instruction, no structure and no guidelines.

KARL: Yeah, it's good.

LOUISE: Why would it be good?

KARL: Because whatever can be confused, should be confused. That which you are can never be confused by any confusion. That which is left over, totally leftover, is always That which can never be and never was and never will be confused, by whatever confusion.

LOUISE: [laughing] Okay, *pa auf* (watch out)!

KARL: You asked for it! [group laughs]

LOUISE: It's always like this—ah ya, ah ya, okay, okay, thank you, thank you, and then boom! Finished.

KARL: Yeah, that's the point.

LOUISE: Machine broken.

KARL: This is not to give you some techniques to occupy your time for years to come, so you can get out of the boredom you are in and have something to do. It's not the right place here. Bang bang bang.

LOUISE: Bang, bang. Yeah.

KARL: The simple answer is, what you are, you cannot find it in time or in space or in any circumstance. So whatever technique, it's nice, it keeps you occupied, but it will not bring you what you are. So, what to do, then? A nice ten to one technique. You count back down to one and then, you begin at one, two, three to ten again, and then? Down again. Infinite.

LOUISE: There's a constant weaving in and out from easy to difficult, easy to difficult.

KARL: There's an ease and there's a disease. Ease and "dis-ease." Health and sickness come together.

LOUISE: Hmm.

KARL: The sickness you may cure always comes back. You are asking for a technique to get out of the disease of ignorance, but the ignorance that can go, can also come back.

LOUISE: Uh-huh.

KARL: So what to do with that? You still depend on something to go. Imagine freedom and the dependency that something has to go for freedom, so freedom can be what freedom is—what an idea?

LOUISE: Yeah.

KARL: Then it will be your freedom, because you had a technique to count down to. You will put it in your pocket, and what then? "Ooh, that's the one who has freedom!" I hope not. So it's . . . "and then."

LOUISE: And then I get another headache, and you say there is no transmission. [laughs] You know, I can feel it right now again. Then you say there is no such thing as transmission or radiation of *shakti.*

KARL: No, it's not a transmission.

LOUISE: What is it then? Why do I feel it right now when you speak to me, and it goes and it goes and it goes?

KARL: And I see it and I see it and I see it.

LOUISE: Yes, yes, and then, boom!

KARL: This is not a transmission, I am talking to That which you are and not to any ghost. So I'm not transmitting anything. There is no transmission, there is no transmitter, and there is no receiver.

And in the absence of a transmitter and a receiver, life wakes up. You feel it as *shakti,* heat, body heat. Then when the resistance of the third eye starts, you get a headache or migraine out of the heat or energy, which simply arises because there's an absence of a transmitter and a receiver, as the awareness of life itself wakes up in every cell. And then the resistance of the controller brings a headache on.

LOUISE: The resistance of the controller?

KARL: Because you want to know, you want to control *your* energy, the idea of "*my* energy," "me," is always a "controller" idea. So whatever comes, you want to make into *your* energy, *your* control system, yeah? Then resistance comes, and you become a little pipe, and when the energy has to go through the little pipe, it becomes a headache. When you control, you are narrow, but you cannot help it.

LOUISE: No. Just breathe.

KARL: Just breathe. [both laugh] No, I tell you, I went through five years of having migraines, and I know where it came from. The moment it went away, it was just gone, because with the controller, everything goes. When acceptance is there without any control system there is simply a total openness of all the parts

I feel your heat here and now, all this energy, but it doesn't bother this [points to his body], whatever is here, at all. It goes in and out, like waves of energy. But its not *my* energy, or anything. It just comes and goes.

Controlling, controlling. [Louise breathes deeply] Intense. You have some question about that?

MATHILDA: Yeah, I was wondering why aspirin doesn't working.

KARL: No. Because it is not a chemical thing that you can solve by another chemical. No, I tried. When the migraine was there, I tried everything. Forget it. Homeopathy, allopathy, blah, blah, blah. Antipathy.

ROSA: [laughing] Antipathy!

KARL: Yeah, sympathy didn't work either.

SOFIA: So the controller can fall down, or not?

KARL: Oh, it was by watching the *Mahabharata* on television . . . going through all the free will, all the Krishna stuff, and the final thing was going with Yudhistara to heaven and hell and being totally identified with Yudhistara, with his character. And then he didn't want to stay in heaven because in heaven there were only enemies, so he went to hell, and Krishna asked him, "Could you accept hell for eternity? Is there any wish to avoid that, any tendency left for you to avoid what is hell, what is separation?"

Then it was simply an absolute no. "I've absolutely worn out that tendency." At that moment there was a total acceptance, a total breakdown of control.

SOFIA: In the total "no," there was acceptance.

KARL: In the total "no way out," there was hell, and there was no wish to get out of it, there was simply no idea of an exit anymore. "If it should be like this, it's like this. Okay." It's absolute acceptance, without even saying it. In total acceptance, the controller is not there. And without the controller, all the resistance and all the migraine dropped at that moment and didn't come back.

But it's not by anyone's decision to drop it. Acceptance is when acceptance is, and not because of any technique you do, because whatever technique you use is against it. Whenever you try to control acceptance, you want it to become *your* acceptance. You even want to control acceptance, and then it becomes even more narrow.

So I say the techniques are all against acceptance, in a way. Because whatever you do is against it. You want to control it by a technique. You want to make it *your* acceptance. So you become more and more the control-

ler— you become even a god, an *avatar* of the universe, by controlling it—
because in consciousness, there's no limit to "controlling." So you become
even the greater god of the universe, but you are still, "an owner of a lonely
heart."

PETE: There's an imagined person who's doing all this seeking and trying
to control—maybe there would be some benefit to just tell this imagined
person, "Yeah, do your seeking, keep trying to control"—until it just collapses, you know? Just keep trying, keep trying—

KARL: No, it cannot collapse because *that* is consciousness already, and consciousness is inexhaustible. If it would be like a person you could exhaust
it, because there's a personal energy you could exhaust, it would be easy.
Then there's the technique of Yoga where you could exhaust that personal
energy. But as the person already is consciousness itself, it's inexhaustible
because it's an inexhaustible energy.

You cannot exhaust absolute consciousness. It will always have another
trick in it's book to avoid exhaustion. Suddenly, there's a second wind, a
third wind, and a fifth wind, and whatever comes for that seeking.

PETE: There's never the collapse.

KARL: It will never collapse, because there is nothing to collapse. There is
absolute consciousness, and the idea that consciousness is so real and so
absolute—you cannot exhaust that idea. Because even the idea is absolute.
These ideas of exhaustion work within certain frames. Say, you're a runner.
You might have the idea you get exhausted after forty miles or fifty miles,
ten miles or one mile, or even a hundred meters. But a marathon runner
might, after twenty kilometers, have a break where he feels he cannot even
walk anymore, but suddenly there's a dead point, a point of acceptance,
and he runs again as if he'd never run before.

You never know—that energy is mystical, miraculous, magical—whatever. Inexhaustible. If it has to happen, if it's meant to happen that you run
again, you will run and run and run.

PETE: I did so many *sadhanas* like a lot of people, and then it seemed to hit
a crisis where I realized the futility of this, you know? But what you're saying is that, as soon as you get some rest, the little make-believe man jumps
up and starts doing his *sadhanas* again. Or maybe not. Maybe he wakes up?

KARL: Maybe not. I don't know. Not because you made *sadhana* will you
resign from it. If it was meant like this, it would be like Ramana saying, "Be-

cause I was lucky, I came into this world and went straight to That on the only 'Who am I?' without first going through all the other things." So you never know. It's a mystery. Absolute mystery. There is no rule in it. Absolute rulelessness.

There is nothing I would say that you could frame into some rule or technique. There is no "because" in anything. There is only, "in spite." Any moment it can change totally to something else. It's not like coming from A to B with all the techniques in between, and then you exhaust your *sadhana* and become more conscious, and then you are more aware, because blah, blah, blah, the house of cards falls down. No? You have to be, in spite of the seeking, in spite of *sadhana*, not because of some stopping. Again and again, I hammer on this—that in spite of knowing or not knowing, you are what you are, not because.

The knowledge you can gain, is second-hand anyway. So forget it. Knowledge that comes because of an absence of mind or a blank mind, is dependent again.

PETE: But that collapsing, where you become completely naked and then you can go through the eye of the needle—I'm not saying that because of *sadhanas* you can achieve something—but sometimes that nakedness point arrives when you've tried so many *sadhanas*, you've poured everything out, and then it's all a big failure for you, and then suddenly sometimes, you get that nakedness right there, there's a moment when you realize—

KARL: But every night you have that nakedness in deep sleep. So you could do *sadhana* to sleep. Do you have a sleeping pill, a technique for deep sleep? Is it because you do *sadhana* that you go into deep sleep? In deep sleep, no one worries about *sadhana* or knowing or not knowing or whatever will come in the next moment, because there is no worrier, there is no question and no answer. So you do your *sadhana* to get sleep?

PETE: [laughing] Unless waking is *sadhana*. I don't know. Once I'm slept out, I have to be awake for a while until I can sleep again.

KARL: So because you sleep, you wake up again. Sounds good. "I sleep so I can wake up again, and I wake up so I can sleep again." Infinite circle— you exhaust yourself so that you can sleep again. This is *sadhana*, even as a spiritual technique. You want to use that technique to get exhausted so you can sleep better, and then you wake up very refreshed for work again. Sounds good.

But this is like it is. Look at the world. So many big masters went into the *samadhi* of awareness, for a thousand years sometimes, but then they woke up again and worked. That dream has all kinds of waking up, of exhaustion and refreshment, of doing and not doing. Your idea of, "total resignation because of exhaustion" doesn't work. You cannot exhaust what you are. It always sounds nice and good and very logical, but it doesn't work. It works if you want to buy a Mercedes or a new house or some goal like that. You can have an, A-to-B, step-by-step approach to reach that. But not for That which you are seeking.

So the precious mind, the precious intelligence, you can dump into the next rubbish bin, because for That it won't work. But it's beautiful, huh, that it doesn't work? You have a tool, you can use it, but it doesn't work anyway. Okay. You play with it. You play with the mind, you play with intelligence, you play with *sadhana*—that is meditation. You simply play. You get entertained.

You are in Self-entertainment only when you have no result coming out of it. At the moment you have an expectation of a result, you're working, then you are working really hard. You even want to have the result of becoming what you are. My goodness! "That will be *my* Self. I reached myself." What kind of self would it be that you could reach?

CHARLES: A limited self.

KARL: Yeah. Relative self, relative freedom, relative whatever. Limited, limited, limited. So what? So what is all this "personal freedom"? An idea. Simply an idea. It's nice, but it's worth nothing. So, you are, in spite, not because of your doing or not doing. If you see it, if you really see, that you are in spite of your *sadhanas*, in spite of what you have done or not done, in spite of your sins or no sins, in spite of your guilt or no guilt, really in spite, always in spite, never because—that's freedom. My goodness.

That Which Is Self Doesn't Know Self

MATHILDA: But can you see that?

KARL: Of course you can see that. You can see that you cannot *be* what you can see. That is being That which is seeing itself. When you are That which is seeing itself, there is absolutely no idea in that seeing itself of what it is and what it is not. You simply exist as that seeing without any concept of what you are and what you are not. Whatever you see, you cannot be. How can you not see that, as you always see that?

You always experience, but whatever you experience, you cannot be. Because what you experience is not a second, is in time, is an idea, an image. The eye of what is seeing, the eye that is sight itself, cannot see itself. So what? You can only see, but you cannot be what you see.

But for seeing, you have to exist. Existence is naked. So whatever you take as a dress of seeing, you're dressed by what you imagine. But it's simply a dress. You're naked, all the time, although you dress yourself with concepts, mistaking those images for real and wearing them. This body is worn by what you are, but the body will be gone like any other dress, you put it on and you take it off, but you still are naked existence. So what? There's nothing wrong with the body, or any dress, but see it as a dressing! But if you take the dressing as real, you are in the salad. [group laughs] No? Quite a big salad!

MATHILDA: Not to identify with it.

KARL: Even that is a concept.

MATHILDA: Yeah. For example, instead of going to a temple, I go to the market, I know I would rather go to the temple, but I go to the market—I am just doing what I'm doing. I have no choice. I'm doing it. I see I'd rather go to the temple, but now I'm here in the market. So I accept this. And it's easy then.

KARL: No. It's not in your hands to accept that. It's still a personal acceptance and means nothing. The temporary little acceptance of seeing something, this is understanding.

But I'm talking about being That which is prior to whatever idea, being the acceptance which has no second, as there is no second anything even to accept. This effortlessness of your nature, the nakedness I'm talking about, is not about understanding that, "in spite of wanting to be there, I'm here." I'm not talking about that "in spite." No, this will come and go. Don't worry. It's not even there. I'm talking about what is understanding itself, knowledge itself, which was never gone.

The knowledge that you exist, in whatever idea or concept—knowledge of that existence was never gone. So you never lost the absolute knowledge that you are. It is in spite of all the relative knowing or not knowing, not because. This is acceptance to be That which is acceptance. As the absolute knowledge was never lost, so you are in the Absolute, but not by knowing or not knowing.

MATHILDA: That's what I mean. You cannot know it nor not know it.

KARL: Yeah. You are that paradox. You cannot *not* know it, but you can neither know it nor not know it. Knowing and not knowing are there because you are. So in spite of the knowing and not knowing, you are. That is absolute existence. So in spite of relative or not relative existence, you are That which is absolute existence.

The relative existence and non-relative existence, the limited and unlimited, are there because you are, but you have no idea of limited or unlimited, because even the idea of being unlimited is limitation. Whatever defining you do, you frame yourself. But in order for you to frame yourself, prior to that, you have to exist. So I ask you to be prior to what is a concept already, of "I," of even awareness, to be That which is the "absolute prior"—that I am speaking to, to the nakedness alone.

So in spite of your understanding, in spite of your little acceptance, you are, not because. A little personal peace or freedom may come with it, but this little personal freedom or peace goes again. You may think it's a way out, but it's not.

LOUISE: It comes in handy. It's like a little toolbox.

KARL: Sounds good.

LOUISE: So if you are in a stressful situation, you can reach out to that part. You know, it's kind of comfortable then. You know, if you are in stress and you know how to relax, it comes in handy.

KARL: Yeah, sounds good. But what can relax is still very tense. Even in personal relaxation, you are waiting to return to the stress. I'm talking about the absolute relaxation, where there is no second, there is no one left to be in any tension, in any relationship.

LOUISE: But meanwhile, what do you do?

KARL: Meanwhile? There is no meanwhile.

LOUISE: [laughing] Meanwhile, I can't go on like this all the time!

KARL: Time is very mean, I know. "Mean-while." Time means there is a second. And after a second, there comes a minute, and after a minute there comes an hour, and after an hour comes a year, and blah, blah, blah. So with the first second, time starts.

To see the first second, stay in That which is prior to the second, to the image. Then you see that time is a child of you, you're not a child of time. That's the difference. There may be time and non-time, and all the experiences and images, but they are all a child of you. You are not a child of time. You are prior to the absolute Source, wherein all the images appear, but you yourself are not an appearance, as you cannot imagine what you are. Whatever you can imagine as a second self—at the moment "me" and "myself" appears—that self is already false. The lie starts, and you are the liar. So whatever comes out of you is a lie. Is that true?

LOUISE: [laughing] Okay. Yes!

KARL: You see, about a lie, you don't care, but about the truth you make a very big fuss. So that's why I am calling you the absolute liar that you are. Whatever comes out of you is a lie. So whatever comes out of you, you cannot be. It's simply a reflection, an aspect, and it's no different from what you are, but it's not what you are, and in spite of that, you are. But it's wonderful. It's freedom. What to do? Imagine that you could control yourself, as you try now. [Louise laughs]

SOFIA: Karl, you said you just have to see. That means intuition.

KARL: Yeah.

SOFIA: Is this the "split second"? You have just to see.

KARL: Just see. Not, "You just have to see." Just see. When you just see, there is no one who creates a concept about anything. Just see, because that seeing is prior to time and non-time. If you just see, you are simply That which is perception itself, and you are prior to time, which is an appearance in That which you are. Whatever appears and disappears in you is simply a coming and going of shadows, but you are the infinite light that all the shadows are by. So what?

FRANCESCO: It's so hard to understand what you mean by "just see."

SOFIA: It is the apperception?

KARL: Maybe.

An Australian MAN: You mean seeing without a seer?

KARL: Yeah, because within absolute perception, the perceiver appears. So the experiencer that wakes up in the morning appears in That which is perceiving itself. You are the absolute perceiver which is never a part of what you can perceive—the separate perceiver, "me," and whatever body, images, appear in That, but you are never part of the appearances. So be That which is seeing itself.

The seer always comes later, is always second. But first there is seeing and then comes "the seer" as an idea. So don't be the idea, be That which is prior to the idea. Prior to the idea of "I" is That which is the "I," what is experiencing the "I." First there is seeing itself, then the seer, or the "I" comes. So be That which is Heart itself, wherein the "I" appears.

FRANCESCO: Too, too, too—

KARL: Too what? It's very easy!

FRANCESCO: No, it's too difficult to remember. Bye-bye, this.

KARL: You can never remember. My goodness.

FRANCESCO: Oh, God, everyday you talk and I don't remember what you said yesterday! Everyday is new, and everyday I think, "What does this mean? I don't remember what you said yesterday."

KARL: Look at the beauty of it, that you cannot remember yesterday, or even the moment before.

FRANCESCO: It's stressful.

KARL: Only if you try to remember, it's stressful. If you see, there is nothing to remember, it's fun, wonderful!

FRANCESCO: But why sit here? I need to remember to understand what you say.

KARL: But you don't have to understand. [sternly] I tell you again and again, you don't have to understand anything!

FRANCESCO: Yes, I know, but this is normal for me! [group laughs]

SOFIA: So in this apperception, there is no witness?

KARL: Even the witness is witnessed.

SOFIA: Yeah, okay.

KARL: So That which is the witness doesn't know any witness. You may call it "the absolute witness," but the absolute witness doesn't know any witness. So what is an idea of "witness" appears in the absolute witnessing. Sounds good.

ROSA: Is it like a baby that doesn't know anything, just opens its eyes?

KARL: No, even prior to that. Because even, in a baby, there is a notion of existence—the notion of existence is already second-hand.

AIKO: It's already lying.

KARL: It's already lying. Lying down. No, you cannot place it in any object or circumstance. It's always prior to whatever circumstance, even the circumstance of the first notion of existence. Prior to that first state of "I," the first baby-like "I"-awareness, is what you are as Heart.

You cannot place it in any circumstance, and say, "As a baby I was better off. I want to be a baby again." You still long for a special circumstance; you think that in the special circumstance you are better off. But you have to be what you are—Heart itself—wherein all these states appear, but you never are an appearance.

So you have to be in any circumstance what you are. If you are only what you are in special circumstances, such as a baby, you are dependent again. And That which is Heart can never depend on any special circumstance. So I am asking you to be That which you are by being That which is prior to whatever you can imagine.

ROSA: That makes me not feel here, right now.

KARL: No. Only you want to understand that.

ROSA: Yeah, exactly.

KARL: Then you have a knot around your heart. You want to make it *your* understanding. You again want to control yourself, but it's unavoidable.

ROSA: Old story.

KARL: Old story. It is called the "heart-knot," the attempt, the intention, to control yourself by the first wish to know yourself. By the wish to know yourself, you step out of the paradise of the absolute "not-knowing" you are. Yeah, stress. As soon as you attempt to know yourself, you create a second self. You imagine a second self you could know, and that is already separation.

But the first notion, the first waking up to that wish, you cannot avoid. You cannot *not* wish a wish. As the wish comes out of the wishlessness, you cannot *not* wish the wish, the wish to know yourself.

ROSA: So it doesn't even need courage?

KARL: No.

ROSA: Even courage is a sensation.

KARL: Nothing is needed. Whatever you create comes out of the idea to wish or to control yourself. Then you need something. But if you are in the total understanding of what is existence, you can never be controlled by That which is existence, as there is no second edition of existence. You are That which has no second edition of existence. Hallelujah. What to do? This controllessness is paradise. But any attempt to control yourself, and then you are in hell. You become a devil who wants to control God. There is a devil in "me," or "me" in God. And the "me" is a devil, and God has to be controlled by that devil, "me." That is how hell appears with the first lie and the first liar, "me." Whatever comes out of it, is a lie.

ROSA: That's the original sin, then, I guess?

KARL: And you are the original sinner. You cannot blame anyone else. You can only blame yourself. But that would be stupid.

ROSA: But it's also yourself.

KARL: It's not myself.

ROSA: It's "our-self."

KARL: It's not even "our-self."

ROSA: It's *myself*?!

KARL: It's especially yourself! [group laughs] As long as you see it as yourself, "our-self," all this comes out of yourself. But I have no idea where it comes from.

ROSA: But there is no "myself."

KARL: No? Who tells you?

ROSA: You.

KARL: Me? There's not even Self, I tell you, because even "Self" is an idea. For what you are, there's not even Self. There's a total Selflessness. That which is Self doesn't know Self, so what to do? There is no myself, there is no yourself, there's not even Self. So there is not my bag and your bag, bag is for everyone. Bag off. Back off. [group laughs]

FRANCESCO: Drink.

KARL: Oh, the famous drink again. Today's looks really good.

THERESE: The color changed.

KARL: Yesterday, it looked like lemonade, but this is brown. Healthy.

MONIKA: Hell-o.

KARL: Oh, hell-thy. Hallelujah.

FRANCESCO: Did you put in sugar?

KARL: No, it's tea or something. What is it?

MAN who made the drink for Karl: Noni juice.

A WOMAN: Nomi juice. Tropical?

KARL: No me?

MONIKA: No me! Finally we know the secret! [big group laughter]

THERESE: We can go out and buy it!

KARL: It's a "no-me" juice. You can buy it in the Ramana Supermarket. Not in the *ashram*, but in the market across the street.

The Idea of "Better" Is Already Quite Worse

LIZ: Karl, I have a question that rolls around my mind. I can't quite get an answer that satisfies me, so I'm sure you'll sort this one out. What is it that reincarnates? If we are never born and we never die—does the Self wait to get into the fetus? I keep wondering what the hell is it that reincarnates, and why do we bother about it?

MONIKA: Yeah, right.

LIZ: If the Self can't be born and can't die, what is reincarnating? The mind?

KARL: Tendencies. Action-reaction of consciousness is transforming infinitely. You can call it "karmic consciousness," "karmic energy." A chain reaction of energy. So there is here, now, incarnated consciousness.

MONIKA: Desires?

KARL: All is consciousness. You cannot say desires incarnate.

LIZ: So molecules that stick together all the time?

KARL: No molecules! Consciousness as That which is molecules, what is the energy of existence which is "pure *shakti*," you may call it, or "consciousness," or whatever.

LIZ: The same self doesn't keep coming back to the same bunch of molecules? It's just there to be used, as it comes through the body.

KARL: What body?

LIZ: The dress.

KARL: So this body is molecules, but this is like an "in-form-ation" in what dream? There are not even molecules that build something. Where are the molecules you're built of? You go back and back and you can't find anything.

The whole scientific world, for centuries, want to find matter, but they haven't found any matter up until now. So it doesn't matter. [group laughs] So first find something that has incarnated and then we can talk about what that is. But as they never found anything that is incarnated, it doesn't matter.

LIZ: It doesn't really matter, I know that. It's just my mind keeps rolling this one around. It won't let it go.

KARL: Enjoy it.

LIZ: Keep it alive.

KARL: Why not ponder about it? If you see, you ponder about matter, but as you cannot find matter, it doesn't matter.

LIZ: It really doesn't matter. I think what's going on is it's an old concept of how it works that I can't have anymore, so I need a new concept.

KARL: You can't get over your Buddhist nature. No, I don't know.

LIZ: I see what I'm doing. It's an old concept that's been killed, and I want to have another one to take it's place.

KARL: You want to have a better one instead.

LIZ: A different one. That void is very hard.

KARL: Only a better one could replace a not-so-good one.

LIZ: One that fits.

KARL: Until now, you've found only not-so-good ones.

LIZ: I've found nothing!

KARL: Yeah, but "nothing" cannot replace something, because "nothing" is again something.

LIZ: Maybe sitting in the void, sitting in nothing, is helpful.

KARL: No.

LIZ: I have to have something?

KARL: No, no. You have to become emptiness itself.

LIZ: It takes some time.

KARL: It doesn't take time. It's here, now. It never takes any time to be That which is emptiness. But to become emptiness, it may take an eternity, because you can never become emptiness. But here, now, you are emptiness, so there is no time in it. And by being That which is emptiness, you are That which is fullness.

If you try to become emptiness, you will never reach it. There will always be one too many—that one who is emptiness. And the one who was never there, you cannot get rid of.

LIZ: There's nothing to do.

KARL: I don't know. Even "nothing" is too much. First find one who did anything at all, who has something to do. So by not finding that, by the question "Who am I?," by not finding the Self which has done or not done anything, by the absolute not finding what you are, there is freedom, there is peace of absolute existence that doesn't even know to exist. But it's not by anything that you can achieve it. *Schief*

Just see here, now, what is there. There is an experiencer experiencing what is there to experience. All this that I just described, like an experience of an image, appears in That which you are. And there is nothing right or wrong with it. It's simply experiencing That which you are in whatever shape and form. So what to do? As there is nothing incarnated here now, where is this idea of "reincarnation"?

LIZ: It's just another concept, just another idea.

KARL: No, the easiest way to find what reincarnated is, is not to find That which is incarnated here and now. I promise you, you will not find what you are, in any circumstance. So by not finding That which you are in any circumstance or any form or anything, who then cares about what you find? You find out—that you cannot find out—what you are. What a paradox, hey?

LIZ: I know. It's always a paradox.

KARL: So what would you gain with all the knowledge in the world, with the understanding of physics and how this works or doesn't work, and what reincarnation is and all that?

LIZ: You're right. It doesn't matter and it's just killing another concept. One more concept—"reincarnation"—gone, or working on leaving.

KARL: You're working on leaving? [group laughs]

LIZ: No, the concepts! I'm not leaving.

KARL: She's looking for a departure plane. It always sounds like, step by step you can become something less, that you reach something. Again, it's a concept. It's an idea. You cannot get "less enough" to be what you are. All the knowledge in the world, whatever you can know, cannot satisfy you.

LOUISE: And yet it appears that it gets better and better as you walk on this path, whatever path it is you are walking. I mean, that's how I experience this journey. It gets better and better.

KARL: But what can get better, can get worse again. That idea of "better" is already quite worse.

LOUISE: But not in the big picture.

KARL: What big picture?

LOUISE: The three hundred sixty degrees, up and down, back and forth, there is some—

KARL: Improvement?

LOUISE: No, I wouldn't call it "improvement," actually. It might even look worse on the outside, but there's a sensation or an image, I don't know what it is, but there is this essence, there is a texture to it. It feels better. I feel better now than I felt when I was sitting with Osho. I feel better now than when I was a suicidal teenager.

KARL: It's a different hormonal circumstance. There are different hormones now than were running your life then. Now the hormones are a bit quieter, maybe. [group laughs]

LOUISE: Sure they are.

KARL: I'm serious about this.

LOUISE: It appears that—

KARL: It's a relative peace now appearing.

LOUISE: Relative peace. Okay.

KARL: A more personal peace comes because your hormones are getting quieter. After menopause or something, they always—

MARY: Men-pause! [group laughs]

KARL: Pause from men!

LIZ: After menopause, you get lighter.

KARL: And the last enlightenment is when you go to the grave—the flash light of the photograph, no. It's still something you can find in the realm of the mundane world. You can get quieter by whatever, but I don't talk that peace, because that is a relative peace. You can become very harmonious, but it's in spite of that.

LOUISE: Yeah.

KARL: In spite of that, you are Teflon. Even that peace will not stick on you.

Only the Mind Minds the Mind

KLARA: I have a question. There's a permanent reporter in me. It reports everything. Changes, blah blah blah, everything.

KARL: Reporting, "Now more peace than yesterday." [group laughs]

KLARA: It's permanent. It leaves me alone in sleep, but I wake, even in dreams, with the same guy. But I have a question—do you still have that?

KARL: The devil in my neck? That always talks to me? No, there is no difference.

KLARA: Who is uninvited?

KARL: Oh my goodness. A guest you didn't invite. What do you do with a guest you didn't invite and cannot get rid of?

KLARA: It's terrible.

KARL: Only because you want to get rid of that guest.

KLARA: Oh.

KARL: If you just let him talk, "Daily report." "Yes, sir." What to do with a guest you cannot get rid of, as you say you cannot get rid of the reporter. The moment the body wakes up, there is reporting. "How did I sleep? What did I dream? What will happen today? Blah blah blah." What to do with it? You kill him by cognizance. You become totally cognizant of the reporter. Because the devil is no different from what you are. This is an experience of what you are. You give yourself a report. There is no difference. All is Heart. All is Self. When there is a second Self, it's no different from the first Self. It's simply two appearances of one and a second.

There's an interaction as consciousness. It's a play. Acting. One role is the reporter, and one role is "me." But in essence both are the Self—the Self taking the image of me, and the Self taking the image of the permanent reporter.

You kill them both by seeing that, in essence, they are no different from That which you are. So by seeing "whatever," or by being That which you are, then the experiencer, that is experiencing what you experience as a reporter, is no different. In essence, there is no difference. So what is the problem then when the reporter reports something? Can freedom be bothered by freedom?

KLARA: No.

KARL: No, see? Freedom is all that is there. There is no moment without freedom. So in freedom, there is an image of an experiencer and a reporter, there is an interaction of consciousness. So what? What to do with it?

KLARA: Just leave it in my head?

KARL: Who is bothered?

KLARA: Me!

KARL: Yeah, "me." So what is wrong with the "me" being bothered by something else? Only you take yourself as a "me" and something else as a second. Then everything is an enemy.

Out of the first lie that you exist, out of first "any-me," you are in an enemy situation. At the moment you are, being born, or "whatever," you create six billion others, and these six billion others are enemies. The first "me" already is an enemy. So by being prior to the first "me," you are prior to those six billion, whatever, images. So they are all living by what you are, but you are not living by them.

What to do then with the first "me" and those six billion other ones, if you cannot get rid of them? You are the helplessness that cannot *not* imagine itself as the one and six billion others. You cannot *not* wake up to the awareness of "I" and, then "I am," and then the world, as you cannot *not* create by being That which is absolute, That which is the manifestation—what to do?

Australian MAN: Have another beer.

KARL: Have another coffee, yeah. And then you have a Shakespeare. When this is gone, when Shakespeare is gone, when there is no question, "To be or not to be?"—

KLARA: So that means that the reporter will always be? I mean, I hear the mystics talking about the "no-mind" state—

KARL: Yeah, if you would recognize yourself in the "me," in the reporter, in whatever you experience, consider it as no different from what you are. You are That which is the experiencer experiencing what is experienced, in essence, as you are That which is. In That, there was never any mind, there is no anything, there is nothing that can disturb you, as That which is freedom itself cannot be disturbed by freedom.

That freedom is the absence of a second. So whatever is there is an entertainment of talking, the Self is talking with the Self. So what? Self-entertainment. And who needs the Self to shut up? What other Self?

So what is with this "no-mind"? The absolute no-mind is to see that whatever is, is the Self and be it. By being absolutely what you are, you are That which is existence itself. So you are That. There never was, never will be, any mind. So then what is the no-mind? There's neither mind nor no-mind. Both are ideas.

And who needs a "no-mind"? The mind. Only the mind minds the mind. Never mind! [group laughs]

Whatever you come up with comes out of the idea that something has to be changed, something has to be different for what you are. It's all coming and going and cannot unmake you, as nothing ever could make you. So what then?

KLARA: Maybe I should try a coffee instead of a tea.

KARL: A coffin? [group laughs] I tell you, at the moment you think you are alive, you step into the coffin and you are dead. Any idea that you are alive makes you dead. So the idea of being alive, of being born, is a "coffin" idea. Right away this is your funeral. Any idea that you are alive is suicide. You become an object. You're stepping out of the absolute existence into the relative idea of "I am alive." So this is all a coffin. All the inmates are corpses.

AIKO: Papaji said "graveyard."

KARL: Graveyard, yeah, shadowland of corpses, those images.

LOUISE: From shadowland to graceland.

KARL: It's graceland, so it's empty.

LOUISE: Crazy.

KARL: That's what Jesus said. "Let the dead bury the dead." Don't worry. By the idea that you are incarnated, that you've been born, you're killing yourself. So being reborn is seeing that what you are was never born. This is a rebirth of what you are.

LOUISE: It's a recall.

KARL: *Total Recall.* Schwarzenegger has to come? No, leave the Governor in California. [group laughs]

Being reborn is a Krishna idea, even Ramana talked about it. The rebirth of your absolute nature is seeing that what you are was never born. Any idea you create about yourself, any way you define yourself, is killing yourself. So any moment you're not the Absolute—the absolute "not-knowing" what you are and what you are not—any moment you give yourself an identity of whatever kind of definition, it's suicide. Hello, suicide! Hello, corpse! Aw, it's not so bad. [group laughs]

LIZ: You give us no hope, Karl.

KARL: Hope? No hope. But that's nothing new.

LOUISE: [laughing] Not so bad. Not so good either!

KARL: It's neither good nor bad, that's the good thing about it.

LIZ: No divine love, no acceptance, no reincarnation. There's nothing.

KARL: No way out.

THERESE: No better life, no relaxation.

MONIKA: No enlightenment.

THERESE: No improvement.

KARL: I would say that you cannot get more enlightened than you already are.

MONIKA: Oh dear!

KARL: You always want to make more.

MONIKA: No, better!

KARL: Better enlightenment. [group laughs] No, it only comes down to the very mind, to the idea of ownership. If this is not there, no one cares. There's a concernlessness. But at the moment you identify with "whatever," "my" comes. This "my" comes out of being born, of being separated. You create a "*my* existence." Whatever you do wants to improve the existence which is yours. That's the nature of it.

But whatever you can improve is dead. It's empty. It's all second-hand. Clothes. Still a headache?

LOUISE: Right now, it's okay. At this very moment, it's okay.

KARL: At this very moment, it's gone. Banishment right away.

LOUISE: Punishment?

KARL: Punishment of controlling. Headache.

LOUISE: Are you working on it again now, hey?

KARL: Am I working on it? [group laughs]

MONIKA: He would send it back.

KARL: No, I have a lot of compassion for this. Normally, really, I don't do anything. But that is something really hard.

No one can take it. If there is one who doesn't want anything from you, nothing to give, nothing to change, nothing to do, it's really hard for a person to stay in that. Because this is the worst thing a person can go through.

There is no one who wants anything from it. You don't have to change, you don't have to improve, you don't have to do anything—this is like it's killing you. It's killing the idea of "you who has to do something." You really resist that, because this takes away all your ideas of being alive, being a person who has to improve. There is no reaction to you. It doesn't even know you.

"Who is this guy anyway? He doesn't speak to me. Speak to me!" "No. I don't even know you." "Acknowledge me! Tell me that I am mature. Tell me that I am maybe a failure, whatever, but talk to me. Tell me something has to change with me, because if I can change, I am still alive. But you talk to me as if I am already dead." "Yes, you are!"

LOUISE: Yeah, it feels like that. This creation of the hammering thing, it draws the attention so I can feel it in the body-mind system. You know, it's like a print. Otherwise, maybe I wouldn't feel it. It's like a trick, with a sense of manipulation.

KARL: What?

LOUISE: [laughing] Every time I think I am on it—da dun da dun da dun da dun!—I fall off the horse, a horse with no saddle or nothing gallops off back to the desert!

KARL: The horse simply disappears from under you. My goodness, you are a flying carpet. You cannot land anywhere. Pad for existence.

LOUISE: A pet?

KARL: A pet of existence. Petal. Hmm.

Absolute Control Is Being That Controllessness

JAMES: Karl, going back to what you were talking about in the beginning, about the seeing. In the seeing, the "I" and the universe disappear, right?

KARL: There is only That which is existence itself, because when you are That which is seeing, then you are whatever is—there is no separation. When you are That which is the experiencer, you are That which is experiencing and what is experience, as you are that existence absolute.

So you are That which is the experiencer, but you are not the experiencer. You are That which is the person, but you are not the person. You are

That which is the body, but you are not the body. So if you are That which is, then you are what is the experiencer, that experiencing, and what is experienced—in the presence of that and in the absence, too. Then there is no difference. In the presence of what is world, or in the absence of the world, only That which is, is.

And That has no idea of being That or not. So even to say you are That which is seeing, you are not seeing, you are That which is seeing. And by being That which is seeing, you are what is seer and what is the whole world. Because then whatever is, is Heart. As you are That which is the world, you don't know the world anymore, because whatever is, is what you are. So in that moment, you are not the seer, not the seeing, nor the seen, as you are That which is. In the presence and in the absence. It makes no difference any more.

In order to exist, the experiencer needs the presence of experiencing and something to experience. But That which is the experiencer doesn't need the presence of an experiencer experiencing blah blah blah. This is absolutely independent of any circumstance. All the circumstances need circumstances, the experiencer needs a circumstance of experiencing, but That which is the experiencer doesn't need anything.

It's too complicated, huh?

JAMES: Yeah, I pretty much lost it.

KARL: It's very easy, actually. It's easy to be it, but not to understand.

JAMES: Impossible to understand.

KARL: But "impossible" is another word of the mind. That which is absolute spirit has no limit of understanding.

JAMES: Right.

KARL: At the understanding of the unlimited spirit or intelligence, there is no "me" anymore. The "me" can only live when there are limits to understanding, as the mind can only be there when there is a limit of mind. In the unlimited intelligence or spirit, there is no mind anymore.

This is like what she was saying, a total "no-mind." Because in the absolute, unlimited intelligence or spirit, there was never any mind. Mind is simply like one aspect of understanding, of the absolute understanding. Mind simply means limitation, a limit of understanding. But there was never any limit of understanding, as the "limit" is only an aspect of experiencing a limit. That limit was never there, except as an appearance of a limitation in

That which is unlimited, which is prior.

Taming the bull, controlling the mind, is not by any control, it's by simply being what you are. And when you are what you are, which is existence itself, there never was, and will never be, any mind. Then the mind is simply only an image, like a dream image or shape, and it is never there. But not by any control, of the mind controlling the mind, of needing a "no-mind" blah blah blah—the absolute control is being that controllessness, being That which is existence itself, which has no second. In That there is no control possible.

There is only control in the idea of "a second self." But by seeing the second self only as an idea, an image, a phantom—what to control? That phantom you cannot control anyway. Anna, everything okay?

ANNA: Yeah, in a sense. but I'm pretty dull today so—

KARL: Oh la. Today's a Shiva day. Very dull.

ANNA: It's just like that.

KARL: No moon. Shiva moon today.

LIZ: Shiva moon? Doesn't exist!

MR. IYER: New moon.

KARL: Or you can call it "no moon." Next month is Mahashivaratri [Night of Shiva]. The big one.

LIZ: Will you be here for that?

KARL: No, I fly out that day. I'd rather not be here because it will be quite crowded. Is *maha* every twelve years?

MR. IYER: Every year.

KARL: Every year. Every twelve months.

MR. IYER: Every month there is a Shivaratri, but that particular month, Shivaratri is celebrated.

KARL: Yeah, it's a *maha*. Every twelve months, the twelfth moon or the thirteenth moon, then many come here.

MR. IYER: But not from outside. Usually from the nearby villages. Not that much crowd.

KARL: Not as many as Deepam [Festival of Lights].

MR. IYER: No.

KARL: But still enough, I think.

THERESE: Last year I was in Varanasi for Shivaratri. There were processions of *sadhus* and elephants and everything.

KARL: Big celebration.

LIZ: That's special.

KARL: So what to do? I remember three years ago, when Yogi Ramsuratku-mar died. Three or four years ago?

FRANCESCO: Three.

KARL: Three. They unplugged the machines.

THERESE: On Shivaratri day?

KARL: Yeah.

MONIKA: Oh, really?

KARL: To make it really auspicious. That's a total teaching of helplessness. Yogi Ramsuratkumar, the biggest *siddhi* master in India, caught hanging on the machines and unplugged on that auspicious day. He could not decide anything, and he didn't care, I tell you.

FRANCESCO: Well, what kind of day do you like?

KARL: Me? Well, whenever you like.

FRANCESCO: Tomorrow? [group laughs]

KARL: If you can find the plug.

FRANCESCO: You don't believe, but it can be possible. Everything can change. Still too much. Still. Oh my God.

KARL: But coming back to the helplessness, it's really like a big teaching, an absolute teaching. Being the biggest master around and lying there, being totally dependent on machines, and then the disciples decide when to pull the plug and make it really auspicious. That concernlessness, lying there, even his arm was lifted by a string. Because there was a glass house all around, everyone could go visit him. Nice scene, huh?

FRANCESCO: I went.

KARL: It was great! I liked it.

FRANCESCO: It was good energy.

KARL: Yeah, but to see that! Then when he went, the corpse was sitting in the chair and the whole room was full of a blueness, totally blue energy, cosmic energy. Whew! It was great. The elephant was released from the corpse.

MRS. ANGELINA: Karl, this apperception, is it there in spite of my seeing or not?

KARL: Do you mean, it's in spite of the action or non-action of seeing?

MRS. ANGELINA: Yes.

KARL: But in the absence of whatever can be perceived, there is simply what you may call "blankness," or the total absence of any dream. But you are still the absolute dreamer. And then waking up to awareness, the dream starts with the relative dreamer. The absolute dreamer is always the apperception, wherein the perceiver appears. With the perceiver comes perceiving and what can be perceived, "I am so-and-so." So the apperception, That which is the Self itself, is, with and without perception or perceiving, what it is. But the perceiver needs to perceive.

MRS. ANGELINA: So when you are saying "just see"—?

KARL: When there is seeing, just see, but without being the seer.

MRS. ANGELINA: Okay.

KARL: Just see. The seer is only there when the seer is defining what he is seeing. So the definer, as the seer, defines what is separate, what is seen.

MRS. ANGELINA: The seen is always there?

KARL: Not always. You cannot say always. The absolute seer, That which is prior to the relative seer, has no coming and going. But the separate seer, which is there when there is seeing and something seen, is temporary. So That which is prior to the relative seer, wherein the seer seeing what is seen appears, is what you call "apperception."

You may say, here, now, is what you are, perceiving what can be perceived, and what is part of the perceiving, what is the relative perceiver, you are not. You are no different from that, but that is already an imagination—the imagination of the seer seeing what is seen, or what can never be imagined. All the imagining is a dream-like imagination of the Self-realization you cannot avoid.

Be That which is prior to what can be seen. That's what Meister Eckhart called, "the eye of God." What the eye of God is seeing is no different from That which is God, but it's not what is God. So even the seeing is not what is God. You cannot define it. But it comes close to the awareness, or canvas state, which is not in time or no-time. Therein all ideas appear, but itself never moves. It's like a pointer to That, but it's actually not it. It's even beyond the canvas, or prior to the canvas, by being That which is the canvas but neither the canvas nor what is shown on it. Question?

A German WOMAN: *Ich verstehe leider kein Wort. Ich kann kein Englisch.*

KARL: Ah, sounds good. She's in the best position one can be in. She doesn't understand English. [group laughs]

LIZ: She'll get it better than us.

KARL: I tell you, many would like to be in her position, out of the fire. *Ya, genie est einfach.* Just enjoy it. *Ich wei niemals was ich sage.* Even I don't know what I say. But this is really paradise, if you don't know what you say. It absolutely doesn't matter—this total being, absolutely irrelevant. I'm totally *Irrer*—crazy. Absolutely crazy.

LIZ: But I enjoy every minute of it.

MONIKA: There must be merit. Otherwise, we wouldn't do it.

KARL: If That which is the Self wants to be reminded by whatever is the Self and places then the Self in front of the Self to be reminded, only to see it doesn't even have to be reminded to be the Self—if that is merit—whew— sounds good.

CHARLES: Maybe you could do a whole *satsang* in German one day, so all we non-German speakers could benefit. [group laughs] Just the Germans would suffer.

KARL: And next day in Japanese.

CHARLES: Zulu!

MONIKA: Swahili!

THERESE: Gibberish.

KARL: I speak all the time in gibberish. Babble-lonian. Out of Babble-lonia.

THERESE: Or monkey talk. Ee-ee-oo-oo-ah-ah!

KARL: Oh, you will sit here! [group laughs]

THERESE: I saw this movie, *Greystoke: The Legend of Tarzan,* and afterwards I spoke monkey. I loved it. You don't think anymore. You just express—ah ah oo oo!

KARL: Oh, they are quite horny, I tell you.

CHARLES: Don't try that here with us. They can understand!

KARL: Thérèse, did you hear? Don't do it in Tiruvannamalai, they might understand you!

THERESE: Yeah, where I live, the roof is quite full of monkeys and I watch them and it's like uh-oh!

KARL: Better speak Hebrew. Oy yoy! Question? You didn't collect some in the last days? You haven't come with a collection of questions for me?

LIZ: She knows better.

KARL: She leaves them at home where they are safe. [group laughs]

There Is No Moment Without That Which You Are

MR. IYER: Can you tell me something about your view about the mystical powers exhibited by the yogis, for example, Yogi Ramsuratkumar? He has cured many people's health problems.

KARL: I would say they blamed him for that, but it was not him.

MR. IYER: Pardon?

KARL: You may say, they are now in good health, but it was not because of Yogi. It's simply like a coincidence. Healing comes from the same source as the disease, and not from Yogi. He never gave them anything, and he always pointed to that. If you call him "Godchild," it's simply his being That which is the absolute Source of the universe, but not by that does anything happen.

The absolute *siddhi*—that you are what is the absolute Source, what is acceptance itself, or what is grace itself—is the Source of both sickness and health. By that, everything comes, but you cannot say what—nothing special comes out of it. You have to take it that you are the Source of war and peace, of ugliness and beauty—whatever—you are the Source of that.

And Yogi Ramsuratkumar was a pointer to that, to be the helplessness which is the absolute Source of whatever you can imagine. But by that, there is no special healing or anything. It even can create sickness, I tell you.

MR. IYER: You don't come across these kinds of events with Ramana or Nisargadatta Maharaj. Only in the case of Yogi do you come across these kinds of events.

KARL: I didn't read Yogi's books or what he said. I just look into That which he is or was or represented. And for me, when I met him and saw him, he represented the concernlessness or ruthlessness of existence. He didn't represent whatever was written, about a beggar or *siddhi* master or I don't know.

MR. IYER: Here is one thing. My brother was attending on him every evening some ten, fifteen years back. So one evening, he said, "Swami, I won't be here for a few days because I need an operation on my throat." Yogi asked about the problem, and my brother explained. Then Yogi didn't say anything. He just called him and he blessed him. Next day, he went for the operation. Before the operation, they did a preliminary check-up, but then they found there was not even a trace of a need for the operation. So they sent him home.

KARL: Magic.

MR. IYER: He came all the way from Pondicherry right away to see *Bhagavan* and tell him what happened in the hospital. He said, "I know everything. You go home, take this, you please come tomorrow."

KARL: They said the same thing about Jesus and others.

MR. IYER: Yeah. In the case of Jesus, he did a lot of healing.

KARL: But still, the one who heals—that, no.

MR. IYER: That's what I'm not able to understand.

KARL: But the final healing is giving you the total knowledge of what you are, by giving you the knowledge of being That, unborn, never dying—and not healing some body. Because the healing, the pointing to the nature of the Heart that you are, that is the absolute healing. The healing of the body is maybe a side-effect, or whatever, but whoever's body was healed is dead now. It's a temporary adjustment.

All these wonders and miracles are temporary too, simply relative, like an amazing show, like David Copperfield, who can make a whole plane disappear, or Sai Baba, who can produce a *linga*. What to do? It doesn't matter. Both mean nothing. Both are the magic of consciousness that can do everything. It can make a mountain appear and disappear; it can make the whole universe appear and disappear.

What is more magical? You are the total magician. You let the whole universe appear by simply taking it as real. You are creating everything simply by looking at it.

A WOMAN: Is this *leela* or *maya?*

KARL: Maya? Hugo? He is a big *guru* here, a German *guru.* [group laughs]

THERESE: Hey, who comes and goes? Hugo.

KARL: Hugo Mayer. Nice name. "Who goes? *Maya.*" So *maya* comes and goes.

BERTA: What about Karl? [group laughs] Renz!

KARL: I rent and rend.

MR. IYER: Another thing. I heard there are some good spirits and bad spirits possessing humans and controlling their activities. Even that kind of thing you don't come across with Ramana or Nisargadatta, but in the case of some yogis, sometimes you come across this. How to take it? Is there a possibility of controlling one by other beings? Is there such a thing?

KARL: If you are in the idea that you are born, that you are a being at all and there are other beings, you are in the ghost shadowland, and you will be controlled by other spirits. As you want to control their spirits, you are controlled by them. As long as there is a second "me," as long as there is a "me" at all as a ghost, you are surrounded by enemies, ghosts. You are full of ghosts, you create six billion ghosts simply by taking the first ghost "me" as real. So in that spirit, then, there are good and bad spirits for you as a spirit yourself. As long as you are the ghost, surrounded by other ghosts, there are good and bad ghosts, like good and bad people. There's simply different realms of material, personal, spirit realms, dimensions. All is there in the dream.

It all comes with the first "I"-thought. With the first ghost, you create all the other ghosts. You are surrounded by good and bad ghosts, because you have to control.

But seeing the first "I"-thought as a ghost, a phantom, you are prior to that, absolutely prior, in the total absence of any idea of what you are and what you are not. Then there is no ghost, no world, nothing anymore, only That is what is. The rest are fleeting shadows or images coming as a dream, and even the dreamer, as "me," is a dream-like figure who comes and goes. But the moment you take the first dreamer as real, the dream is real too. And in this dream, there are spirits, ghosts, good and bad boys, whatever. So it all depends on the first root of "me."

When a yogi tells you that there are good and bad spirits, and you can be occupied by them, he himself is still a ghost. He can only talk out of what he knows. Whatever he knows, then, in the spirit—ghost, magician, sorcerer, blah blah blah—he becomes. Maybe he can control energy, maybe he becomes a big master of whatever. But it's still—

MARY: Projection.

KARL: Projection, and it's like one shadow controlling another shadow. That's all.

SOFIA: But what about Ramana who appeared to Papaji and told him—

KARL: Why not? Still there. It's not a ghost appearing to another ghost, it's simply one image appearing to another image, like giving some hint. Like the mountain. Is there a mountain? Sofia, is there a mountain? One sees a mountain, and another sees pure light. What's the difference?

So there is Ramana, there is light taking the image of Ramana, as a symbol, like a hint, like the mountain being a total pointer, an absolute pointer to That which is prior to the mountain. So if the whole existence, That which is existence itself, takes the mountain as being a total pointer to That which is existence, so what? When Ramana, as an image, is taken as a symbol for Papaji in that appearance, so what? As that image was an aspect, it was never alive, so it cannot go. Even here, now, Ramana is still alive as images.

FRANCESCO: Yeah, but in that incident, Ramana appeared in front of Papaji and told him to go to Tiruvannamalai and see Ramana, that that was for him.

KARL: Yeah, so what? Consciousness cannot do that?

FRANCESCO: It helped him, because he had travelled around India for many years looking for a *guru* and he didn't find one.

KARL: He was always dancing with Krishna.

FRANCESCO: Yes, but that is different.

KARL: What different?

FRANCESCO: Well, Ramana appeared right in front of him and told him to go to Tiruvannamalai.

KARL: And Ramana asked him where is Krishna now.

FRANCESCO: Yes, but when Papaji actually went to Tiruvannamalai and was in front of Ramana, Papaji said that Ramana looked in his eyes and gave him the possibility to understand what he is.

KARL: I was not there.

FRANCESCO: Me neither. But I hope.

KARL: I hope one day it will happen for you.

FRANCESCO: That's what I come here for. Every day!

MARY: Hint, hint!

FRANCESCO: Look in my eyes! [group laughs]

KARL: In spite of what you just said, in spite of "whatever" Ramana figure, in spite of the mountain or whatever you imagine, you are. I can only point again. In spite of your understanding that "why," you are, not because.

Afterwards, there will be not more understanding. There is maybe some controlling of some understanding of some circumstances, but it cannot control That which is you, as That which is understanding. You cannot add something to the absolute understanding that you are, by any relative understanding, of why Ramana appeared to whom, of whatever, tralala.

FRANCESCO: Yeah, but it's nice, if I were in Italy, and Ramana was outside the door and he said to me, "Oh, Francesco, how are you?" It would be nice, you know. It's only like, "have another coffee."

KARL: If it would be, then you wouldn't talk about it. I don't say there's anything wrong or right with it, I just say, it's nothing special to have some visions of someone.

SOFIA: So, if you dream about the master, or have some vision of the master, or the master is there, it's exactly the same?

KARL: Again and again, I can only tell you, there is no moment, there is no thing, without That which you are. And That is the master himself. You are That which is the master. The master you can experience is simply a reflection of it only. So those images you call your master are only images. But the master you are, which is always there in whatever given moment or circumstance—without that, what is the master? There would not even be a circumstance, and no Ramana appearance, and no dream of any one master, and all this. So the master, the grace, that is what you are, is always there without any coming and going.

Any master of images coming and going is maybe like a nice extra or something, but it cannot add something to what you are. If you enjoy it, okay. But if you make it special and make it *my* experience of a master, and "I'm specially chosen because the master comes to me at night," and you take it personally, then you are in the shit hole again.

MARY: It's false.

KARL: False or not. You simply take something personally. Like the experience of enlightenment. The moment you take it personally, you run around and want to sell it. "My experience!" What is that? But that's what happens.

BERTA: We are talking about That which you are established in.

KARL: No, I'm not talking about anything. Forget it!

BERTA: You are talking about something that is impossible to talk about.

KARL: Yeah, and I say I am talking about what I cannot talk about.

BERTA: That's what all the masters do. So that's another word for "master."

KARL: It's your problem if you call me "master." I don't know any master.

BERTA: But that's what masters do. They talk about what cannot be said.

KARL: Yeah, I'm a talk master. [group laughs]

THERESE: A head master.

MARY: No head!

KARL: I'm the revenge of Germany on Holland! [group laughs]

MONIKA: No, the revenge of the Dutch on the Germans! Other way around. [more group laughter]

MARY: Someone gave a beautiful image the other day. They said that Ramana Maharshi and Arunachala were one. Arunachala is the potential, totality, electricity, and Ramana is the light bulb, kinetic, the shining, the radiance. And that they are one and the same. I thought that was good. It's just an image.

KARL: Nice image. I would say, there's a stable light and a running light. That's all. Both are light. Like, Mount Kailas is the home of Shiva, and this is Shiva himself.

That Absolute "No Way Out" Is Peace, and the Rest Is Trying to Escape

A French WOMAN: About the creation, the sense you use it—I create the world by using the senses?

KARL: No, you are not creating something. You cannot create what is already there.

WOMAN: Yeah, but you say we are the creator.

KARL: But the creator is part of the creation. The idea of God as "the Creator" is part of creation. That Creator God is part of the manifestation of Self. But there is nothing created, so there is no one who creates anything by giving his attention or seeing something. There is only Self, only Heart, and there is no creator and no creation. So you can never create anything by your giving attention to something.

WOMAN: Before you said, by looking, you create, you make this world real.

KARL: No, by taking the creator as real, there becomes a creator and some creation. But actually, it's all Self, and Self is infinite and never comes and goes. In becoming the creator, as "me," by taking the creator as real, you are separate from what you are already. You take an image, a form, as real, but even the "Creator God" is an image, simply an idea. You're still stepping out of the Godlessness you are, out of the paradise of not knowing, into some idea.

Out of the "creator" idea, you create images and forms. So you become the formless consciousness as a creator, creating all kinds of "in-formation." But already that is a dream. It's fake. It's false. So you never created anything, as there was never any creator nor any creation. All that is, is Heart or Self. And in That, there is nothing ever coming or going. So there is no creating, there is not even an appearance and disappearance. What to do with that?

WOMAN: Nothing.

KARL: Then you see that whatever comes out of the dreamer, out of the idea of an image of a dreamer who wakes up in the morning, is simply part of the absolute dream, which is absolutely there without any coming and going. As there is no difference between That which is the absolute dreamer and the absolute realization, there is no coming and going in it. Nothing happens. Nothing can ever disappear, as nothing ever appeared. Nothing is ever created, so there is nothing that can go.

There is not even the illusion of coming and going. Even the illusion is infinite. Nothing is by you.

WOMAN: When I say it, the "me" is not a small me.

KARL: Even the big "me." The giant "me." [both laugh] No, That which is Self never created anything. There is no such thing as creation or creator in whatever is existence. There is only the absolute existence with no coming and going. Nothing is ever created by anyone, not even by That which is the Creator. All this is the dream-like realization, and the dream is as solid as it can be, as a manifestation or realization of absolute existence. There's nothing to see or understand. Simply be That which is never coming, never going, ever unborn, which can never be created or create anything. [Silence.]

MONIKA: I thought it was all my fault! [group laughs]

KARL: But even that is not your fault, that you think everything is your fault. But that is a total pointer—and that is peace—the rest is fiction. The rest is, again, trying to understand and control what is existence.

Existence, the mystical existence, the mystery of absolute existence, you can never reveal as it is. You have to be it. By being it, there is no knowing of it and no not knowing. There is simply That which you are as what is. And never in That is anything created, or comes or goes. So nothing ever happened to That which you are. So all these happenings, dream-like ideas of coming and going, cannot touch what you are. And that is peace itself—the rest is fiction!

A British MAN: How do we realize that peace, then?

KARL: That peace is ever-realized and doesn't need your realization of it.

MAN: How do I realize that this is the case?

KARL: There is no "how" to it. It will never be in time. It will never be in any idea. It will never be owned by anyone. So the nakedness of existence cannot be owned by anyone. You have to absolutely be it. You have to be the nakedness, which is an absolute absence of any idea of what you are and what you are not. Even the absence of the absence, you are, which is the omnipresence of That which is existence itself, and which has no experience of that presence.

MAN: You seem to be giving me an objective, in a sense, to be what I am, to be existence prior to phenomena.

KARL: Whatever you can leave, you cannot be. To exist, you cannot leave. So you cannot *not* be what you are, but whatever can leave you, you are not. Whatever ideas come and go, they are simply concepts. They may leave you. So you may believe in them or not, but they will leave you anyway. Whatever you "be-leave" in, will leave you.

In order for you to believe or not believe, you have to exist prior to both. And That which is prior to a belief system of being and non-being, you cannot reach. But in spite of knowing or not knowing that, you are the absolute knowledge, never because of any relative more or less knowing. So I tell you, you cannot *not* be what you are, as you have never lost yourself.

MAN: But you see, I'm so habitual—I feel I have to have a technique. It's just so ingrained. I can't escape this feeling that I need to know how to do it.

KARL: Good. You can do techniques. Why not? I have nothing against it.

MAN: But what you seem to be saying is that I don't need any technique.

KARL: No, That which you are doesn't need any technique. And what you are *not* needs all the techniques just to stay alive. [group laughs]

You cannot mix it. That which you are never needed any technique, but the false "me" needs all the techniques just to survive. So whatever the false is doing, whatever technique is keeping the false alive, the false "creator" idea, "I am," consciousness, does everything, whatever tactic, to get out of the tick-tack. But by trying everything to get out of the tick-tack, it's attaching the tick-tack to time.

Whatever you do to get out of time makes sure that you are in time. And as a person, as a "me," you have to make time real. Otherwise, there would be no "me" anymore.

MAN: Yes.

KARL: So whatever you do, it's a survival system.

MAN: Well, I do understand you, but it hasn't clicked.

KARL: No, it will never click. That's a click. Never ever. You are never-never! But you will never, ever hear the click. Because when the click is there, there is no one to hear it.

MAN: Is it like shooting yourself? You never hear the bang.

KARL: Something like this. You're already dead before you hear the bang. [group laughs]

Sounds good. It will always be too fast or too slow for what you are. I tell you, you cannot *not* do *sadhana*, but in spite of *sadhana*, there is That which you are. But *sadhana* keeps whoever does the *sadhana* alive.

A MAN: Why not?

KARL: Yeah, why not? I just point out that you cannot become what you are by ending *sadhana*, just as you cannot become what you are by doing *sadhana*. Both are okay; both are irrelevant.

That's the beauty of *sadhana*. You do it, but no one is doing it. It's simply Self-entertainment, all the way—this is meditation! This is freedom, even in meditation. There is meditation only then when there is no expectation of results. Without intention, there is no person anymore. So when there is meditation, there is absolute cosmic consciousness, as That which is consciousness meditating about That which is Self.

But with intention, when there is action with intention, it makes you a person. The intention keeps your "me" alive, because there's an advantage idea, meditating to get something out of it—more personal freedom, peace, whatever you can name.

There's nothing wrong or right with it. I'm simply pointing out the functioning of it, of the experience of "me" [holds up thumb, index, and middle fingers].

The function of "me" haves an intention to keep itself alive. And then comes "I am," simply meditation without intention [holds up thumb and index finger]. And prior to the "I am" is "I," awareness [holds up thumb], and prior to that is Heart [fist]. Heart never needs "I," "I am," and "me," but all of these appear in That which is Heart. So nothing is ever created because Heart is the first and the last.

So in every realm, in every dimension, in whatever world, time, it all needs intention, because there's only time when there's intention. There's only "me" when there's intention. So whatever you do keeps it alive. It's a survival system of that [thumb, index, and middle fingers]. When there is no intention, there is the formless "I am" [thumb and index finger], meditating. By no intention, it keeps the "I am" alive. And then prior to that is the pure consciousness as "I" [thumb], simply awareness. And awareness keeps awareness alive, it's simply automatic.

But prior to that is That which is awareness and That which is "I am"-ness and That which is "I am so"-ness. This [shows fingers and then closes them back into fist again and again] is always That which is Heart [fist] and this [shows fingers and then closes them back into fist again and again] is the realization of this [fist], and there is no difference.

You cannot create any need for That [fist] which never needed "I" [thumb] or this [thumb and index finger] or this [thumb, index, and middle fingers]. But this [thumb, index, and middle fingers] needs intention, this [thumb and index finger] needs no intention, and this [thumb] needs being the Source of no intention and intention. So timelessness creates time and non-time. But timelessness needs That which is timelessness, as non-time needs That which is non-time, and what is time needs That which is time. And That is Heart. Very simple! So be That, as you cannot *not* be That.

British MAN: Yes. The way to be it, is to be it.

KARL: There is no other way.

LIZ: Very simple!

An Irish MAN: This "no intention" keeps "I am" alive? This happens very naturally. There is no effort in it.

KARL: Yeah, but "no effort" needs no effort to be no effort.

MAN: I don't deny that.

KARL: Yeah, but it's still a definition, "no effort."

MAN: But I was listening to what you were saying—"no intention," keeps "I am" alive.

KARL: But the "no intention" is only because there is intention of the "I am so-and-so." Otherwise, you would not define it. There's only non-time because there is time. There is only "no intention" because there is intention.

MAN: No question, no question.

KARL: I'm just pointing to it. It's like a survival system because there are polarities that keep both alive. Emptiness is only there because fullness is. So fullness is empty, and emptiness is full. Form is non-form, and non-form is form. The survival of "non-form" is to be non-form. The survival of "form" is to be form. The survival of "I" is to be *I*. But for this [fist], there is no survival.

MAN: But it feels that there is no one.

KARL: There was never one. But there is still one. Even to say, "There is no one," there is still one. Who is experiencing the "no one"? [laughs] Nice trick. Nice bush and no bush. The no-bush trick. A notebook trick. A laptop.

CHARLES: Can you now not answer the no-question?

KARL: [laughing] That will be the final trick. You have to see even the dependency of "no-dependency."

Irish MAN: [laughing] What does that mean?

KARL: An idea of "no dependency" needs no dependency. So it's depending on no dependency.

MAN But there is no idea of "no dependency."

KARL: But you just talked about it.

MAN: I listened to you! [group laughs]

KARL: But even the "I am" depends on the *I am*. "I" is depending on *I*.

MARY: What about "is"?

KARL: What "is"?

MARY: Just "is."

KARL: "Is" is depending on *is*.

MARY: "Is" is better than "I am."

KARL: Better? [group laughs] You cannot get out of the dependency of existence. This is a "no way out" that you depend on what you are. You cannot escape existence as you are That which is existence.

So there is an absolute dependency as you cannot escape what you are.

This is the absolute no way out. A bit more or less dependency, who cares? That's the point. There is dependency in the "I," there is dependency in the "I am," and so on, all depends on the absolute dependency that you are That. So the absolute "no way out" is peace, and the rest try's to escape.
MRS. ANGELINA: Not possible.
KARL: Whatever attempt you make to find an exit out of what is, is suicide, and then you complain that life is a misery. Any moment you want to escape what is, you want to escape what you are, and then you suffer because of that. That is the beginning of suffering, stepping out of acceptance of being That which is existence. You step into objective life, and then you want to escape objective life. But even that you cannot escape, even that is an experience of what you are.

You cannot *not* experience what you are. You cannot *not* realize what you are, so there will never be any escape in any sense. Hallelujah! Bye-bye. Finally, amen. Thank you, thank you. I'm always amazed that someone listens to me. Total amazement. [group laughs]

"Silence is all there is. Nothing happens in That. Nothing comes or goes in That which you are."

January 22

You Are That Which Is Home; or, the End of All Ends

"Disappearing" the Teacher

KARL: Windy, a bit. *Kommt die Katze* (the cat's coming) today.

GEORG: *Hier kommt die Katze* (here comes the cat)! Kamikaze!

MONIKA: Comfy cats, comedy cats. *Sie kommen wie Kätze* (they come like cats).

THERESE: Kamikaze! Meow!

[Karl is not usually surrounded by any of the indications of respect that customarily accompany spiritual teachers in India, such as garlands of flowers and incense. There is only a simple chair set at the front of the room for him to sit on when he arrives. But on this day, someone has placed two flowers on the bamboo beam behind and above Karl's chair and two flowers on the arms of the chair.]

KARL: Here and here—what?

FRANCESCO: [pointing to Monika] She did it.

KARL: Oy, my, my—

GEORG: Flower power.

KARL: Flower power! Back to the sixties.

GEORG: California, yes.

MONIKA: That's from Holland, the flower *Bauer* (farmer).

THERESE: I have good news. Today is a confusion day.

MONIKA: That's good news?

SOFIA: Only today?

THERESE: Even more today. This Indian man gave me a ride from Mountain View, and I said to him, "Oh, I am a bit late today," and he said, "Oh, don't worry, today is a confusion day, because of astrology." So even if you have plans, they will all be confused. I said, "*That* Karl is going to like—confusion day!" [group laughs]

KARL: So you get an infusion from confusion. Okay. Confusion again. What to do?

KRISTOPH: Mind is confusion.

KARL: Then there would be some mind. To give it another name doesn't make a difference. First, you have to find mind, and then you call it something. So that's confusion, what you cannot find?

KRISTOPH: Just a play with words.

KARL: That's what I said.

THERESE: Hey, Karl, it's getting dangerous. You are getting flowers around you. Respect is coming!

KARL: Yeah, I have to watch out.

THERESE: Respect, authority.

KARL: I did something wrong, I think. [group laughs] Something went wrong here. [looks around at the flowers that mark four corners of a square around him] Four.

GEORG: Framing you.

KARL: Framing. Everyone wants to frame me, for sure! [group laughs] It's really dangerous. The "divine love" frame.

JAMES: The reason they want to frame you, Karl, is because they know it's all your fault.

KARL: Okay, crossed! Nail me. Frame me. It's the same.

JAMES: I didn't bring any nails.

KARL: No? You didn't bring any questions?

JAMES: I've got a question, for entertainment. From the point of view or perspective of Self-realization, it would seem that an individual who is Self-realized wouldn't be critical of manifestation, and in particular, of other teachers.

KARL: Who says so?

JAMES: Well it's just an idea, but every teacher that I have known criticizes other teachers.

KARL: Yeah, that has to be.
JAMES: Can you explain that. Why does that have to be?
KARL: Because the Shiva aspect has to destroy all, even himself as a teacher. This teaching is to destroy all the teaching and teachers and whatever can be said. This is not criticism or being cynical; it is simply that nothing can be left over. No teacher, no teaching, no disciple. That is the Shiva aspect of destruction.

So this is not a critical point of view. It is simply that you take everything that can be taken away. All the teachers, even, because you point out, "Look they cannot help you. There is no one who has it more. No one has that nectar to give you."
JAMES: Yeah, I mean, it sounds good to criticize other teachers.
KARL: It's not criticizing anything. It's destroying them—in front of you.
JAMES: I mean it's fine to be criticizing other teachers and then at the same time criticize oneself. But some of them just criticize other teachers.
KARL: Some. Then they have to go one step further. Because the teacher that's in front of you has to "disappear," too. So they have to destroy the whole world and then themselves in front of you. But maybe that's what comes next. Who knows? Why do you question it?
JAMES: I see it brings up another thing and that is, some people they take a teacher or guru and they place them on this pedestal, you know that's way, way, way up there.
KARL: Then they think they are safe or what?
JAMES: It's projection, right?
KARL: Just fun. No danger.
LOUISE: Is there anything besides entertainment in that?
KARL: Entertainment.
LOUISE: Is that all—entertainment?
KARL: Yeah, besides entertainment, there is entertainment.
LOUISE: Besides that?
KARL: There is entertainment.
LOUISE: Keep on going, keep on going.
[Karl sits silently for a moment. All eyes are on him. Suddenly, one of the flowers falls from the bamboo beam above Karl's head and lands on the floor with a small bounce. Several people exclaim "Ah!"]
KARL: See, and then it comes down. [group laughs]

LOUISE: Then you have a hangover.

KARL: From what?

LOUISE: From too much entertainment?

KARL: Of whom? Entertainment is the absence of one who gets entertained or not entertained. Then there's only entertainment and there is no hangover. But as you see it as a personal entertainment, there is always a hangover afterward, because you make a difference between entertainment and something else.

But if there is nothing but entertainment, there is no one who is entertained anymore. There is no hangover from that. Only when there is a polarity of entertainment and non-entertainment, happiness and unhappiness, then you get a hangover of bliss, of nectar, of entertainment, of divine, blissful—

LOUISE: Infinite entertainment!

KARL: Okay. But maybe there's not even entertainment.

LOUISE: Oh!

[Suddenly, from the beam above Karl's head, the second flower falls to the floor. The group explodes with laughter.]

KARL: So I'm getting out of the frame again—by doing nothing. They just drop by themselves.

FRANCESCO: [picking up flower and offering it to Karl] Want this?

KARL: No, it looks better on you.

FRANCESCO: Thank you. Tomorrow I change *gurus*.

KARL: Tomorrow you, change *gurus*? Okay.

FRANCESCO: Okay? One second! Now it's "okay," before you told me "no," why?

KARL: You think you would get that from me?

FRANCESCO: I know. I'm joking.

KARL: That would be something. "Please, stay!" So maybe it's not even entertainment. [covers his head] Something has to drop now? [group laughs]

MONIKA: The roof!

JAMES: Would you say Karl has to go?

KARL: No. How can something go that was never there? First find something that is there, then we can talk about something that has to go.

JAMES: That's a good answer. [group laughs] I think that probably for some of us, myself included, I still think of there being a "Karl."

KARL: Yeah, have fun with Karl, as this [points to himself] has fun with Karl too.

JAMES: Another good answer.

KARL: It's all "fan-tastic." All "fan-tasy." Everything is "fun-tasy." Everything is "fun-tastic," and everything is fun.

Sofia, something to add to that? [to the rest of the group] Sofia now wants to urgently take peyote and really fly away. [Sofia laughs] "Once and for all, I want to break out of the bondage of—"

THERESE: Entertainment! [group laughs] This morning I was thinking how I have to go to another teacher, and then I was already missing the fun here. I don't want to sit in silence.

KARL: You can never sit in silence anyway! What an idea, that someone would be left in silence. "I'm sitting in silence."

BERTA: Yeah, but that was also Ramana's teaching.

KARL: But not sitting in silence.

BERTA: He was silent.

KARL: No, no, he was not silent. There was silence, but there was no one who was silent. That's the difference. As what you are is silence too, there is no difference. And the noise, the movement, or whatever, cannot disturb the silence, that's all. He was always aware of the silence, but there was no one aware. There was simply the silence aware of itself.

BERTA: I think that was what delighted me so much with Papaji.

KARL: I have no idea.

BERTA: Because he also was what you said but cannot say. It is like he also was in silence.

KARL: But there was no one in silence.

BERTA: That's what I mean; I cannot say it like you.

KARL: Forget Papaji, the form, the name, whatever. There was never any Papaji. Silence will be there, with or without that name of Papaji or whatever master or anything. Silence is what is existence itself. It doesn't need any name of Papaji or Ramana or anything, even Arunachala.

BERTA: If you never heard about it, it's great to have a man like Papaji with whom you sit in silence, and then you become aware of That which you are already.

KARL: No, he may show you that *you* will never sit in silence. It will not be *your* silence—that he can show you. But you can never sit with anyone in silence. No one can give you the silence that you are, not even Papaji or Ramana or any form. He can point to that he is no different from what you are, that silence is your nature, your very nature. There's nothing to come, nothing to go for it, and he cannot bring it to you, and he cannot give it to you. There is nothing to give, nothing to teach, nothing to get, from "whatever," not even from him.

I tell you again, if you really respect Papaji, let him die as a figure, as a name. Be what is Papaji, forget him totally and don't make him into an icon, he asks you this, now.

KRISTOPH: If you meet Buddha, kill him.

KARL: If you really have respect for That which you call your teacher, let him die in front of you, because he wants you to let him die, so that you die with him, at this very instant, into That which is silence, where there is no Papaji, no you, no nothing else anymore—where there is pure silence, That which is Self, without any second.

KAATJE: So we just have to relax and let go.

KARL: You can never relax! You cannot get more relaxed than you already are. You are relaxation itself. What an idea, that you can get more relaxed or a person can ever be relaxed enough that it can go to the silence. Never, ever can any form reach the silence. What an idea that you can relax! [pause] Nothing to hope for.

And the new relaxation, what will it bring to you? What is new, gets old and can go again. Forget it. That which is your nature is here, now, absolutely relaxed. And the new relaxation is simply like an idea, a fantasy, of one who is himself a fantasy.

Blowing Away Belief Systems

PETE: Will you talk about the difference between the "I" and the "I am"? I'm confusing these two. You were saying the "I am" is formless and the "I am so-and-so" is form—

KARL: Yeah, and what is the pure "I" is formlessness. This is the Source of form and non-form, which is awareness. There is not even the idea of "non-form." There is no second in awareness. There is not even space. The "I am" is already space-like, formless consciousness. And out of that space, or emptiness, comes form. "In-form-ation." Both come together at once, as polarity, form and non-form, as one. Both come together out of what is awareness.

PETE: So the "I am" is potential form?

KARL: No, even the "I am" already is form-like. Even the non-form is a kind of form. They both come together. There is no form without non-form. There is no emptiness without fullness. Both come together at once out of what is the Father, the awareness.

In Christianity, you might say the Father [holds up thumb] is awareness as Source, and then the "I am" [thumb and index finger] is the Holy Spirit, and out of the Holy Spirit there comes information as "I am so-and-so" [thumb, index, and middle fingers]. So the formless "in-forms" itself into "in-form-ation." Both come together as the "in-form-ation," of manifestation, as form and formless. Both come out of the Father, out of what is awareness. So Father [thumb], Holy Spirit [thumb and index finger], Son, or world [thumb, index, and middle fingers] is like another trinity.

But That [fist] is what you are. So even with awareness, you are That which is awareness. Then "I am"-ness comes, and you are That which is "I am"-ness. And then comes "I am so"-ness, or the world, and you are That which is the world. And you are here, now, That which is Heart itself, as awareness, as "I am"-ness, and "I am so"-ness [fingers up—one, two, three— then back into fist, in quick succession again and again].

And there is silence in all this. Because silence is all there is. Nothing happens in That. Nothing comes or goes in That which you are.

THERESE: [showing fingers and then drawing them back into fist] But from there, it goes to there—something happened.

KARL: Nothing happened. This awakening of the awareness is infinite. It never started. As this is [fist], these are there too [thumb and fingers]. There's no waking up from this to that [finger to finger]. You cannot wake up, because it never happened.

There is a totality as Heart and the manifestation. It never comes and never goes. As infinite as is That which is Heart, is That which is manifestation. There is no coming and going in anything. It never wakes up to anything. Awareness is as infinite as That which is awareness, and "I am"-ness is as infinite as That which is "I-am-ness," and "I am the world" is as infinite as That which is the world. There is no coming and going in anything.

So there never is any waking up. You cannot put some time into something where there is no time. There is never any such thing as time, something creating, something created, because nothing ever is created. Whatever is, is. There was never any point of the big bang. Maybe there's a Big Ben in London but not a big bang in existence. Hope that it's clear! [group laughs]

But that alone is peace, this absolute, immense peace of That which is Heart, never coming, never going. Realization is no different from That which is Heart, as everything that is, is Heart, or Self. That is as solid as solid can be. Never changing, never coming, never going. This moment is as infinite as That which is Heart, because the essence of this moment here, now, is That which is Heart.

JAMES: Those three states, they exist simultaneously? They exist simultaneously and don't exist simultaneously?

KARL: They are, but they are not.

JAMES: And there is no one in any of those three states?

KARL: No, you are That which is Self in any circumstance, but yourself, you don't have any circumstance. You're never in any circumstance. All the circumstances are your infinite realization, but there is no one who is in any circumstance.

That is what is meant by *If You Meet the Buddha On the Road, Kill Him*, because Buddha cannot walk the earth. It's never some form or name or anything. It's a nice book title. It helps you see what your nature is, That which is Buddha himself, Buddha nature, can never incarnate into anything. It's never in any circumstance or walking the world or whatever. It's never a part of anything, because it cannot be divided from something to another thing. So it is never in any place, but there is no place without it.

JAMES: Which is why there is no one that gets enlightened?

KARL: No, never was, never will be. Again, when Ramana was asked about his realization, he said that the Self is ever-realized and Ramana is no different from the Self, so That which is Ramana is as ever-realized as That which is the Self. There is no question. There is no new realization of any kind. So you realize that you are realized. But this is nothing new. There is no one who is realized more than another one.

Come in, then you can look out. Have a seat. Have a sip? [drinks from his bottle of juice] Thank you.

FRANCESCO: I love you. [sound of water trickling is heard] Oh, very quickly you— [group laughs]

KARL: So, very quickly it goes! Is there some question about this, about personal entertainment?

KRISTOPH: At some point the personal story has to end. Isn't it like that? How can you say there's no personal story?

KARL: Nothing has to end. You may say at the end, in what you would call "end," you see there was no beginning.

KRISTOPH: Okay. You see it from the point of the Absolute, but there's also the personal view, no?

KARL: Yeah, I heard about it. [group laughs]

KRISTOPH: But if you remember your story—maybe you cannot remember anymore—you were also once in the state where you were identified with your form.

KARL: No, I was never in any state. That state of ignorance appeared in That which I am, but That which I am was never ignorant. So I was never in any ignorant state. That ignorant state, what you would call "a person," appeared in That which I am. And then it may disappear. But there is no need of it, because it was never there. That appearance of personal ignorance, whatever state, is there or not, but who cares about it? And who needs it to drop? And who needs what to end? I have no idea.

KRISTOPH: So its just fleeting— like a leaf in the wind. You get identified or not.

KARL: Yeah, it's a "be-leaf" system. It's a leaf in the wind, because it's a "belief" system. [group laughs] "Be-leaf" it or not!

As long as you are in a belief system, you are like a leaf in the wind. And then, "Oh, existence is blowing me! Maybe where I don't want to go. Maybe blowing me away." So you are blowing in the wind.

And then you come to this point, "Oh, I am the wind. I am consciousness. I am the all-creator." From one "be-leaf" system, you've gone to another "be-leaf" system, of being the creator of the leaf and the belief system. Then you think, "Oh, maybe this place is a better place for me to land. I am not a leaf anymore, I am the wind who blows the leaf." It's a big blow system, a blow job. [group laughs]

Yeah, because you're still quite dependent. It's a dependency. First you are dependent on the wind that blows you, then you are the blower, but you are still depending on blowing the leaf, because you cannot do otherwise. You have to create. You have to blow because you are the wind. The function of the wind is to blow, the function of the leaf is to be blown—blown away.

KRISTOPH: But in reality, you are both?

KARL: You are neither one. You are neither the wind nor the leaf.

KRISTOPH: You are that one who sees that? You are the one in whom this is happening?

KARL: No. You are That which is that. But there is no one who sees it. Even the one who sees it is part of the belief system. Even the relative seer, that perceiver or experiencer, is part of the absolute experience. So I am not whatever you call the "experiencer."

You may call it, as Ramana did, "the absolute dreamer," and the relative dreamer, as an experiencer, is part of the dream, the absolute dream or realization, but That which is the real, That which is the Self, is never a part of the dream. So there is neither the subject nor the object nor whatever you name or frame it. All that is dream-like in it, or no different from what is the dreamer, but it is not That which is Self.

A truth you can talk about is not the truth. The truth you can frame by any name, even "the witness," whatever you call it, cannot be That. The Taoist would say, "The Tao you can talk about is not the Tao. But there is nothing but the Tao." So you have to become the paradox, as you are That already.

KRISTOPH: So even if I wanted to find a name for it, that's a problem.

KARL: It's fine. That's what we are sitting here for. You bring something up, and I *klopp* (beat) it. Then it's *kloppt* (beaten, broken).

But that's the whole thing. You want to imagine yourself, and by imagining yourself, you want to frame yourself, maybe, because you want to know yourself. Then you are in the imagining, so you become one who is imagining himself, wanting to know himself. So you become consciousness meditating about what you are. You are in the seeking, the Self-inquiry business of consciousness always looking for That which is consciousness.

And one moment or one split second, consciousness becomes totally aware that That which is consciousness cannot be in any frame. Then it's full stop. And then in that full stop, that split second, it simply is That which is Self having absolutely no idea of even existence or non-existence. It's a total absence of any absence or presence.

That's the life experience of Ramana, when everything drops whatever can drop as an idea or belief system, of being a body, being spirit, whatever comes up, everything leaves you—every belief system is seen as only a belief system, a concept, but you are in spite of it. That which is Absolute, in spite of any belief system or even awareness—That you are. That is life itself.

But this is not an experience; this is an absolute non-event. This is an absolute non-happening, as whatever can happen, you can drop as an experience. Even the experiencer gets dropped in That. What is left is home itself. But no one is at home anymore.

TOMAS: And in which sense is that now different from any other belief system? Isn't that also a belief system?

KARL: That's another belief system. It has to go, too.

TOMAS: So there is no qualitative difference there?

KARL: This is a pointer to the quality you cannot frame. So even the frame cannot fit That. You cannot frame it.

TOMAS: Even the pointer is a belief?

KARL: The pointer is a pointer. You can make it a belief system, if you like, if you make it *my* belief system and say, "by the pointer I will become something," then it becomes a belief system. If you take it purely as a pointer, then there is no belief system because this pointer is now, not in any time-frame.

TOMAS: The pointer doesn't point to a belief system?

KARL: No.

TOMAS: So there is something different from a belief system?

KARL: There is something different. That which is a belief system, you cannot believe in. You have to be the belief system itself.

TOMAS: As you are all beliefs systems anyhow.

KARL: Whatever you believe, you are.

TOMAS: So it makes no difference.

KARL: It makes no difference. Only that you may totally see, by getting the pointer, that whatever difference may be there, it makes no difference. Whatever comes and goes will never make any difference for what you are. It never made, and it will never make any difference.

So all the differences, and all the different flavors and shapes of existence, and states of coming and going, are there, wonderful, unique. Every moment is as unique as can be. Every snowflake is as unique as you can get it. There are no snowflakes the same as any other. There is only the Self in a unique expression, at any moment. It's fantastic. So enjoy yourself.
TOMAS: Thank you.
KARL: There is no other Self that will enjoy you.

Not Finding the Sufferer

SOFIA: [quietly] I am just, uh, realizing that the mind cannot cope anymore with all of this that is going on.
KARL: Yeah, that's what I'm here for.
SOFIA: Sort of—I don't understand—No. No, not today. Just—
FRANCESCO: For me, it's normal.
KARL: For him, it's normal.
SOFIA: Full, full—I don't know.
KARL: In German we say, it's like a universal—[asks the group] What is a universal answer? *Was ist eine universale Lösung?* Yeah, its a solution, a universal solution. The mind gets into a universal solution from the pointer to the absolute silence, and it becomes a total solution, an absolute solution.
GEORG: Absolution.
KARL: Absolution! You're in the church here, now. Every morning you go to church, whether you like it or not. [group laughs]
　　But I don't sell the letters, the absolution letters. In the Middle Ages it was well-known that the Church sold letters for the sins you had not even done yet, the sins you would do the next day or next week. It was the best and biggest business the Church ever had. Most of the churches in Europe were built by those letters. It was a thriving business, to create a sinner, and then to give him absolution.
MONIKA: In advance!
KARL: In advance, even, until you die—but it's very expensive. [group laughs]

KLARA: But this is also a game of the Self.

KARL: Yeah, it's fun, isn't it? The Self gets paid by the Self. It's a joke anyway. But if you don't laugh about the joke, no one else will laugh about the joke you are. [group laughs]

THERESE: It's easy to laugh about the joke everyone is—except mine.

KARL: Oh, we can help you!

THERESE: [laughing] That's why I come.

KARL: You need a good mirror to laugh?

MONIKA: Such a happy failure!

KARL: Every morning, "Thérèse!" [group laughs] Your name? I always forget your name.

MRS. ANGELINA: I have no name.

[The group reacts with a big "awwww!"]

KARL: They call her "a nobody." Oh, it's a big name—No Name. Well, we found the No Name.

MRS. ANGELINA: Indian people call me "Auntie."

KARL: Italian Auntie. Auntie is good. "I'm Auntie—I'm not pro, I'm anti. I'm against everything. I'm anti!" [group laughs]

MRS. ANGELINA: Anti-work, anti-meditation, anti-realization, anti-master—

KARL: You're the Anti-Christ! [group laughs] We found the devil! Coming from Italy. Diavolo. Oh, so your name is Diavolo.

MRS. ANGELINA: Yes.

KARL: Ah, now we see. The Anti-Christ.

MRS. ANGELINA: [quietly] Anti-*crisi* (crisis; epileptic seizure).

KARL: The Anti-Crisis?

MRS. ANGELINA: [very seriously] I don't want any more crisis [seizures], any more suffering.

KARL: [with mock sympathy] Aw!

MRS. ANGELINA: I am here for peace, for not suffering anymore.

KARL: But as you don't want to suffer, you suffer.

MRS. ANGELINA: I know, but I am very—

KARL: Consistent, and stubborn.

MRS. ANGELINA: Yeah, yeah.

KARL: You always think, "I have a nail and I have a hammer; I have to do something with them. Otherwise, I wouldn't have them. I have a mind; I have to do something with it. Otherwise, I wouldn't have it. It has to be used. The system doesn't give anything for nothing. If there is a possibility of suffering, I have to do it. Otherwise, there would be no possibility." Yeah? Hallelujah. You are a good dummy. They call it "crash test dummies for existence." [group laughs]

FRANCESCO: It's a test. [explains to Mrs. Angelina in Italian]

KARL: Test dummy. It tests if the car is stable enough, or if the safety belt is working. Or enlightenment—is this way or that way good enough? [group laughs]

GEORG: So is every suffering actually optional, or is there a physical component to suffering, and you only create a belief system to deny and get out of this?

KARL: No, suffering starts with the first idea that there's an individual "me," your "I" is already a psychic problem, a crisis, so with that, suffering starts. Whatever you do out of that manages the existential crisis of that, even to exist. Because it began as an existential crisis, whatever you do afterwards try's to manage the suffering, because by taking the image of existence as what you are, giving some reality to experiences, even to the first notion of awareness—you are in separation.

There is me and myself, in a very subtle way. There is Heart and the idea of "Self" as awareness, as a notion of existence. And out of the notion of existence, taking that as real, you fall in love with what you are—and then you start managing the crisis of existence.

So suffering starts at the moment you take awareness, or whatever image, as "I," as real. That's the moment you fall in love with the second self, you fall in love with the image, even of awareness. You're in the potential of suffering and the potential will always show itself.

With the beginning of taking whatever as Self, even the idea of "Self," the "I" starts, the "I"-thought is there, and out of the potential "I"-thought, the Source of "I am" and the experiencer starts. Whatever is an experiencer is, in a way, suffering, because there is separation. In whatever you find yourself, in whatever way, whatever image you take as yourself, whatever form or name you give yourself, it is suffering, because you step out of the Absolute you are.

GEORG: Yeah, I think I understand that, but I'm trying to apply it to practical matters. If I get hit by a truck, let's say, I'm in physical pain and—

KARL: That's not suffering, that's pain. Suffering starts if you call it, "*my* pain.*" If you make it minute by minute *my* pain, "I have a history of pain," and "the history of pain comes by me, who has a history of pain," then it becomes suffering.

Without the ownership idea that it is *your* pain, there is simply a vibration of energy, what you would call "pain," of some body having pain. And without the idea of "*my* body," without the ownership idea of any kind, or without the experiencer taken as real, there is no suffering. There is simply one experience of That which is existence.

There's an absolute acceptance of That because there is no way out of it. You see the experience of pain as unavoidable, as it is what you are, and it simply shows one aspect of your infinite nature. Only if you take the body as a separate individual body, as *my* body, then whatever comes to this body is suffering.

From birth, the first mistake, taking the "steak" as real, you become a sufferer. First you seek the breast of your mother to become satisfied in your stomach, but even then there is no "me," there is no ownership. It only starts at three years, when you say "my body," because your mother told you that it's *your* body, it's *your* toy, and it's *you* who did it, so take care!

The caretaking starts at three years; before that there is no caretaking. There is an experience of being hungry and then looking for milk to get a normal working energy. Action-reaction. But at three years old conditioning begins. It's finished, and then the "me" is there, completely developed as ownership—*my* body, *my* individual existence, then suffering is really established.

KRISTOPH: One needs the individuality to function, or what?

KARL: Oh, I'm not saying there is something wrong with it. It's simply for you to see the functioning of what consciousness is, coming out non-identification into identification. Again, I want to point out, it's unavoidable that consciousness does this. This is a functioning of consciousness—stepping out of the formless into form, "in-form-ation," and identifying with that.

Still, there is something prior to consciousness, wherein all this happens, which was never touched by that, never involved in anything, which is perception itself, you may say. That which is the absolute dreamer was never a part of any dream that identifies itself with consciousness.

It's not you, but you're taking the awareness—the second self—as what you are. You're falling in love with it; you're glued to it. And the only solution is the heartbreaking thing, because heartbreaking means you drop out of self-love. By accident, you love some image, "whatever," even light, you take the light as an image of what you are, as a second one, and you fall in love with yourself, and out of that love all the rest comes. The love then becomes love and hate, the polarity and all the suffering.

The source of suffering falls in love with what you are not, an image of yourself—as even the first image of awareness, of light—and out of that first "I," all the rest comes. So by seeing awareness is there because you are, as you are That which is awareness, then even awareness cannot touch you. Everything is because of you, but you have no cause.

Then who cares about what comes after the first awareness as "I am"? All that is a dream-like realization, and it cannot touch what you are. So as you are never born, That which is not born cannot suffer from something that is objective experience. That's all.

So you're the total "split second." For That which you are, nothing ever happened at all. There is no birth, no death. Everything comes as belief systems, but only That which you are is life itself. So whatever you can experience is dead, is empty. And That which is an absolute experience of life itself, you can never experience. You simply are the unimaginable, unexperienceable Self. Whatever comes out of That is imagination coming and going, but there is no caretaking. Because whatever you can imagine is simply an imagination.

This simply points to the absolute unborn you are, which is never in any suffering system. But the first moment you step out of that, by taking any idea or belief system as real, the suffering starts. For you, it's unacceptable that there is a second, because you step out of that absolute peace, out of the freedom from a second, into the idea of "a second," and then there is war. Even if you call it "love," that love is war. The defense system starts, the conserving of whatever is there then, as you make it an individual existence, a separate being.

Even this idea becomes so real, because whatever you give your attention to is reality. Whatever you take as real is real. So at the moment that you take separation as real, it is as real as it can get. Only when That which is awareness turns to That which is awareness, it's like a mirror that totally mirrors That which is prior to it. They call it "the inner sun rising," but it has no cause, it comes and goes, it's not by any effort, not by any doing or not doing in front of it. So in spite of all your effort, you are, but you cannot avoid any effort. This is a paradox you cannot solve.

That helplessness—to see that as paradise—that's what I'm sitting here for. I'm pointing to That which you are, the helplessness, as there is no second.

Whatever you like to control, you are controlled by. Whatever you see, whatever you experience, is no different from what you are. By trying to control what you see—and thinking that by controlling it you are getting out of it—what an idea! So whatever you like to control puts you in that frame, and you get imprisoned by the idea or belief system, whatever you do. Whatever definition you start with is imprisonment.

Only the absolute absence of any idea of what you are and what you are not, and even the absence of that, is That which you are. That is silence and That is peace—immense peace which you cannot experience, because you are That. That is why it is called "the nakedness of existence."

MR. RAO: Is it what you call "the natural state"?

KARL: You can say it's the statelessness that is your natural state, That which has not, and never will have, any state. All the states are from the absolute Source, but That which is the absolute Source has no source. So it's a statelessness wherein all the other states and ideas and images appear.

There is no state without That, but itself has no state. You may say there is no place for it, but no place is without it. It is always the absolute essence of existence, never the form or non-form, or whatever name or frame or belief system you give it.

I Am That means "I am that—question mark." Absolute question mark. That absolute mystery of what you cannot frame, and as much as you try, you cannot put it into any system. By not finding what you are, whatever you found, in whatever experience, drops. By not finding the absolute experiencer, as the relative experiencer which rises in the morning and is already part of the experience, you cannot be the experience of the experiencer. Absolute experience has to be prior to that. That's all.

Always prior, prior, prior. It's a pointer, but simply go to That which is prior, what they call "the total abstract," "the total substratum." It's a concept, but a concept that you cannot be a concept. In German, they call it "*kotzept*" (vomit; play on *Konzept*). So it is an outbreak of all ideas at once. It's even the outbreak, the vomiting out, of any idea that you even exist. It's an absolute diarrhea of concepts. [group laughs]

MRS. ANGELINA: [with deep anguish in her voice] But Karl, when strong pain comes—

KARL: You cry.

MRS. ANGELINA: What can I do?

KARL: Cry.

MRS. ANGELINA: I have to make it something.

KARL: What?

MRS. ANGELINA: I don't know. Karl, I ask you because you can answer maybe.

KARL: Well, I answer you—cry. What to do?

MRS. ANGELINA: [crying pleadingly] But you have to make it something when you have this big suffering.

KARL: Whatever you do, you feed it. Whatever you want to avoid, you feed by avoiding it. You cannot avoid the avoidance.

MRS. ANGELINA: I cannot?

KARL: [sternly] You cannot avoid the avoidance. You cannot avoid the pain.

MRS. ANGELINA: [weeping] I cannot?

KARL: No!

MRS. ANGELINA: It's not possible?

KARL: But that is the "no way out," and that's the only way out of that pain.

MRS. ANGELINA: But I want to have the suffering stop!

KARL: There is no sufferer. Simply try to find the sufferer. Full stop. And I promise you, you will never find that bastard!

MRS. ANGELINA: I will never find—

KARL: You will never find the bastard of suffering. As you cannot find the sufferer, there never was any suffering.

MRS. ANGELINA: [quietly] You sure?

KARL: But if you try to stop the suffering, you feed the sufferer.

MRS. ANGELINA: Because I see my suffering increasing.

KARL: Yeah, it's a crisis. Always increasing. As much as you want to avoid it, it is increasing. And I'm asking you, as Ramana would ask you, to find the bloody sufferer.

The ultimate medicine to whatever is suffering is trying to find the sufferer, and by not finding the sufferer, there was never anyone that suffered.

It's part of history. And if you could not find that ownership of history, of "me" being in any history, what is the history of suffering? A joke. An idea suffered by another idea! [sarcastically] Oh my goodness, I'm really full of compassion for the idea who is suffering about another idea!

[Seriously] I absolutely don't want the pain to stop for you. Absolutely not. As every pain, whatever aspect of existence, is there to be experienced by the absolute experiencer you are. There is no avoidance. You cannot escape what you are. And every pain is a Self-experience of your infinite nature. There's nothing to get away from. You cannot escape what you are. Never, ever!

[Suddenly, Mrs. Angelina smiles through her tears.]

KARL: Ah!

MRS. ANGELINA: I like this!

[The group, which had been utterly silent witnessing Mrs. Angelina suffering, now erupts in loud laughter.]

KARL: As you feel— That is paradise!

[The group is delighted and amazed. People are clapping and sighing with relief.]

MRS. ANGELINA: Because everyday I try to feel better, and I don't feel it.

KARL: You feel worse. That's the thing of it—by trying to feel better, for sure you feel worse.

MRS. ANGELINA: And people tell me, "Take this pill, or take this, or take that," and every day it's worse. [with lightness in her voice] But now, I don't know, something—

FRANCESCO: For now, it's okay.

KARL: Here's the devil again. He just said, "Don't worry; it will come again." [group laughs] He knows himself. "Mea culpa!"

This ultimate medicine is the only pointer I can give you. The ultimate medicine—find the sufferer, or find the one who could be sick. And by not finding one who could be sick, because That which you are cannot be found in any circumstance, this is the absolute end of suffering. The end of the sufferer is the end of suffering, because by not finding the sufferer, there was never any suffering. That's all. It's not even ending anything, because there was never anything to end. So enjoy yourself.

MRS. ANGELINA: Karl, you see, sometimes I lose consciousness. I have epileptic seizures.

KARL: Yeah, I like it.

MRS. ANGELINA: And when the epileptic crisis arrives, I feel, "O my God, all is finished!"

KARL: You will be finished.

MRS. ANGELINA: It's very strange because I don't have any control over my body.

KARL: But that is great. This is a total pointer of grace to your helplessness. Enjoy it! There's nothing that can harm you. There's nothing to lose by losing that which is being conscious, losing control of whatever kind. There's nothing better than losing the bloody controller. Then grace comes and hellfire starts. By giving you an epileptic experience of pure electricity, electricity from the whole universe going through your little body—ohhhhah-hhh! That's grace! You get shocked out.

MRS. ANGELINA: It's grace? You tell me it's grace?

KARL: Yeah, I tell you.

MRS. ANGELINA: Oh, I am happy! [group laughs]

KARL: Believe it or not, this electricity is what you are, is consciousness. Pure electricity. All the forms, everything, is electric, so when the armor breaks and the electricity goes through you, it's like an epileptic seizure, because you cannot keep alive the individual armor around you, as a body-mind organism.

I had so many dreams, reality dreams, in the seventies, where I went to different teachers. They all came and said, "Blah, blah, blah," and in the very end there was always an electric shock that touched my elbow. Boom! That was like epilepsy, as I know it fully. Then you are totally shocked for hours, in that electricity, pure "bvbvbvvvvv," it alway gives you what you cannot take. Yeah, sounds good. Ah, I'm very happy for you.

MRS. ANGELINA: Thank you very much.

KARL: No, this is actually only so you get used to what you are, in a way, by becoming That which is energy. You see that whatever high electric voltage, whatever goes through you, cannot touch you, as you are That already. Whatever can be touched is an experience, but it cannot touch you as That which is perception. That perception here, now, is no different from that perception in your childhood, or as a baby, or even before. It was never touched by anything. Not even the high electricity can touch That. So you're not shocked by this shock.

FRANCESCO: Just have another coffee.
KARL: Just have another coffee, yeah. [tenderly] Francesco!

No Avoiding the Void

LOUISE: But with that electricity, don't you have to be plugged in? Like, you know, this *Tauchsieder* (immersion heater) thing? You plug it in and then it boils the water.
KARL: But you're never plugged out. How can you plug out of existence?
LOUISE: But nothing comes out if you don't plug it in.
KARL: There is no plug! How can you plug in, when there is no plug?
LOUISE: Well, let's say I'm the *Tauchsieder*.
KARL: You're the *Tauchsieder*? Oh my goodness.
LOUISE: I mean, just talking about that electricity. Dreaming about that thing. Electricity itself is nothing.
KARL: What nothing?
LOUISE: You have to plug in and use it.
KARL: It's nothing? Put your finger into the plug and you will see what electricity is. Nothing?
LOUISE: Well, there's something at the end.
KARL: At the end?
LOUISE: There's first water, and then there is electricity.
KARL: Did you see the film *Matrix*? You saw that they were using bodies of humans as batteries, giving electricity to the whole system. So you already are electricity; you don't have to plug into it.
LOUISE: Okay.
KARL: So what, okay? Where is the *Tauchsieder* now?
LOUISE: I just got stuck.
KARL: You got stuck in the *Tauchsieder*, yeah.
LOUISE: [laughing] I started boiling!
KARL: You are boiling. Let's see where the *Siedepunkt* (boiling point) is reached. Steams up.
JAMES: In Buddhism, there is a kind of ongoing discussion about what en-

lightenment is. In one school, they point to a refining of awareness to the point where one maintains the experience of awareness.

KARL: In German they call it, "*die Scheidewand der Wahrnehmung.*" Sounds good. What's that in English?

MONIKA: The wall of perception.

KARL: No, the border, the border of perception. Like the borderline. In the Bible, they would say "the youngest day." Stay on the youngest day, before time, before any idea of time and non-time—be on the border, the judgment border, before judgment.

So it's judgment day. The youngest day before any judging, any time or non-time, before any concept happened. Stay in That which is prior, simply prior, to what wakes up in the morning, not going with the body waking up and its experiences. That is what is meant in Buddhism, no?

JAMES: Well, the other school says that—in a sense, what I'm hearing from you—it's prior to awareness.

KARL: They call it "awareness of awareness," "emptiness of emptiness." They always put two things on it. And for me, it's the same. That which is awareness, is the awareness of awareness, it's like the fullness of fullness, the *I am*-ness of "I am"-ness. It's always the pointer to the absolute Heart of existence. So there is no difference.

JAMES: So from that you come into this thing you talked about, this non-event and the non-experience. Can you talk a bit more about that?

KARL: By the way. Not on the way—by the way. In spite of the way. In spite of what are fleeting experiences in front of who you are. This "in spite" is the "split second," and then there is nothing to add. In spite of all the history, in spite of all that ever happened to what is in front of you, to the body-mind, or whatever, as an experience you can experience—in spite of all that, you are. But That which you are, you absolutely don't know.

JAMES: But still, this is tricky.

KARL: Tricky?

JAMES: There was a time when the non-event, or non-experience, happened.

KARL: You may say, for the body-mind organism, there is still time, because without time, without separation, there would be no form or non-form. But there was not a time. It is here, now. This body needs time. This imagined object needs a subject in a circumstance, simply to be experienced. So you need the imaginable time, frames, bodies and objects, so that experiences can happen.

JAMES: So the non-event, the non-experience—

KARL: Is here, now.

JAMES: All the time?

KARL: There is no time in it. Not even non-time. Time and non-time appear in That.

JAMES: So that's the reality of what Karl is, constantly?

KARL: No, this is the reality of That which doesn't know reality. And That doesn't want to know it, because there is nothing to know.

JAMES: The thing I was trying to get from you—which I haven't succeeded in getting yet [group laughs]—is—was it, a one-time event? I know there's no such thing as time, but time does seem to continue.

KARL: No, no. This—to be That to which nothing ever happens—was never different. In That, there is no coming and going. So it's here, now—or never.

JAMES: Yeah, but in that, in what you say—

KARL: No, its simply a pointer. It is never, never! That's a split second of being never-never. Not even ever. It's never-never. So what you are is never-never? Are you ever? No. You are never-never.

JAMES: That's why I asked the question yesterday. In the non-event, in the experience, does the world disappear?

KARL: It's not a non-experience. It's the experience that, what is an experiencer and whatever you can experience, you are not. It's an absolute experience of being absolutely independent of whatever you experience, even absolutely independent of the experiencer. It's an absolute experience of That which you may call "freedom," but having no idea of what is and what is not freedom. It's simply being That which can never be touched by the senses or by anything you can sense of objective life.

So you are as That which is ever in no sense. All the senses are there, but you are never in any sense—never was and never will be. And for That which was never in any sense, which was never born and may die, in that moment, the idea of "death" is dying. That's all. You see what you are is never-never. But this is nothing new or old; this is never-never. So that anything can be there—any concept, any belief system, any image—you have to be there first as That which is never-never. That which is never-never is the substratum that you cannot reduce anymore. At the moment of total reduction, you reduce yourself to the max. So, in the moment, you become emptiness and fullness together. As you are in the emptiness of ideas, the Heart is so empty in itself that only then can it contain the fullness of absolute existence. So you go back to the maximum reduction to become the maximum of absolute existence.

The other way is simply impossible. That is why the Buddhists often point to this emptiness, to go into the emptiness. To reach the absolute aspect, to become the oneness with everything [makes a big exhale], you cannot reach. But to get to the emptiness of Heart, there's a natural pull from inside. You just see the pull as what you are, and then you simply rest in that. And the void which is there, simply becomes a best friend—paradise.

So you don't want to avoid the void anymore. Maybe before you wanted to avoid the dying, or "whatever," because the void means dying, dying of objects. But if you see the void is what you are, by becoming aware of the void, the emptiness, then you simply rest in that—by the seeing that there is nothing to fear. That is what Jesus was saying—don't fear what you are. Because the absence, the absolute absence of any idea, you are, the absence of any idea is the void. That darkness of knowledge, you are.

You are not the light of anything, because that is called "Lucifer." Whatever will bring you light is Lucifer. Whoever brings you something, promises you some knowledge, even if it's what is consciousness or light, promising some knowledge that can add something to your nature—it's all a lie. It cannot add something to whatever is you. So the lie of light, the Lucifer light who tells you, "I can bring you something. I can help you. I can make you more happy than you are. I can bring bliss, whatever, heavenly bliss of the god tralala, divine," even the "divine love" idea—is the devil's idea.

All the imagined belief systems and enlightenment—even the idea of "enlightenment"—comes out of the devil. As if enlightenment can add something to your nature! What an idea? Always a joke! You are talking to yourself, and you're creating the devil imagination, and then it talks to you all the time, and it's promising something, but it never can keep the promise.

It will never deliver the treasure you are. You are That which is God itself. All the ornaments—whatever it says, even the promises—are still gold. They cannot touch you.

So don't believe yourself. You cannot even trust yourself. That's the beauty of it. There's always this image of yourself—"Trust me. I lead you. Trust me." Always talking. "Trust me. I can deliver." Hah! No. You cannot even trust yourself, as there is not even a Self to trust, even the idea of "Self" comes out of the same "whatever."

"Whew. Absolutely alone. No one to trust. No God, no Self. Whew!" But that's paradise, Godlessness, helplessness, the "one without a second," that's paradise. Not even knowing yourself, a total absence even of an idea of "Self" or "God" or anything, you are That which is.

FRANCESCO: Whatever! That's paradise.

KARL: Ah!

JAMES: Now you've got flowers. Next there will be candles and incense.

FRANCESCO: Tomorrow, that. No, the flowers were from her.

MONIKA: In spite of myself! [group laughs]

Dropping the Whole Existence

KARL: *Tauchsieder*, something?

LOUISE: I find it sometimes more difficult to be in the world, with what can't be known, the void you are speaking of, and so this body-mind functioning, anywhere, everywhere, nowhere, it appears sometimes one is not so much in it, or one can step out of it.

KARL: Who can step out of it?

LOUISE: I don't know.

KARL: Yeah, I don't know either! I don't see anyone in the world. I don't see anyone that can step out of it. What an idea that you can step out—of what?

LOUISE: Well, I do that.

KARL: So you are still in. You did not step out. Because of the stepping out, you are still in.

LOUISE: I know, and I find that sometimes harder.

KARL: What? Stepping out? Because the stepping out makes you in. You trick yourself.

LOUISE: When this woman walked in, you said, "Come in so you can look out."

KARL: Yeah. There is no difference.

LOUISE: So there it is. "Again and again, nothing to gain!" Well, what am I asking? I don't know. [laughs] I'm not asking anything. I just, you know, could also bring you roses and flowers, and I could just kiss your feet, or not, or throw tomatoes.

KARL: You don't dare. [group laughs]

LOUISE: Tomorrow I bring tomatoes.

KARL: I will never wash my feet again.

LOUISE: I do have a question, but I don't know how to ask it. Sometimes I find it hard.

KARL: What?

LOUISE: What? Yeah, really—what? What is hard?

A MAN: "I have to suffer! I have to suffer!"

LOUISE: You're not helping. [laughs] Bail me out!

KARL: I see the controller, and by controlling suffering, being in. Then controlling, getting out, and then still controlling. Controlling, controlling. Yeah. Enjoy your controlling.

LOUISE: But this is an old number now, when you tell me that.

KARL: Yeah, I tell you every day, "Enjoy your controlling."

MAN: Until you believe it.

LOUISE: Until I believe it!

KARL: Until you have gotten enough about controlling? No, you'll never get enough control.

LOUISE: How come?

KARL: It's part of the game.

LOUISE: But why me?

KARL: "Why me?" Take another "any-me." Take your enemy.

LOUISE: No, why do you tell me this? Is there nothing else?

KARL: Because I see the controller. By whatever you do, you control.

LOUISE: Any idea?

KARL: To step out of it? The moment you want to step out again you want to control. You cannot escape the controlling. There's no way out of controlling.

LOUISE: Ooooh. [group laughs]

KARL: Until the brain is—
LOUISE: Bursting.
KARL: Bursting.
LOUISE: To pieces.
THERESE: That's why she put the scarf on.
LOUISE: It's a bandage!
KARL: Bandit. She's the bandit now.
LOUISE: [laughing] Bandito!
KARL: But you feel it. You just feel the heat.
LOUISE: Yeah, I do.
KARL: This is like the controller, here [points to forehead], the third eye. And this is always controlling. Whatever it does, it controls. This is the devil, controlling.
THERESE: So the one who doesn't have pain there is no controlling? I don't have pain there.
KARL: She can simply not avoid the energy anymore, because there's too much energy. The life energy wakes up, and then the controller is really in trouble, because the resistance gives us a headache, a migraine.

So it doesn't work anymore, the controlling of "whatever," because this "energy hell" comes, the life energy that shows you your control. It's teaching you. "Oh, you are controlling; let's see what we can do about it." That brings on a headache. Then even she wants to control the headache or the energy, and then it becomes more of a headache. Like a self-running system, feeding itself. As I would know it, eh?

But it's actually not so bad. Because only by the hellfire, by the pain, by the "me-graine," the "me" is grained away by the life energy itself. The total awareness annihilates the idea of "controlling," because there will be a point when you see there was not any control in controlling, so even the control you cannot control. So what to say? Grace all the way.
THERESE: But Karl, when I hear about this migraine— I don't have migraines.
KARL: Oh, now you want to have migraine?
THERESE: Yes. [group laughs] It seems like it's a stage, it's a great step, you know, if you have migraines, lots of energy coming out.
KARL: I never say it's a great step; I just say it's a functioning. I just speak about the energy, how it's functioning. I don't say it has an advantage; I

never say that. I just say how it works. There's no advantage.

THERESE: There's no rule, because many people don't have migraine and they still have life energy. Life energy is still in movement, and not everybody has migraines.

KARL: No? But it may come.

THERESE: I sound like I'm saying, "Oh, I want a migraine."

BERTA: Oh, terrible—migraine.

KARL: Yeah, I tell you. If you look into that, there is a whole library in the Vatican, rooms full of stories about sages with an inner fire arising, and always with inner fire comes body fire, and then heart fire, and then migraines, body-aches, and whatever you can imagine. It all comes with it. It's very famous. I don't say it's an advantage. I simply say it happens like this. I don't say it's a necessity.

THERESE: I'm missing all the time, then—

KARL: You're missing everything! You're a happy failure! [group laughs]

THERESE: [laughing] On my death bed—

KARL: Now she's complaining again, "Oh, poor me. I have no migraines!" That's a perfect example of individual personality.

THERESE: I'm having migraine now. Stop. [group laughs]

MONIKA: She's happy!

KARL: It's in the Bible. If you ask for it, it will be given.

BERTA: Yeah, and if you never heard about it, it will not happen, so I don't talk about it anymore. [group laughs]

KARL: When it will happen, it will happen; if not, not. It simply means there is no disadvantage or advantage in anything. But if it happens like this, this is part of the entertainment, whether you like it or not. But again, there will be no advantage for whomever, because there is no one who could have an advantage by anything. Not even by the migraine. I know there are many people who then think, "Oh, I am now in the energy thing, with *kundalini* and migraines, and I am now mature and ripening."

MONIKA: At least something's happening.

SOFIA: But sometimes it doesn't lead anywhere.

KARL: It never will lead anywhere, not just sometimes. There is never anything; it never leads to anything.

SOFIA: But sometimes it's the "split second," and sometimes not.

KARL: The split second is never. I'm not talking about something that will come. The split second is here, now. If it wouldn't be here, now, it would be never. So there is nothing to come. That which cannot happen, will never happen. You'd better not wait for it, because it will never come.

That's the good news. It will never come. With or without a migraine, it will not come.

If it really would help existence to become That which is the Self, it would stop right now, because there was Buddha, there was Jesus, there was Ramana, there were so many sages. If it really would help—those experiences of "whatever" transformation, coming from identified consciousness into cosmic consciousness, all that energy happening, then back to it—if it really would help, this would simply stop. It could not continue. For one Self, that would be the end. By whatever transformation or transmutation into something else, the whole existence would simply drop.

If you could control That which is existence itself, as That which is the Self, by whatever experience of heat or transformation, what kind of freedom would it be? So all this is part of the show, but it makes no difference. There will be Thérèse forever, Thérèse still waiting for a migraine. [group laughs]

THERESE: It's new now, a new migraine.

KARL: Then there could be one who gets this experience, the split second, blah, blah, blah, and then he goes, "Oh, what have I done before this split second?" And then it becomes a religion or a technique of Yoga. "Because I, by doing this and that, had this and that experience of my body, of heat, so it all has to be connected to my previous experiences." He even takes the experience of non-happening, as a personal experience. Then whatever was prior to it is taken as, "because of that, I came to this point."

But it is never because of any step before, That is. In all of the steps, it was already there, so it's nothing new. I'm always pointing only to That. Never because of any doing or not doing, in spite of the heat, in spite of the migraine, in spite of all the sensations and happenings and stories and histories, you are what you are, never because.

So forget it. It may happen or not, but who cares? It's not an advantage or disadvantage. It's simply a different body sensation in what you are.

And by seeing that, for what you are, there is never any such thing as an advantage in anything, the disadvantage drops too, and then you are what you are, in spite of whatever, never because of any body heat, or anything to drop. There is nothing to drop. This is part of the show. You may enjoy it, but it will not help you.

You Cannot *Not* Realize Yourself

BERTA: Utterly hopeless.

KARL: [laughing] Isn't it fun? Imagine there is hope! Hope is hell. The devil is always there, the devil who wants to pick something up and say, "Look, maybe this will help. If you do this, I promise you paradise."

BERTA: That's also why I'm sitting here, not only because you take this hope away, but because you have the ability to talk about That. Then if I don't hear this for a long time—when I meet you after three years, it feels like I have forgotton. I cannot get it out of books or tapes. Hopeless as you are, somewhere there's hope.

THERESE: Hopeful hopelessness.

KARL: Hopeful hopelessness! There is still hopeful hopelessness.

MONIKA: But there must be something. Someone, somewhere, must be getting something out of this, because really there's no logical reason to sit here. [group laughs]

KARL: Yeah, I'm a running advertisement. "Look at me. I should be the most frustrated man on earth, because I'm sitting here talking to shadows, and they cannot understand anything, and it's all irrelevant, it means nothing, nothing has to be helped. I should be totally frustrated."

MONIKA: Yeah, so are we. I mean, I am. [group laughs]

KARL: But I tell you, the helplessness, the total irrelevance, is paradise. Because this is freedom. Absolute freedom. There's nothing to get out of any circumstance. So it's absolutely irrelevant what I say or not say. But this is absolute freedom—in spite of what I say or don't say, I am what I am.

MONIKA: But in this association, of no expectation, no getting—

KARL: No, it's not "no expectation, no getting." I'm not talking about "no expectation."

MONIKA: Okay, expectation, but not getting.

KARL: There may be expectations, but who cares?

MONIKA: Some merit, or some thing is there.

KARL: Maybe not.

MONIKA: It makes no difference. But I don't even understand.

KARL: She thinks, "If that German can do it, I can do it too." But there is no one who has done it. I tell you this over and over again, I never reached anything, as I never left anything. I cannot reach that what I am, so I didn't reach anything. So for sure, from me, there is nothing to get.

FRANCESCO: True.

KARL: You cannot get anything out of emptiness.

MONIKA: Emptiness?

KARL: Maybe That is what you are, but you cannot get That, because by seeing that out of emptiness nothing comes, that you never left emptiness and you are That, you see emptiness cannot be given. You are the emptiness. This is the paradox I point to. You may see it, out of emptiness but nothing comes and nothing goes back into the emptiness.

You are the emptiness itself, which has nothing to reach, nothing to gain, by anything, as you have never left emptiness, you cannot gain it back. So the pointer is that you can get nothing from That which I am, as emptiness points to That which you are. So the nakedness talks to nakedness.

MONIKA: It's a pointer.

KARL: Sometimes they call it "the divine wedding," when you see the beloved is emptiness, and the lover is emptiness too, and in the emptiness, both disappear. But this is also a concept.

I'm always pointing to that "no way out." There is never anything that comes from what you are, and as you have never left whatever it is, there's no going back to it. But this "no way back to it," maybe that *is* a way back. Who knows? Simply by seeing that you never left, you are That which is already home. You never left home. There is no one at home. Never was anyone at home, as you are That which is home. All this is a pointer. Maybe on one point, pointing to That which you are totally, you will be pointed out.

MONIKA: And then I'm pointless.

KARL: Then you are the pointless point. You are not pointless; you are the pointless point.

MONIKA: But it has been pointless?

KARL: Before?

MONIKA: Before. [both laugh]

KARL: So you have pointing. Sometimes there is a nail and a hammer, hammering it in. "There is nothing to hammer! I'm hammering, but there's nothing to hammer. There's not even a hammer. "

TOMAS: I'm wondering about how somebody could take this split second personally. It doesn't make any sense.

KARL: It makes sense.

TOMAS: It makes sense?

KARL: Yeah, because it doesn't make sense. Everything is possible, as no one could ever experience this split second.

TOMAS: That's what I mean.

KARL: A person will always make it into an experience.

TOMAS: But the person cannot take something personally that he or she didn't experience.

KARL: I tell you, the person always takes everything personally even if there is nothing to take personally. What is here? Everyone is—there is nothing personal here, but you still take it personally. So even this split second—the experience of non-experience—you take personally, for sure. How can you not take it personally?

TOMAS: Well, for sure, it is not for sure.

KARL: Not for sure? Maybe. Maybe not.

TOMAS: So it's not sure?

KARL: But that's sure. [group laughs]

TOMAS: So even the split second is not a way out?

KARL: No.

TOMAS: Well, I'm waiting for it, whatever you say.

KARL: Yeah, you're *Waiting for Godot*, but Godot never comes. You cannot *not* wait. But you can see Godot never comes, so you wait, but without waiting. That is meditation.

When you meditate because you want a result of some knowledge of what you are, it's action with intention, which makes it personal. It's like the advantage idea. "I'm doing something and want to get something out of it, even the knowledge of myself."

But if you see that That which is what you are cannot be known in anything, and you still meditate, without expectation, then there is doing without doership, there is action, without intention. There is no one who is acting. So there is still action, but there is no active one or non-active one. As nothing can come out of it for what you are. So it unfolds itself by itself.

The infinite realization of what you are as Self-experience can never stop, as you cannot *not* experience what you are. So even the non-experience is an experience, as you cannot step out of That which you are, you cannot step out of the Self-experience. By Self-experiencing, you realize yourself, and you cannot *not* realize yourself.

Whatever aspect of life, whatever moment, is part of Self-realization and Self-experience. And this will never stop. There are all kinds of experiences—heat, sensations of what can happen with the body—whatever in this time frame of the dream of experiences, can happen. But even as they can happen, they are not real.

Finally, There Is No "Finally"

A Latino MAN: I have a question. It's sort of personal. Are you happy in your life? Do you have any suffering? And has your life changed after you have come to realize your true Self?

KARL: I'm sitting here. There are always changes. For the body, "whatever," everything is changing every moment, but not because of the split second. There is no cause and effect in That.

MAN: My question is—

KARL: If I'm more happy after that?

MAN: If you are just happy.

KARL: No. I have no idea of happiness.

MAN: Do you have an idea of suffering? Do you cry?

KARL: Crying? I cry often. When there is a sad movie, I cry. How can I not cry when there is a tear-jerker movie? [group laughs] Really. It's made by me. They call it "tear-jerker," and so I have to cry.

If you see, the compassion you cannot avoid, you are that. Whatever you see, you are. There is no difference between the experiencer, the experiencing, and what is experienced. Whatever sadness is there, you are. Whatever happiness is there, you are. Whatever you can bring up, you are.

How can you not be in compassion with what you are?

MAN: Let's take this on a large scale, for the whole planet, for humanity.

KARL: For humanity? Oh. First you have to find humanity, and then we can talk about it.

MAN: Anyway, there is what there is. Okay? Each week, every day, people give more pain to one another.

KARL: Since humanity has existed, there has been war, pain and suffering. You're right.

MAN: But it's getting more and more now.

KARL: No. Look at the Middle Ages, I tell you, there was enough pain and suffering. Maybe because there are more people now, you think there is more pain and suffering. So what's your question? What shall we do with humanity, or what? Don't fuck anymore, because then there will not be more pain, maybe, because there will be less people.

MONIKA: *Brahmacharya!*

KARL: No, if you ask me what to do with humanity, with all the people, I would tell everyone, "Don't fuck anymore," so there would be no people anymore, and then there's no suffering. Make a really radical cut.

Another MAN: Then you have a different kind of suffering!

KARL: You suffer for a while, until you die, because you don't have sex anymore, but you simply stop the population from growing. Stop popping, then there is no population. [group laughs]

Latino MAN: So you're saying, there will always be suffering and pain.

KARL: No, there was never any suffering and pain. That's the problem. You cannot stop something that was never there.

MAN: But you see the woman crying. She will cry tomorrow and the day after tomorrow.

KARL: Yeah, she will always cry; it's her nature. [group laughs]

MAN: What's the ultimate goal?

KARL: That there is no goal. That's the ultimate goal—that there is no goal. Finally, there is no "finally."

MAN: But the fact is still there—

KARL: What fact?

MAN: The fact—

KARL: Yeah, "fack-ing" around, it's still there.

MAN: We are not happy.

KARL: No? You can never find anyone who is happy. You're right. As there is no one who can be happy. You cannot find anyone. First find one at all; and then can we talk about happiness and unhappiness.
MAN: It depends on the definition of happiness—
KARL: Only by definition, you create an idea of one, that's all. If you simply stop defining, who is there? You have to define "humanity," so that there is humanity.
MAN: Buddha, Krishna, Rama, Ramana Maharshi, they say there have been few, very few people who really became enlightened.
KARL: No. All of them you just mentioned said there was never anyone who was enlightened. Buddha in the *Diamond Sutra* makes it totally clear. He said that there was never any Buddha walking the earth and never will be. So there will never be anyone enlightened. He said he'd preached for forty years and hadn't said one word to anyone. That's Buddha.

And that's what Ramana says—That which is Ramana is the Self, and the Self is ever-realized. What you may call "Ramana" will never realize the Self, as the Self is ever-realized.

So there has never been any realized person on earth, as there is never any person at all who can be realized. That which is any person is ever That which is Self and is ever-realized and doesn't need any more realization than it already has. The pot never will realize That which is a pot. So what is it about enlightenment? First find one who is unenlightened, then we can talk about enlightenment.
MAN: We are all unenlightened.
KARL: Who is here anyway? I'm not talking to ghosts! I don't see anyone here, as ghosts can never be enlightened or unenlightened. I see the Self here, now, as That which is. There is no one, any *one*, here who is enlightened or not enlightened. And I'm not talking to shadows. I'm not talking to ghosts who come and go. I'm talking to That which I am.
MAN: But—
KARL: But? Yeah, but, ahh, ahh, brings but.
MAN: You said that there is an armor through which we cannot penetrate toward realization.
KARL: No, no, I didn't say that. In spite of the armor, you are what is Self. Not because of some armor that drops. Then you didn't listen. I never said that realization will come by anything. I always said realization is your na-

ture and that you cannot add something to realization. So with or without
armor, you are what you are. Whatever circumstance you are in, the circumstance is because of you, but you are not because of the circumstance. So
in spite of the circumstance of armor or no armor, you are what you are.
So having an armor is part of the realization, and there is nothing right or
wrong in it.

MAN: So you might call some maniac or mass murderer—

MAN: So there is a sort of action, which is called "seeing"—

KARL: Yeah, and you see, maybe by action, there is nothing to gain. Again
and again, I tell you, there is nothing to gain.

MAN: There's nothing to change?

KARL: First show me something that is there at all. The whole scientific
world, since the beginning of scientific experiences, wants to prove that
there is matter. Until now—there's no proof. They cannot even say if there
is anything at all. They can only say, "Oh, there is quantum physics. There
is a wave or a particle, but we don't know what it is. It's always changing." So
now all the scientific people become Buddhists because they cannot find
out what God is. So they look into mysticism, they've all become mystics.

THERESE: So now they look for techniques to find what they already found.

KARL: Yeah, you are that. You are that! By you thinking you are alive, you
are creating six billion others, and by making them alive, you are killing
yourself. You are the mass murderer by saying there are six billion people.
You are the biggest mass murderer I know. Simply by thinking you're alive,
you're killing six billion.

MAN: I don't think so—

KARL: You create them! And by creating them, you kill them.

MAN: Then how to uncreate them?

KARL: You don't have to uncreate them; just stop creating. Be what you are,
and there is no one left.

MAN: And how to be what you are?

KARL: How? There is no "how."

MAN: You say, there is the emptiness of emptiness and stuff, but you don't
say, do this or do that. Why?

KARL: No. Because you cannot get more empty than you already are. Whatever you do avoids that. Whatever technique, or meditation, by Self-inquiry,
whatever you do, is like avoiding the void. And by seeing the futility of any

technique, maybe, by seeing that nothing can come by any technique, by any meditation, nothing can add something to what you are, you cannot find yourself in any circumstance. So by not finding yourself in any circumstance, by looking or seeking, it *may* stop. In the full stop, you see you never lost anything, and as you never lost anything, you cannot gain back something.

They didn't find anything by anything. By any electron microscope, nothing was found, because you always can split it again, less, less, less. Infinite less.

A WOMAN: Infinite parallel universes.

KARL: Whatever, but there is not even one you can find. So many parallel universes, but there is not one you can find.

Latino MAN: So Karl, you told me, stop creating murders?

KARL: Yeah. Stop creating murders by imagining that you are alive. You stop taking as real something that you imagine. You imagine you're alive, and this is a concept. When you stop taking imagination as reality, at the moment when you are not, when you have absolutely no idea if you exist or not, there are no others anymore. At the moment you take yourself as that imagination, as real, you create six billion others, so by your stopping—full stop—being That which is prior to any imagination, there is no you and no others anymore. But at the moment there is you, there are six billion others. So you create six billion others. So you are the mass murderer here, now.

MAN: And so you.

KARL: No, not me. You! Especially you. [group laughs] There is no general relation. Look only to yourself, there are no others anyway. I ask you, look at what you are, not at what anyone else is. It's only you that counts. There are no others anyway. So be totally shellfish in that. Shellfish? [group laughs]

Try to fish that fish you are. Become the fisherman who tries to fish the fish you are. And as you cannot fish the fish you are, you become the fisherman who cannot fish the fish the fisherman "ish"!

MAN: The thief cannot catch himself.

KARL: Yeah, but that's what you try to be. First you are a thief, and then you become a policeman by saying, "I know the thief has to go." The mind first becomes a thief who steals your attention, and then, by your not wanting to give it attention, it says, "Okay, now I'll become a 'no-mind.' I'll make sure there will be no mind anymore," says the mind, "so you will be not bothered anymore, so I don't steal your attention anymore."

So after being a thief who steals your attention, then it becomes the policemen who tells you, "I'll make sure now there will be no thought anymore that will bother you." So then the "no-mind" is there. What to do?

MAN: Nothing.

KARL: Nothing is quite a lot, I tell you. Even nothing is too much.

KARL: Hit, hit, hit. Hit machine. This song is a hit. [group laughs] Ah, it's not so heavy. It's so light. *Unbearable Lightness of Being.*

An American MAN: Not being. The unbearable lightness of *not* being.

KARL: No, of being.

[Silence.]

THERESE: So, Karl, with quantum physics, they have the answer, so-called.

KARL: No, they have no answer—that is the answer.

THERESE: But then they go to Buddhism to understand what they saw or they didn't see.

KARL: First they go into the scientific thing, into the belief system of scientific proof, and then they go to the opposite, to another extreme of another belief system that there is—what? So they come from something into nothing. First they want to find something, and then they want to find nothing. That's Buddhism then, or whatever religion.

First you go into the world, to the outside, you want to find matter, or whatever matters on the outside, happiness. And then you don't find matter, you can't find it, so you go within, you go to the inside, and there you cannot find it either.

And by not finding, outside or inside, what you are, you stop totally—full stop. So by not finding existence on the outside, you drop the idea of "outside," then you go inside, but by not finding existence inside, you make a full stop.

First out and then in, but by no way do you find yourself. Neither the outer nor the inner. There is neither outer nor inner Self, as there is never any in or outside for what you are. So by absolutely not finding what you are and what you are not, in any circumstance, you rest in the "not finding." And by not knowing, you know that you are not something you can know.

This is the Absolute itself. This is the freedom of the knower who knows or doesn't know. Because in the absolute not knowing of what you are, you rest, in That which is, the absolute knowledge that cannot be known by any relative knowing or not knowing. So in spite of knowing or not knowing, you are the Absolute you are, which is knowledge itself, but not by knowing or not knowing.

Clear?

GEORG: Hammer.

MAN: Okay. Being and not being.

KARL: There is no "not being."

MAN: There is no being.

KARL: But when there is no "not being," there is a being.

MAN: There's no being and there's no "not being"?

KARL: There is still a being. Even when there is not a being, there is still a being. You cannot get out of being. You try hard. [group laughs] Here's another one who wants to land in the "never" land.

MAN: [laughing] Never-never land.

KARL: In the "not being" land.

MAN: Okay, then practice being?

KARL: Whatever. Can you practice being? A practical being. Can you put being to practice? "Now I want to learn how to be." Would you ask for that? Being is your nature. It's totally natural. You are. You don't have to practice That. But then you mediate on it. "How can I be That which I am?"

Ah, okay. Thank you very much.

GROUP: Thank you!

THERESE: Survived one more!

KARL: Survived another time. [sings] "This won't be the last time, this won't be the last time—"

[Everyone is laughing.]

Glossary

All terms are Sanskrit unless otherwise noted.

Advaita: non-duality; philosophy of non-dualism

ashram: hermitage; place of spiritual striving and retreat

avatara: divine descent

Bhagavan: Lord; revered person

bhakti: loving devotion

Bodhisattva: awakened one; compassionate one

Brahmachari: a person who follows the spiritual path of *Brahmacharya,* which can include celibacy

Chi Kung: exercises to increase vital energy (Chinese)

dharma: "what holds together;" order; duty

ghat: landing place along a waterway

guru: teacher; spiritual master

Hari Om: Indian salutation; *Hari* is a name of Vishnu

Jin Shin Jitsu: energy work; a form of acupressure (Japanese)

jiva: individual soul; life; embodied self

jivanmukta: a person who is liberated while living

jnani: knower; wise one

karma: action; cause and effect

koan: paradoxical statement or unsolvable riddle (Japanese)

kundalini: life force; primordial or cosmic energy within the body that, when dormant, lies coiled like a snake

lassi: Indian drink made with yogurt and sometimes fruit

leela: divine play

linga: symbol of Shiva

maha: great; mighty; noble

maya: appearance; illusion; mysterious power of creation

moksha: liberation

Namaste: Salutations; I bow to you

neti-neti: not this, not this

nirvikalpa samadhi: non-conceptual state beyond all thought; *samadhi* without any mental modifications

Om: the primordial sound

puja: worship; ritual

sadhana: self-effort; spiritual discipline

sadhu: a holy person; monk

sahaja samadhi: natural, spontaneous state of one-pointed concentration or meditative oneness

samadhi: one-pointedness; absorption; union

samsara: empirical existence; objective universe; worldly illusion

sat-chit-ananda: being-consciousness-bliss

Satguru: teacher of reality

satori: insight; a state of spiritual enlightenment sought in Zen Buddhism (Japanese)

satsang: holy company; spiritual talk

shakti: power; energy

siddhi: attainment; supernatural powers

Tai Chi: supreme ultimate (Chinese)

tantra: rule; ritual; scripture; often used to denote "sacred sexuality"

tapas: austerity

Vedanta: end of the Vedas; end of knowledge

Yoga: union; a process leading to oneness

Zen: meditation (Japanese)

Zazen: sitting meditation (Japanese)

Glossary Sources

Godman, David, ed. *Be As You Are: The Teachings of Sri Ramana Maharshi.* London: Penguin Books, 1992.

Grimes, John. *A Concise Dictionary of Indian Philosophy: Sanskrit Terms Defined in English.* Albany: State University of New York, 1996.

Nisargadatta Maharaj. *I Am That.* Durham: The Acorn Press, 1973.

Ramana Maharshi. *Talks with Sri Ramana Maharshi* (Second Edition). Inner Directions, 2000.

Seung Sahn. *The Compass of Zen.* Boston: Shambhala Publications, Inc., 1997.

About the
Author

During the 1990s Karl Renz encountered a moment of clarity in which there was no desire to change anything or to avoid pain or suffering. He felt, "If I must remain in this condition for the remainder of my existence, so be it." Karl later described it this way:

"At that moment there was an absolute acceptance of being. Time stopped. Karl and the word disappeared and a kind of 'Is-ness' in a glaring light appeared—a pulsating silence, an absolute aliveness that was perfect in itself—and I was that."

Karl travels throughout the world sharing with spiritual seekers. He doesn't give instruction in a traditional way, but his paradoxical logic works brilliantly to help the mind relax, to let go of its grasping and seeking, so that we may recognize the changeless, absolute freedom that is our true nature.

To find out more about Karl's schedule, and to view some of his artwork, please visit his website at www.KarlRenz.com

Aperion Books

Book Publishing for the Digital Age

Aperion Books is dedicated to producing high quality publications that help people facilitate positive change in their lives. We specialize in publishing titles on spirituality, wellness, and personal growth.

Our unique Collaborative Publishing Program is specifically designed to help writers and authors expand their personal and professional horizons through creatively designed books that are distributed to national wholesalers and leading retailers.

CPSIA information can be obtained
at www.ICGtesting.com
Printed in the USA
BVHW072001080421
604501BV00003B/253

9 780982 967843